RT HON HENRY MCLEISH began his political career ⟨in⟩ local government in 1974, and was leader of Fife R⟨...⟩ years. In 1987 he was elected as a member of the UK ⟨Par⟩liament and acted as Minister for Devolution and Home Affairs in the Labour government from 1997 to 1999. In the first Scottish Parliament he was Minister for Enterprise and Lifelong Learning from 1999, and in 2000 he became First Minister of Scotland until 2001. Retiring from politics in 2003, he is now an adviser, consultant, writer, author and broadcaster, and lectures in the USA and elsewhere on a variety of topics.

In 2008, Henry McLeish chaired the Scottish Prisons Commission, which produced a report into sentencing and the criminal justice system entitled 'Scotland's Choice'. In 2010 he conducted a major report on the state of football in Scotland, which had been commissioned by the Scottish Football Association.

Luath Press is an independently owned and managed book publishing company based in Scotland, and is not aligned to any political party or grouping. *Viewpoints* is an occasional series exploring issues of current and future relevance.

Scotland
The Growing Divide

Old Nation, New Ideas

HENRY McLEISH

Edited by Tom Brown

Luath Press Limited

EDINBURGH

www.luath.co.uk

First published 2012

ISBN: 978-1-908373-45-8

The paper used in this book is acid-free, neutral-sized and recyclable.
It is made from low-chlorine pulps produced in a low energy, low emission
manner from renewable forests.

Typeset in 11 point Sabon
by 3btype.com

Contents

Acknowledgements

The author wishes to place on record his thanks to Michael Keating, Professor of Scottish Politics at the University of Aberdeen for his generous cooperation and permission to quote extensively from his book *Plurinational Democracy: Stateless Nations in a Post-Sovereign Era.* (Oxford University Press, 2006) and *The Independence of Scotland* reviews Independence and devolution options (Oxford University Press).

The author would like to acknowledge the Independent and non-party think tank, Reform Scotland, for its excellent work in compiling a glossary of Devolution terms and for their insights into the concept of Devo-Plus.

The author would also like to thank Dr Fiona Davidson, Associate Professor, Director of European Studies at the University of Arkansas for the design and development of the political maps used in Chapter 11, and Mr Tom Brown, one of Scotland's most respected and experienced political commentators for his advice and editorial input.

Introduction

2007 WAS A MOMENTOUS political year, with the commemoration of 300 years of the Treaty of Union, the tenth anniversary of the devolution referendum in which Scotland said 'Yes, Yes' to its new parliament with tax powers, dramatic political events in Wales and Northern Ireland, and the appointment of Gordon Brown as Prime Minister of the UK. Of greater significance for Scotland was the election of the first ever Scottish National Party government and a First Minister determined to ask the Scottish people to vote on Independence. The SNP with 47 seats, one more than Labour, formed a Minority Government and embarked on governing Scotland for the first time in their history. This extraordinary political event has transformed Scottish politics, ignited the debate about Scotland's political and constitutional future and left some searching questions to be asked about the Unionist parties and particularly of Labour who had dominated Scottish politics for over half a century.

All of this focused attention on Scotland's place in the United Kingdom; indeed, on the question of whether Scotland should remain within the Union – and, if so, on what conditions. This should have been the time for an understanding of Scotland's devolution journey so far and a careful examination of the arguments about where it may take us in the future. Instead, much of the debate at both UK and Scottish levels was poorly-informed and predictable. For the first time in a century of Scottish politics, the Unionist parties were on the defensive. They seemed unable or unwilling to face up to the stark reality of a new politics in the making. Furthermore, they were at a loss to understand the importance of the constitutional question and the reasons why the SNP had moved from a party on the fringe to a party of minority Government under Alex Salmond.

Writing in *Scotland: The Road Divides*, Tom Brown and I believed this massive political wake-up call would be heeded by the Unionist parties. It wasn't.

Five remarkable political years on from 2007, and one year on from the spectacular SNP victory in the 2011 Holyrood elections which propelled them to a majority government, very few lessons have been learned. There seems to be a disconnect at the heart of Scottish politics where the Unionist parties have, at least for now, lost the constitutional plot and cannot seem to recognise or grasp the most basic idea of modern political engagement – Scottishness.

The period between 2007 and 2012 has been eventful, with a string of dramatic political developments north and south of the border, in some cases of seismic proportions. Election results at Holyrood, the defeat of the Labour Government at Westminster, the election of new political leaders in Scotland, major shocks to our politics, our institutions and our democracy, major crises in banking and finance, the worst economic slump for a generation, the Murdoch media and phone hacking crisis, the battle to save the Euro and the arrival of the Conservative-led Coalition at Westminster are changing the politics of Britain and undoubtedly reshaping and reframing the relationship between Scotland and the Union.

Amidst all of this upheaval and transformation there is one factor that screams out loud and clear – the relentless rise of the SNP and their determination to 'set Scotland free'. More recently, the Coalition budget and tax cuts for the wealthy, the cuts in welfare, the attempts to franchise the NHS, the cash-for-influence exposé of Tory fundraising and the alleged help from Jeremy Hunt for the Murdoch bid for Sky Broadcasting – now part of the ongoing Leveson inquiry into the relationships between the press and the public, police and politicians – have not only exposed the weaknesses of the Conservatives but inevitably reinforced the view of most Scots that Conservatives are pursuing alternative policies and politics which are alien to traditional Scottish views. This can only feed a sense of the Union and the Westminster Parliament being out of touch with a different kind of Scotland. What happens in London is likely to have a direct bearing on the growing sense of Scottishness in the run up to the referendum in 2014. There is little doubt that politics, government and democracy north and south of the border are diverging and this is feeding into a stronger sense of nationality, identity and diversity.

This new and substantially altered edition of the book considers the condition of Scotland's politics, the Home Rule story so far, the change and challenges of the past five years and their impact on Scotland today. It also updates the narrative on Scotland's constitutional and political future and assesses the prospects for the Unionist parties and the SNP as they face up to the prospect of a referendum within the next two years.

What is remarkable is the fact that the predictions and insights given in the 2007 edition about the fortunes of the Unionist parties, especially Labour, have been largely confirmed by what has actually happened since. The Unionist parties may have wasted five precious years. This raises the question of whether recent political changes in Scotland are merely significant blips in the normal cycle of events, or developments with long term significance for our political parties and our country. Is there a fusion of identity and nationality politics with traditional politics and priorities taking place in Scotland? Is this creating a serious realignment of political thinking and ideas and the possible demise of the old politics of both the UK and Scotland?

Writing in 2007 the authors said,

> Devolution *is* a process, not an event. There can be no going back to entrenched positions of old-style Unionism; yet the Nationalist goal of separation is unacceptable to the clear majority of Scots.
>
> Despite the narrowness of the current debate, the hope is that it can be opened out to include the 'third way' of a more flexible modernised Union that is confident enough to embrace the new politics of the 21st century. This requires the 'Mother of Parliaments' to understand that transferring more powers is not a sign of weakness but of strength and confidence in the constituent parts of the United Kingdom. Without that, the paradox is that the impetus for the break-up of the Union may be created at the very heart of Unionism itself.
>
> There is also a desire to shift the debate from the preserve of professional politicians and link it more directly to the aspirations and everyday needs of ordinary Scots.

These comments are even more relevant today than they were in 2007. *Scotland: The Road Divides* remains a warning about the need for change, and acknowledges three key issues. First, the danger of the Unionist parties continuing to ignore the realities of change and seeing the constitutional and political future of Scotland as some kind of unwelcome distraction from other political concerns. Secondly, the growing influence of the SNP and their current domination of the politics and governance of Scotland and the impact this is having on the mood of the people. Third, in the context of progressive sub-national politics, illustrated in other European countries, the concepts of identity, nationality, diversity and difference are increasingly important considerations in the vision and values of any aspiring nation and will influence the way Scots are likely to vote.

At the heart of this book we also deal with an extraordinary paradox. In the run-up to the 2014 referendum, the Scottish people will be forced to debate and then vote on a choice of two options, status quo Unionism and Independence, despite the fact that a majority of Scots may support another alternative which will not find its way on to the ballot paper. The reason is simple: the three Unionist parties, who would be the main beneficiaries in the long run, will not, at least at this stage, allow this to happen. Scots will be offered instead the promise of jam tomorrow but only if they defeat Independence in Scotland today!

This new narrative, *Scotland the Growing Divide*, rejects this dismal idea and argues instead for a new vision, a new alternative and a second question on the referendum ballot paper. This would lead to a positive rethink of the Union and a transformation of Scotland's role within it. Of the people, by the people, for the people should not be conditional on being told by Westminster what to do first.

CHAPTER I

Westminster We Have a Problem

2007 WAS A REMARKABLE year in which the political landscape of the United Kingdom and Scotland was transformed. The 2007 change of power in Scotland, formerly Labour-dominated, to a Scottish Nationalist minority government; the unlikely coalition in Wales between Labour and Nationalists; the remarkable power-sharing by former enemies in Northern Ireland; the appointment of a new Prime Minister, a Scot representing a Scottish constituency; the publication by the UK government of a Green Paper on 'The Governance of Britain' and by the Scottish government of a White Paper on an Independence referendum, 'Choosing Scotland's Future – A National Conversation – Independence and Responsibility in the Modern World', have all contributed to constitutional flux. Much of this has now been overtaken by the Westminster elections in 2010 and the Holyrood elections in 2011. What does remain is the threat to the Union.

One symptom of the uncertainty about 'the state of the Union' was that the 300th anniversary of the Treaty of Union in 2007 was not marked by a celebration. Instead, there was a low-key 'commemoration' of the survival of the institution which has held Britain together for three centuries.

After four Scottish Parliament elections, we seem to be at the end of the beginning of devolution. Scotland and the UK have reached a constitutional and political crossroads and to all but the most rigidly unbending Unionists, it is obvious that the Union must adapt to survive. Again, it currently shows no sign of bending to the inevitability of change

On 11 September 1997, Scots – despite their long history of dissension, a remarkable degree of party political tribalism and their modern political divisions – came together as never before. By an overwhelming majority they voted across party lines and social boundaries with a decisive double-affirmative 'Yes, Yes' for the restoration of the Scottish Parliament with tax-raising powers.

Their votes in that devolution referendum paved the way for a bold new constitutional settlement, realigning the 300-year-old Union, creating unknown and unforeseen risks, but at the same time opening up promising possibilities for Scotland and the United Kingdom.

Written at the time of the 10th anniversary of that referendum, *Scotland: The Road Divides* was not a history of those ten years. It was an attempt to take a close-up and politically honest look at where the devolution journey has taken Scotland and the United Kingdom. It asked searching questions about the future: is it the status quo, is it a further development of devolution, or is the Scottish Nationalist dream of Independence a possibility?

Nor was this an anti-Union treatise, since the authors were both Unionists at heart and our hope was to show alternative ways in which the bonds and structures of the United Kingdom can be preserved and strengthened. Questions about 'Britishness' and 'Scottishness' were not merely the preoccupation of a Prime Minister of the United Kingdom who happened to be a Scot; they are of concern to us all. We, too, are proud of our Scottish nationality and heritage and prefer, along with the majority of Scots, to have the best of both worlds.

Meanwhile, traditional loyalties to party and class are less strong – as was decisively shown in the May 2007 and 2011 Scottish Parliament elections. The advent of a Scottish Nationalist government – and, perhaps even more, its display of confidence and competence – along with Labour's loss of control of all but two of the 32 local authorities, created a radical realignment in the political control of Scottish institutions.

Only time will tell whether this – and the change in the Scottish mindset – is permanent. There is a distinct possibility that, as Scots become more sophisticated in the practice of devolution and the use of proportional voting, they will continue to develop a political 'split personality'. The clearest demonstration of this is the election of two SNP governments with their platform of separation from the UK, when the overwhelming majority of Scottish voters have declared they are anti-Independence.

Depending on the nature of the UK government, Scots seem prepared to wield their votes to gain the best advantage for their country. Thus, Scots set aside traditional ties and even ideologies to vote differently in UK and Scottish elections, returning an SNP-led coalition in the first instance and then a majority Government at Holyrood. In sharp contrast Labour had a resounding victory in Scotland at the 2010 General election. The danger is that, after a period of seemingly-effective Nationalist government, sufficient voters will be prepared to support full Independence in a future referendum – in line with First Minister Alex Salmond's all-too-obvious 'softly softly' strategy for achieving separation. We should not underestimate the virtues of 'soft politics' in the hands of Scotland's SNP First Minister.

The only safeguards against this would be more subtlety in the approach of the UK government to constitutional change (certainly more sensitivity than has been shown by certain UK government ministers and a surprising number of MPs) and a bolder response to the dangers by those Scottish political parties that support the Union. None of this is obvious from a Westminster whose embrace of sovereignty and indifference to the devolution idea is deep and unwavering. Britain remains one of the most highly centralised nation states in Europe, despite the devolution of some power to Scotland, N. Ireland and Wales over the last 13 years.

The ousting of Gordon Brown and the Labour Government in 2010 changed considerably the Westminster-Holyrood dynamic. The Conservative victory and the arrival of David Cameron as Prime Minister installed, as far as Scots are concerned, a traditional enemy at Westminster and, for the SNP, held out the prospect of more alienation of the Scottish people as a right wing Government – propped up by the Lib-Dems – continued to see Scotland on the edges of their radar.

This split personality voting and the return of the 'auld enemy' at Westminster presents a real danger of further polarisation of two extreme views: this is not stable-state politics. It does, however, reflect the tribalism in politics, which is a tried and tested way of unifying the party faithful, and in this case the populations of two nations.

An increasingly potent factor over the last few years has been the growing English resentment at the Scots getting self-government while Scottish MPs and Scottish ministers of the United Kingdom government rule and decide on purely English concerns. 'English votes for English laws' has become an effective slogan but the paradox is that, although it has become the chant of the arch-Unionist Conservative Party, it is potentially damaging to the Union.

It was said at the time that devolution was not an end in itself, but a continuing process. It is clear that many wish that process to continue and gather speed; yet it is also clear that others fear it will take Scotland and the UK on the wrong path.

The late Labour leader John Smith famously described devolution as 'unfinished business' and, 13 years on from delivery, it remains unfinished. There are those who will strenuously dispute this, fearing that any further tinkering or more drastic alteration to the delicate balance of the Union will damage it beyond repair. However, any realistic assessment shows that maintaining the status quo without further adaptation, evolution and modernisation is not an option. The politics of common sense suggest that the constitutional question will continue to evolve and deepen its impact on the way Scots think of their future. This is particularly relevant to the current debate about the second question on the referendum ballot paper.

In the current circumstances, in 2012, it is not overstating the case to say that the maintenance of Scotland within the Union can only be achieved if politicians across the Unionist spectrum are prepared to be open-minded, face up to uncomfortable truths, shed out-dated prejudices, realise the need for new political ideas and accept pragmatic solutions.

And, despite their understandable euphoria of their accession to power, Scottish Nationalists must recognise the cold reality that though they are in government they have not won the hearts and minds of Scots for their core belief in Separatism. The results of the 2007 and 2011 Scottish elections cannot be interpreted as an endorsement of 'capital-n' Nationalism; to a large degree it was Scotland's expression of disillusion with New Labour, and the way in which the SNP Government has become populist in its approach and competent in its delivery of policy. Scots have also become more aware of their Scottishness and the powerful attraction of the saltire wrapped around issues of pride, passion and patriotism; identity and nationality are coming to the fore as election issues. These issues and symbols of a modern country are not complex or the monopoly of one party so it is all the more remarkable that the SNP has cornered every aspect of the idea of Scottishness without a struggle! The SNP have demonstrated their potential as a competent, credible and popular party of government – with or without their ultimate aim of Independence. This is the factor that the Unionist parties should fear most.

However, in the case of Scottish Labour, it takes more than the shell-shock of their loss of power to explain their muted performance in their first months of the 'new politics of the SNP'. It was even more remarkable that, between the defeats of 2007 and 2011, Labour failed to recover, or to gain any political traction and seemed stranded in a political no man's land of denial and an inability to assess the enormity of what had happened to them.

After 2007, the Scottish Labour Party had a new leader in the energetic and accomplished Wendy Alexander and she conducted a post-mortem on the demise of its domination of national and local politics, which had lasted for half a century. It seems the party that delivered devolution had not come to terms with its consequences. Writing back then we said,

> In addition to producing a strategy for electoral recovery and over-hauling the party machine, Labour should be redefining its mission in post-devolution Scotland, re-thinking the party's identity and whether it should or can be more 'Scottish'.

By the time of Labour's defeat in 2011 none of this had happened. It is worth pausing to ask, why not?

The only thing of consequence to emerge between the two Holyrood elections was the Calman Commission which was set up to look at the devolution powers. This was a solid piece of work, created to give some purpose to the collectivist Unionist effort at a time when the SNP were movingly swiftly and confidently forward. The contents of Calman are now part of the new Scotland Act 2012. Once again, this seems to be too little too late, as they have been overtaken by events and history.

Labour's problems have not eased with the passage of time between 2007 and today. Does it want to create a distinctive political culture and identity for Scottish politics – or does it want to continue to look over its shoulder to Westminster? Does it really understand devolution? Is it prepared to lead the debate on an evolving constitution? In effect, can Scottish Labour win back Scotland, not only in its once-traditional and narrowly-based heartlands but on a wider national basis? Put simply, what does Labour in Scotland stand for at the start of the 21st century? Can it produce a progressive left of centre platform which contributes both to the wider ambitions of Labour in Britain and to creating a winning appeal in Scotland by embracing Scottishness, nationality and identity?

It should go without saying that the challenge is every bit as serious for the other Unionist parties; in fact their survival depends on how they face up to the post-2011 situation. The Tories are still seeking their way out of the Scottish wilderness into which they condemned themselves in the 1980s and 1990s. Like the Labour leadership, David Cameron has to decide whether he will allow his colleagues north of the border to be 'Scottish' or whether, for political expedience, he will pander to the Little Englanders and the anti-Scottish sentiment which has always blighted Toryism.

The Scottish Liberal Democrats now find themselves in a political no-man's-land. Their electoral prospects in Scotland in 2007 were not helped by being too close to Labour. The 2010 election left them providing cover for the hugely unpopular Conservative dominated Coalition government. The drubbing they received at the Holyrood elections of 2011 simply confirmed, in dramatic style, how unpopular they were with the electors. It is not a question of 'Whither the Liberal Democrats?' but 'What is the point of the Liberal Democrats in Scotland?'

Underlying all of this is the basic question: What is the future of Scotland within the Union? After 305 years of the Union, 12 years of Devolution, five years of SNP Government and with the prospect of a referendum on Independence in 2014, there is a real opportunity (so far ignored) to take stock and initiate a more inspired debate acknowledging the new realities facing Scotland. For far too long the debate has been dominated by the SNP, now the Government of Scotland. But this debate is not about the future of the SNP, it is about the future of Scotland and the kind of country we want to live in. The debate is not just about Independence; it is about the powers, ideas, ambitions and other alternative visions. If the SNP did not exist, the nation and the political parties would still be talking about Scotland's future and our role in the UK.

Above all, we have to free ourselves from the highly polarised and narrow debate on the future of our country which still sees constitutional politics as an inevitable choice between the status quo (no more devolution!) and the Separatism of the SNP (no more Union!). There is much more to the future of Scotland and the United Kingdom, for the future is not one Union but many unions. Despite the blinkered view that sees only two options, we have much wider choices, for which we only have to look at the diversity of constitutional alternatives in Europe. Britain didn't invent sub-national government, federalism or devolution!

What about our future in the European Union?: Scotland could play a more significant role alongside sub-national governments, small nations and regions.

What about our future in the United Kingdom?: Relationships with England and the other devolved areas will change, with the possibility of a federalist pattern of governance emerging as Westminster revisits the whole question of devolution. England remains one of the most highly centralised countries in the Western world, with no law-making outside London.

What about our future in the global union?: The revolution in communications technology and the breaking down of boundaries and barriers all offer a different world, in which Scotland can have a greater role in climate change, trade, immigration, energy and development aid.

And what about our future in terms of our own domestic agenda? Economic, institutional, social, environmental, educational and political challenges in Scotland demand distinctive solutions. New powers and responsibilities from Westminster will be part of this.

The world is changing. Sometimes we seem more bewildered than understanding of what is happening. Scotland and the UK cannot simply watch and wonder. The Union is in danger of losing a great opportunity to reconnect with the Scottish people and renew the relationship. In turn it makes little sense for the Union to frustrate Scotland as it builds on devolution and demands a greater say in its own future.

None of this requires us to leave the Union, nor to accept the current constitutional settlement. But it does require us to create a distinctive Scottish political culture and an identity for our parliament and Government that commands broad support. This will provide the confidence and the tangible results that will help the electorate see the benefits of further constitutional change: but we have made little progress on this front. Scotland needs a world view not just seen through the prism of London and Westminster. Scotland needs nation-building. Scotland needs to build capacity to deal with change and help transform its future. Scotland needs a political and constitutional consensus, which it currently doesn't have. This is absolutely vital. Both the status quo and Independence are divisive scenarios, Scotland and the Scots are capable of building a better vision for the challenging times ahead. BUT currently there is nothing new on the table as the Unionist parties seek solace in trying to kill off Independence without worrying a great deal about what happens the day after the referendum.

New thinking is required which sees the world in different ways, with new solutions to old and enduring problems. It is inevitable that Scotland's role in the UK will change significantly in the first half of the 21st century; the first decade has only served to illustrate what a remarkable journey the country is on, with little indication that the momentum is slowing. There is a great deal we can learn from social and constitutional changes in Europe but only if we can break free from the debate of extremes and the constraints imposed by the Unionist parties.

What now for Scotland? Thirteen years on, we are surely at the end of the beginning of devolution. Again writing in 2007 we said,

> As the clash between an apparently inflexible Union and a seductively harmless-seeming form of Independence takes shape, it needs to be pointed out that constitutional and political roads need not lead to such a stark choice between two extremes. It should not be too much to expect that the futures of Scotland and the Union can be built on enlightenment and hope, not misunderstanding and political prejudice.

There are signs that for the first time in post devolution politics, Scotland's role in the Union is now higher up the Westminster agenda. In the first few days of 2012, the media – including the English press – was full of comment on the back of David Cameron's intervention into the referendum issue and for all intents and purposes looking like a 'Westminster, we have a problem' moment. Mirroring the Tom Hanks crisis in the film *Apollo 13*, David Cameron had lost patience with the failure of the Unionist parties to stop the SNP juggernaut and he was clearly worried by the fact that Westminster had lost control of the constitutional debate. The future of the Union went viral and, for the first time in a decade, devolution and Scotland's role within the United Kingdom was centre-stage.

This was probably not the intention of the PM, whose intervention was probably more opportunistic than considered and more about Westminster exercising its legislative muscle, but it certainly focused the minds of the Unionist parties north and south of the border, generating some real debate about the forthcoming referendum, the nature of the question and the issue of whether the Scottish Parliament could lawfully hold such a vote.

Consultation papers on the referendum from both governments quickly followed and although the intense and frenetic debate that followed has subsided, we are now at the start of what is likely to be the most momentous period in the political and constitutional history of Scotland since the Act of Union in 1707. The result of the referendum in 2014, regardless of the outcome, will change the future of Scotland and its relationship with England, Wales and Northern Ireland. Scotland is now preparing for its date with destiny. This book discusses the political and constitutional future of Scotland as the journey continues. The report from the House of Commons Scottish Affairs Committee, published in early August 2012, confirms the Westminster obsession with Referendum legalities. Most Scots will be content and relieved to accept that Scotland's ultimate future will be decided by themselves in the court of public opinion, and not in the law courts by advocates and QCs. These are exciting times for our nation. It remains to be seen whether the author is being too optimistic about the future of a country he passionately believes in.

CHAPTER 2

The Road to Home Rule

AN UNDERSTANDING OF the emerging 'new politics' requires an understanding of how the politics of devolution and Independence have evolved, and the modern political parties have reached their present positions.

Labour's involvement with the constitutional question, leading ultimately to the embrace of devolution, started in the early part of the 20th century when a number of speeches by key people such as Keir Hardie floated the idea of 'home rule'. Keir Hardie first pledged the Labour Party's support for Scottish home rule in an election address in 1888 and the Labour Party went into the general election of 1918 with Scottish home rule as the third priority in its manifesto, ahead of housing, pensions and education.

Gordon Brown wrote in 1993:

> There's a joke in the Scottish Party about our 1918 manifesto. Then we promised home rule, proportional representation and the prohibition of alcohol. And in more than seventy years we have managed to secure none of them.

It can now be said that two out of three is not bad, but the third is still highly unlikely...

Over the years, Labour's commitment waxed and waned. By 1929, home rule had fallen to the bottom of the 63 priorities in Labour's manifesto. It formed no part of their manifesto in 1945 and in 1958 Labour formally dropped any commitment to devolution.

Interestingly, in Labour's early days, there was a socialism and nationalism debate within the party and in Scotland, also involving the movement that led to the SNP and the Liberals. A number of home rule bills were submitted to Westminster but, although they affected Scotland, their primary aim was to deal with the Irish question. A number of backbench bills on home rule for Scotland were submitted, but these never had any chance of success.

These formative years also saw the genesis of Labour's continuing difficulties with constitutional questions. Because of socialism's tenet of centralisation and command of the economy, there was hardly any further discussion for much of the first half of the 20th century. Many Labour Party stalwarts believed that any form of nationalism or home rule cut across Labour's wider political aspirations and was a distraction from the main political battle, which focused on dealing with class and the excesses of capitalism. Surprisingly, much of this argument remains today.

Basically, throughout the last 100 years, there has not been a body of fundamental and coherent philosophy or strategic thinking about territory, sub-national government, federalism, nationality or identity within the Labour Party. Instead, policy on this subject has evolved incrementally, often hesitatingly and sometimes acrimoniously, over the century, with understandable highs and lows in the party's interest. Labour, for much of its history, has viewed the devolution of power as a distraction from the main UK struggles and as a sop to the Nationalists. This suspicion of constitutional change remains deeply embedded in the psychology of the party and remains today a major obstacle to modern and progressive thinking on the matter.

As a result, Labour's engagement with devolution has ebbed and flowed, reflecting Scotland's national mood, the varying political fortunes of the Nationalist party, the campaigning zeal of devolutionists within Labour by groups like Scottish Labour Action, and the impact of the economy and unemployment in Scotland on leadership thinking in London.

It was not until October 1974, after the strong showing of the SNP in the February 1974 election, that the first full manifesto commitment at UK level was given: 'The next Labour government will create elected assemblies in Scotland and Wales.'

From 1974 through the five general elections to 1997, there were reaffirmations of the commitment to devolution in the UK. Prior to 1974, the economic, industrial and employment problems of sectors of the UK were the focus and at that time Scotland was still classified as a 'region'. Significantly, in a section of the 1955 UK manifesto entitled 'Scotland, Wales and Northern Ireland', the concern was identified which heralded a great programme of decentralisation of industry and subsidies for the 'economically deprived regions'.

The manifesto said:

Under the Tories, there had been hunger and misery, idle pits and shipyards and bankrupt farms. Labour in power brought new life to Scotland and Wales. Thriving industry justified triumphantly Labour's systems of controls and priority. But unemployment in some parts of these countries remains high. Labour will ensure full employment in Scotland and Wales and will begin to overtake Tory neglect by bringing new industries to Northern Ireland.

But, of more interest and for the first time in a UK Labour manifesto, there was a comment: 'We respect and will safeguard the distinctive national cultures of these countries.' Until then these countries had been termed only as 'regions' and the use of the words 'distinctive national cultures' and 'countries' was telling.

In the 1970s, the SNP did so well that in February 1974, Labour quickly got to work on a response and produced the commitment to Scottish and Welsh Assemblies in their October 1974 manifesto.

On 22 June 1974, Labour's Scottish executive met to ratify the Downing Street proposals on devolution. Unfortunately, this was also the day of the Scotland–Yugoslavia World Cup football match and only 11 members of the executive turned up. Most of those who stayed away to watch the football were pro-devolutionists and this allowed the anti-devolutionists to throw out the proposals. Labour leader Harold Wilson was enraged and at the Dalintober Street meetings in August, Scottish Labour put devolution back on the agenda, even though many members were against it. In October 1974, the SNP won 11 seats, the highest number they ever achieved at Westminster.

The matter remained reasonably high on the agenda until the 1979 referendum debacle. At that time, Labour was split between devolutionists and Unionists, while the SNP was split between devolutionists and those who favoured complete Independence.

In the referendum, 1.23 million Scots voted 'For' and 1.15 million voted 'Against' the Scottish Assembly, with a turn-out of 58.8 per cent, but with the Cunningham Amendment (stating that a 'yes' vote would only be valid if 40 per cent of the total electorate voted for it) creating another obstacle, the vote represented only 32.9 per cent of Scotland's electorate and, as a result, devolution for Scotland fell. This was a tipping point for constitutional change within the Labour party.

The referendum defeat foreshadowed the downfall of the Callaghan government and the election of the Conservatives, leading on to the Thatcher years. As a result, in the immediate aftermath of the 1979 Labour defeat, the Campaign for a Scottish Assembly was launched by home rule politicians, academics and activists. The early 1980s were lean years for devolution and it was only in 1989 that the Scottish Constitutional Convention held its inaugural meeting to reactivate the fight for devolution. Despite the election defeat of Labour in 1992, a firm commitment to a Scottish Parliament was reinforced and the election of a Labour government in 1997 ensured that, after nearly 100 years, Scotland would have its own parliament. Scots are now living the legacy of those early struggles.

The Scottish National Party, in sharp contrast, has had the idea of radical constitutional change for Scotland at its heart since its formation in 1934 – through an amalgamation of the National Party of Scotland, founded in 1928, and The Scottish Party (a 1932 breakaway from the Cathcart Conservative Association). It has to be said that the growth in nationalism, or the fear of it, often resulted in a flurry of political activity from Labour and the Conservatives.

Always a fractious party, it has ironically (but not inaccurately) been said that the SNP's first split occurred when it enlisted its second member. There were initial disagreements over whether to concentrate on electoral politics or wider cultural aims, followed by arguments over relations with other political parties, especially the Labour Party. Despite little success in the polls, the SNP's very existence sustained the concept of a separate Scottish state in the public mind.

Over the years, supporters of Scottish Independence have continued to hold mixed views on the home rule movement, with three strands of thinking: those who wanted devolution within the framework of the UK, those who saw it as a stepping-stone to Independence and those who wanted to go all-out for Independence.

From opposition to European integration – because it was perceived as an assault on sovereignty – the SNP moved to a positive policy of 'Independence in Europe' and cited the prosperous Scandinavian countries and Ireland (the 'Celtic tiger') as models.

When the SNP declared itself for outright Independence 50 years ago, a moderate element would still have joined in any all-party action to achieve a substantial degree of home rule. Interestingly, this half-way position is where the SNP found itself in 2007 – in power under devolution but, because it was a minority government, it was unable to push for Independence. Four years later in 2011 – as a Majority Government of Scotland – the SNP made a firm commitment to pass a Bill and put the issue of Independence to the Scottish people in the first officially-sanctioned vote on the matter. In a curious way and capturing the essence of democracy, only the Scottish people now stand between Scotland being independent and the Treaty of Union being rewritten. Beneath the surface, the divisions between 'softly, softly' gradualists and 'big bang' Separatist radicals still exist, making full Independence a less certain outcome for many in the SNP. This stopping short of Independence may provide a natural bridging point to link the gradualists with those in the Unionist parties who wish to move on from the status quo and the first phase of devolution. This area of common ground remains to be explored in the ongoing debate. Once again there is no progress on such an agenda, especially within and between the leaderships of the Unionist parties in Scotland. There are, however stirrings of new thinking outwith traditional party politics.

There is no great corpus of Conservative Party thinking on constitutional change or the politics of devolved power. The party formerly known as the Conservative and Unionist Party, now simply 'Conservatives' or 'Scottish Conservatives', has in the past been robustly opposed to devolution – never more so than under Margaret Thatcher's leadership. It was conveniently forgotten that in 1968 Edward Heath promised, in his 'Declaration of Perth', a Scottish Assembly indirectly elected from members of Scottish local authorities, and when Mrs Thatcher reversed this policy in 1976, the Shadow Scottish Secretary, Alick Buchanan-Smith, and Shadow Minister of State, Malcolm Rifkind, resigned.

However, having been saved from electoral extinction by the Holyrood Parliament and proportional representation, the Tories are now grateful, but reluctant, devolutionists. The 2007 Scottish leader Annabel Goldie paid tribute to the Union as 'a 300-year success story' but the May 2007 manifesto promised the Scottish Conservatives would 'make the Scottish Parliament work better for Scotland'. Ms Goldie followed this up by meeting First Minister Salmond to discuss drugs policy, one of a number of issues on which consensus might be achieved, explaining: 'It reflects a new political will and a desire to take forward a new agenda in Scotland.' This was very much the pattern between 2007 and 2011 where the SNP, lacking an overall majority, were happy to get Tory support and in turn secure some tangible political benefits, especially at budget times.

Goldie's party also participated in a meeting with Scottish Labour and the Scottish Liberal Democrats, to issue a joint statement rejecting the SNP government's proposal for a referendum on Independence. The Unionist parties also came together in the agreement to set up the Calman Commission to inquire into further powers for the Scottish Parliament. This was possibly the only time in the five wasted years that the three Unionist parties came together in common cause; occasioned by the total domination of the SNP, the need to remain connected to the constitutional issue and to start to look like a credible alternative to an SNP Government that was digging in and looking more competent and confident by the day. After the 2011 Holyrood election, the SNP's overall majority negated the need for them to cultivate allies, build any consensus on issues and make budget concessions to the Tories or indeed any other party. There is no doubt that an overall majority in a Parliament, where the voting system was deliberately designed to ensure that never happened, is not good for consensus or cross-party agreement or bipartisanship. Tribalism rules and the opposition's task is made much more difficult.

Any prospect of a change in Scottish Conservative Party thinking on devolution disappeared during the Tory leadership contest after Annabel Goldie stepped down. The fight that followed had Ruth Davidson taking on Murdo Fraser for the Conservative crown in Scotland. The views of the candidates could not have been more different. Murdo Fraser wanted to scrap the party name and all the post-war baggage that went with it. A new start for Scottish Tories was advocated and to the impartial observer this made a great deal of sense for a party that seemed to be in terminal decline and had not stopped falling in the polls since 1955. With no MPs at Westminster after the 1997 General Election, only proportional representation (PR) at Holyrood saved the party from total oblivion. There was no doubting the fact that Scots were embarrassed by the Tories and their perceived anti-Scottishness which was at its most virulent during the Thatcher era. Not surprisingly Tory party members did not share his radical vision for the renewal of Scottish conservatism and Ruth Davidson was elected leader. In sharp contrast, she embraced the Union flag and seems determined to resist further calls for radical constitutional change, instead working to defeat Independence and keep Scotland within an unchanging Union. Few people see this as a step towards renewal or reform. Most people see this as a lost opportunity to halt a decline covering nearly half a century.

The Liberal Democrats are committed to a federal United Kingdom, with elected regional assemblies throughout the country. In 'Here We Stand' (1993) they proposed that a federal framework be put in place 'that regions may or may not take advantage of immediately', and in their 1997 election manifesto they remained committed to regional assemblies.

In the joint Labour–Lib-Dem statement of March 1997, the Lib-Dems indicated that, despite their disagreement with Labour's intention to hold pre-legislative referendums in both Scotland and Wales, they would not seek to frustrate or delay the referendum legislation and would campaign for a 'double yes' in the referendum.

Their 2007 Scottish election manifesto said: 'A growing number of people support more powers for the Scottish Parliament – many more than support Independence.'

This followed the report 'Moving to Federalism – a New Settlement for Scotland' by the Steel Commission, set up by the party and chaired by former Scottish Parliament Presiding Officer and former leader David Steel. Its terms of reference included:

1   To examine the powers, responsibilities and financial powers of the Scottish Parliament and its relationship to the United Kingdom Parliament and government and to the European Union.

2   To consider how to move forward to a fully federal structure for the United Kingdom (including consideration of the relationship between the Scottish Executive and local government in Scotland).

3   To identify what changes to the powers and legislative competences of the Scottish Parliament are desirable.

4   To identify the potential advantages of greater fiscal and economic powers for the Scottish Parliament.

In his introduction, Lord Steel wrote:

It has long been accepted that the Scotland Act should be reviewed a decade or so after it came into force in 1999.

It has also been accepted that the so-called 'Barnett formula' under which Scotland has, since the 1970s, received its share of public expenditure is due for re-examination. In my Donald Dewar Memorial Lecture three years ago, I said that no self-respecting parliament could exist permanently on a grant from another parliament.

The Commission called for a second Constitutional Convention to consider the best ways to devolve new powers, including taxation powers, to the Scottish Parliament, as well as the creation of a joint committee of the Scottish and UK Parliaments, and a new category of powers in which the two parliaments should work in partnership. The new convention would consider the case for applying this approach in areas including regulatory powers, misuse and control of drugs, control of firearms, asylum and immigration, strategic planning of welfare services and aspects of employment law. The Commission also believed the Scottish Parliament should have exclusive competence over the electoral system, the operation of the Scottish Parliament itself, the civil service, energy policy, transport powers and marine policy. Other extended powers might include betting and gaming, public and bank holidays, human rights and equalities, and an increased role in governance of broadcasting.

As expected, the Commission rejected full fiscal autonomy, and preferred 'fiscal federalism', believing that:

> The time is right to move the debate on fiscal powers forward and fiscal federalism offers the opportunity to Scotland to bridge the gap in accountability seen in the current system but within the framework of a renewed and refreshed set of relations for the UK.
>
> It is instructive that full fiscal autonomy (where Scotland raises and retains all tax revenue and remits an agreed sum to Westminster for shared services) does not operate in any industrialised country. In contrast, fiscal federalism can be seen to work well in countries across the world. There is no doubting the constitutional credentials of the Lib-Dems. They have consistently advocated a form of federalism and have been highly critical of a situation where Devolution and the Holyrood Parliament could continue with a hand-out from Westminster. This was in their eyes a Parliament that could not win

trust and confidence without the respect and responsibility of fiscal federalism. Of all the Unionist parties, the Lib-Dems are the radical party. But in recent times that radicalism has been rather subdued as they battle the twin problems of their so-called allies in the Coalition Government at Westminster and their electoral unpopularity caused by signing up to Austerity Britain. But being seen as providing a cloak of respectability, for the right wing ideology of a Conservative led Government, has not been helpful to the Lib-Dems.

From a tentative start, or even outright opposition, the parties have all made a political journey that has ended in recognition of the inevitability of the new constitutional settlement that is devolution. The next stage in that journey is equally inevitable. For the SNP, the journey is to Independence, whatever that means in a world of growing interdependence. For the Conservatives, Labour and the Lib-Dems there is much less certainty and a great deal of confusion. Listening to Radio 2 the words of a song captured my concerns, 'They're talking, but they're not saying anything. They're listening but don't hear anything. They're moving but not going anywhere' The Lib-Dems and Labour should be in the forefront of constitutional change and a positive force for a federal Britain.

CHAPTER 3

Referendum 1997

IT IS USEFUL TO LOOK back at the 1997 referendum, both to understand why things happened as they did and to see what lessons can be learned for the future. The debate surrounding the referendum in 1996 and 1997 still has importance for a number of reasons, mainly because they have not been properly addressed by the UK parties.

In the pre-referendum tensions of that time lie the roots of the disputes and suspicions that plague politics in the post devolution era. Labour's fraught relationship with the constitutional question continues to cast a shadow over the party's ability to win success in the new era of Scottish politics. Little has been done to create working relationships and trust between UK politicians and devolved parliaments. Instead, there has been resentment and some MPs have been openly scornful of their MSP colleagues, as was shown by the infamous 'White Heather Club' jibe which originated among Scottish Labour MPs at Westminster.

Furthermore, the parties themselves have not come to terms with the new politics or created true devolution in their internal structures. The doggedly centralist attitude at Westminster has not only created unnecessary strains, it has been self-damaging for the parties. For Labour in particular, there are unresolved questions to be answered before the UK Party can be comfortable with devolution. Despite having delivered it, large sections of the Party still appear uneasy about the consequences of devolution. For some members, the arrival of the Scottish Parliament was a grudging response to a 'Nat' led threat and never part of a longer journey.

The debate of a decade ago reveals the doubts and misgivings about devolution within the Labour Party then and now. The prevailing psychology of that period may help explain the defensive and negative attitudes within the Westminster parliament; why some members of the party are uncomfortable with devolution; why today's Labour Party in Scotland can seem ambivalent and uneasy about where devolution goes from here; and why UK Labour has been slow to allow the Scottish Party to respond to the new realities of devolution 13 years on. After nearly 100 years of discussing some form of home rule, the Labour Party in Scotland remains uneasy about any real debate about the constitutional future of Scotland.

The referendum itself was a symptom of that uneasiness. Devolution was a huge issue in Scottish politics and Labour accepted that it was what John Smith had described as 'the settled will of the Scottish people' and 'unfinished business'. In England and at Westminster, however, there was a feeling of indifference and certainly ambivalence. Devolution had never been part of the DNA or the soul of an institution which had ruled without disruption for centuries.

The majority of the Blair shadow cabinet accepted that devolution was 'unfinished business', but no more than that. It was largely regarded as a Scottish affair, for some a distraction from mainstream politics, and key Unionists such as Derry Irvine, Jack Straw and David Blunkett did not disguise their misgivings.

At Westminster, there was little awareness that each minor turn in the winding road towards devolution could attract outsized headlines in the Scottish media. Devolution was not recognised as something that would change the face of British politics and was not taken seriously enough, and there is ample evidence to suggest the Unionist parties continue to pay a heavy price for this. Nor was it recognised as having repercussions for England, despite the consideration of assemblies for the English regions, which collapsed after a disastrous referendum in the north east of England.

While not being seen as integral to the future of the UK, devolution was a method of showing that Labour could be more Scottish and served notice on the Scottish National Party that there was an alternative to Independence. However, within Labour it was felt – mistakenly – that completing the 'unfinished business' by delivering the Scottish Parliament would be a one-off event and not a continuing process.

In the summer of 1996, with the increasing prospect of a general election victory, there was still deep concern within Scottish Labour about the merits of devolution. The internal debate tended to focus on nationalism versus socialism and the argument was made that by 'selling out' to appease nationalist feeling, Labour was betraying its traditions and principles. This was the classic 'the poor in Newcastle are the same as the poor in Glasgow... they need socialism not nationalism' argument. Although basic, it typified the Left's argument against political and constitutional change in the UK, traditionalism blinding them to any notions of how devolution could help to achieve some of the historic goals of Labour. Because of the narrowness of this argument, there was no possibility of tackling these wider issues. The debate also highlighted our isolated British mentality and our sense of exceptionalism by refusing to learn from the experiences of other European countries.

It is important to realise how these historic exchanges are still relevant to the problems of the modern Labour Party, north and south of the border, adjusting to the realities of post 2007. There was sentiment and emotionalism, but no intellectual, international, political, constitutional or democratic depth to the argument. It was a functional approach to business that had to be finished, without recognition that it was business that would change the face of British politics forever. Hatred of the SNP and the excessive tribalism which has characterized devolution thinking, has deprived the Scottish people of any serious debate on constitutional change.

In practical terms, there was the question of whether a referendum was necessary or whether, as a constitutional issue, it was similar to the votes on Europe in 1973 and 1975 and the people should be allowed to decide.

Labour's U-turn

Since the publication of the 1990 document 'Towards Scotland's Parliament' by the Scottish Constitutional Convention, in which Labour was a full participant, the Labour Party had been committed to legislating for a Scottish Parliament within its first year in government. Repeated assurances were given, not least by Shadow Scottish Secretary George Robertson, that success in the general election would be taken as the mandate for a devolved Scottish Parliament.

Robertson said it was 'clear party policy' that there would be no referendum because the party wanted to legislate early and quickly, stating unequivocally: 'The referendum will be the general election, when there will be clear alternatives on offer.'

The Shadow Scottish Secretary was accurately reflecting party policy and a widely-held Scottish view. It was reasonable to assume that a majority vote for Labour could legitimately be taken as a majority for its declared policy of devolution, and this was in line with the national mood in Scotland, where the devolution bandwagon had been gathering pace and popular support throughout the years of Tory government.

However, under pressure from the New Labour leadership, Robertson found himself having to perform a humiliating U-turn and, somewhat unfairly, underwent what one academic has described as his 'days of debacle'. From his previously-stated position, Robertson was forced to accept a referendum and defend it against ferocious criticism from all sides in Scotland.

The leading Scottish figures in the shadow cabinet – Gordon Brown, George Robertson, Donald Dewar and Robin Cook – were all consulted at various stages, but it cannot be said that there was ever a vote, nor that there was any formal agreement to have a referendum. In an interview with Brian Taylor, the political editor of BBC Scotland, for his book *The Scottish Parliament* (Polygon, 1999), Robertson is quoted as saying it became 'absolutely blindingly obvious' that a new Labour government would have 'a serious problem with the implementation of the Scottish devolution promise.'

There were obvious concerns and arguments on both sides. It was felt a referendum would improve the prospects of the legislation having a trouble-free passage through the House of Commons if the people of Wales and Scotland had given it their prior blessing. This could be presented as acknowledging the sovereignty of the Scottish people, in effect, for the first time in the 300 years of the Treaty of Union.

By historic custom and practice, every stage of a constitutional bill would have to be fought on the floor of the House and not be sent to committee. Blair and the party managers were worried that the devolution legislation would take up too much parliamentary time and overshadow other new pieces of legislation which were of more immediate importance and were desperately needed after 18 years of Conservative government.

A referendum would also give both the Leader and the devo-sceptics in his shadow cabinet the convincing evidence they wanted of the public acceptance of devolution by both Scotland and Wales.

While there was disappointment in many quarters in Scotland, the straight single-question referendum – 'Yes' or 'No' to a Scottish Parliament – was generally acceptable. But this disappointment turned to fury when Blair/Robertson announced, without consultation, that there would be a second question on the power to vary taxes in Scotland by 3p in the pound.

In a chaotic and acrimonious few weeks, Labour stumbled from no referendum (the question is settled and a general election vote will be enough), to a referendum with two questions (principle plus tax), then two referenda (the second one to sanction the use of the tax power), and finally back to one referendum with two questions.

How this came about is still a mystery. It is generally accepted that the referendum proposal first surfaced in a committee set up under the chairmanship of Lord (Derry) Irvine, Tony Blair's legal mentor and future Lord Chancellor, to review the legislative programme of the Labour government.

Blair was clearly concerned that, having committed Labour to no tax increases, he would face a major crisis of confidence if the Scots in the first term of a Labour government decided to use their tax powers. Tory attacks on a 'Tartan Tax' were having an effect.

He also sensed that a move beyond the block-grant funding to income tax powers would be breaking new and dangerous ground and, at a later stage, could lead to more demands for further fiscal powers, including fiscal autonomy. Even if Blair thought Scots might reject this question, it was worth asking for a variety of reasons.

It may also have been the case that the future PM was beginning to appreciate the seismic changes devolution would bring and the possible difficulties that would ensue and was in need of the reassurance that a referendum would bring.

Part of the background to this extraordinary turn of events was sketched by Alistair Campbell, Blair's former director of communications, in the edited extracts from his diaries in *The Blair Years*. The entry for Monday, 24 June 1996 reveals how Blair clashed with Donald Dewar and George Robertson:

> TB was adamant he was going to make clear his view there should be no tax rise, there should certainly be a referendum and it should be made clear that Westminster was the ultimate constitutional authority.
>
> George Robertson's reaction was not dissimilar to Donald [Dewar]'s, that yet again TB was provoking unnecessary fights, though when you got on to the substance of the arguments they were not far apart. TB said he could only promise what he intended to deliver, this was the best way to do it. He said every home rule

effort up to now had failed because of over-ambition. GR said for some, it would be a political nuclear explosion. TB said I know I am right, and I know it must be done sooner than later. GR could see TB was moving. He felt you could do the tax and referendum bit, but not the third element. TB said it was a statement of the obvious, power devolved but power retained.

Thus, concern about the potential impact of these changes in Scotland was over-ridden, possibly because the ideas were mainly from London-based politicians who had no understanding of what they would mean in Scottish politics so close to the general election.

There was no cognisance of the mistrust that had been created in Scotland by the failure of the 1979 home rule referendum on a Westminster-imposed technicality, and the festering frustration caused by Scotland's treatment by a Conservative government which Scotland had overwhelmingly rejected at successive elections.

All of this surfaced in the outrage which met the announcement that there would be a second question on the referendum paper. Blair, who repeatedly had to refute allegations that he was lukewarm on devolution, was accused of a betrayal of the John Smith legacy and even of being party to a plot to undermine the scheme.

What followed was a period of bitter recrimination in Scotland and feverish activity within the Labour Party to resolve the differences. In the knowledge that a general election could only be months away, the party was anxious to avoid recreating the old image of the Labour Party at war with itself and, still worse, of a traditionally loyal Scottish membership rebelling against the new leadership.

The first attempt to allay Scottish fears was spectacularly unsuccessful. The new line on devolution was leaked by Alistair Campbell to a London paper, the *Independent*, triggering a wholly predictable outcry on both the Scottish backbenches at Westminster and north of the border. A news conference was hastily called at Glasgow International Concert Hall on 27 June, at which the Scottish 'big guns' – Robertson, Brown, Dewar and Cook – attempted to silence the critics of the new line. But it turned into an ill-tempered affair, at which members of the Scottish media did not bother to disguise their scepticism (or, it has to be said, that of their readers and listeners).

Suspicion was heightened with the realisation that the second question had been finalised in discussions at Robertson's home in Dunblane during Blair's visit for a memorial service for the victims of the school massacre, a national tragedy which was still raw in the Scottish consciousness. The line of questioning showed that the reporters found this either hard to believe or in profound bad taste.

The row escalated to such damaging proportions and the split within Labour became so deep that Blair flew to Scotland again on 28 June to address the party's Scottish executive in the old Lothian Region HQ in Edinburgh. It seemed that a truce had been brokered when, after several hours, the executive backed the Leader's change of policy by 20 votes to 4.

This did not end the dissent, however. The second question was still viewed as a 'wrecking device' and MPs, unions, pressure groups and leading Labour members united in a campaign to scrap it.

Scottish Labour Action, the home rule pressure group within the Labour Party, argued:

> The well-financed Tory 'Tartan Tax' campaign would target the second question. All existing evidence suggests that our party leadership's response to the Tory/anti-devolution onslaught would be muddled and apologetic.
>
> The way in which our u-turn has been managed has destroyed much of the goodwill and unity built up over seven years in the Constitutional Convention. The two-question format is perceived by many outside the party as a 'rigged referendum', and if the second question remains it would be more difficult to motivate many of the voters that we need to win.

At yet another Scottish executive meeting, at Stirling on 31 August, there was stalemate until Mohammed Sarwar put forward the unlikely compromise that the two-question referendum should go ahead but, before the tax-raising power was used, another referendum would have to be held by the new Scottish Parliament. To widespread amazement outside the meeting, the compromise was accepted – and the Labour leadership found itself in another fine mess.

Scottish Labour Action spoke for many when it described this as 'a complete fiasco' and a disaster for Scotland:

> The last two months have been the most dispiriting for Scottish Party

activists since our defeat in 1992. Not only have we seen our devolution policy chopped and changed on a completely unnecessary
basis, but we have also had a first- hand experience of all that is
worst about 'New Labour'.

The Convention process has all but been destroyed and any
illusions about the autonomy of the Scottish party put firmly in their
place. At the end of this process it is not only Party activists but also
the wider electorate who are beginning to doubt if the 'unfinished
business' will be finished in our lifetime.

There was general relief when Robertson sensibly (if undemocratically)
dropped the second referendum. The entire episode had resulted in what
should have been Labour's flagship policy in Scotland descending into
an undignified and unnecessary shambles. Fortunately, devolution was
significant and serious enough to survive even that – but the lesson
should have been learned that constitutional change has to be above
suspicion, clear-cut and with no hint of ulterior political motives.

In fairness, devolution would not have been delivered without Blair's
continuing commitment. When questioned on the eve of the referendum
about suspicions that he lacked enthusiasm for devolution, he replied:

> I keep denying it but it's one of these 'when did you stop beating
> your wife?' questions. I have always made it clear I am committed
> to Scottish devolution; I was committed to Scottish devolution when
> it wasn't very fashionable to be committed to it.
>
> Decentralisation is an important part of the programme of my
> government. I said that I would introduce it and the proof of the
> pudding is in the eating. If we win this referendum and deliver a
> Scottish Parliament, then I will be the Prime Minister who delivered it.

Despite the criticisms of Tony Blair's lack of enthusiasm for devolution,
there is no doubt that he remained faithful to the John Smith legacy.
During the preparation of the White Paper in 1997, Blair remained
entirely supportive of Donald Dewar in ensuring the White Paper was
the best it could be. Blair made it clear to many of his cabinet colleagues
that there would be no watering down of the content. The committee
working on the White Paper was a tough and bruising ordeal for
Donald Dewar as he faced up to the critics and sceptics within his own
party. Any informed comment would confirm though, that these were

Donald Dewar's finest moments. He delivered for Scotland a remark-able White Paper. It should also be said, however, that in the later years of Blair's Premiership, having given Scotland its parliament (on his terms), he seemed content that the matter had been dealt with, and when UK Ministers raised doubts about different policies being followed in Scotland, he was wont to shrug and say:

'That's devolution for you...'

'A Grown-Up Parliament'

On 24 July 1997, Donald Dewar introduced the devolution White Paper at Westminster, then flew north (on what was erroneously dubbed the 'freedom flight') for a launch party in Edinburgh Castle. The slogans were deployed: 'a new parliament for the new millennium' ... 'a grown-up parliament with a grown-up role' ... 'the people of Scotland now hold the future in their hands' ...

But that parliament would not be allowed to vote on Independence; only the Scottish people in an election, not the politicians, would be able to do that.

> If people in Scotland want to move in another direction, they are entitled to do so', Dewar said, 'but they show no signs of that. Practical politics means that if Scotland's voting position changed then politicians of every party would have to address that. But I think that the referendum will end that argument and we will be able to move forward.

He also warned that the hardest task would be to convince the Scottish people to vote for the new parliament, but among ministers the feeling was that the proposals would receive overwhelming support. Their real concern was that apathy and a low poll might undermine the credibility and authority of the devolution settlement.

Publicly, the normally lugubrious Dewar sounded an optimistic note: 'In my time, I have seen many devolution schemes. I genuinely believe this is the best – and right for Scotland. As someone who has seen devo-lution measures come and go, I think this one is going to come and not go.'

The sense of anticipation and excitement, however, was not shared by a number of Scottish Labour MPs who had campaigned on anti-devolution platforms in the past and had to be persuaded, at a group meeting at the Scottish Office in Whitehall, to give the referendum a chance. The unspoken bargain was that they would not speak against devolution but neither would they be expected to actively campaign for it.

The weakness of the Conservative Party's position was shown by the contrast between their anti-devolution rhetoric and their lack of a single Tory MP in Scotland – and they failed to see that the new scheme would have benefits for their political survival in Scotland

Tory constitutional affairs spokesman Michael Ancram, MP for Devizes in Wiltshire, said the scheme was 'dangerous, damaging and dishonest – today is a sombre day for Scotland.' Their English-based Scottish affairs spokesman, Dr Liam Fox, struggled without much support and blamed the Liberal Democrats: 'It cannot be long before they are sued under the Trade Descriptions Act for calling themselves an opposition party.' In a typical put-down, Dewar retorted: 'You were unwise to talk about the Trade Description Act – you do, after all, describe yourself as a Scottish Opposition spokesman!'

Tory peer Lord Mackay of Ardbrecknish, a former Scottish Office minister, lamented: 'This is a day of great sadness for our 300-year-old Union. I fear indeed that this marks the beginning of the end of Britain.'

At a Labour rally in Glasgow the next day, Chancellor Gordon Brown warned the House of Lords not to try to block the new parliament, saying that unelected peers had no right to interfere with the clear will of the people. He had reason for issuing his warning: the Lords had already attempted to vote down one part of the Referendum Bill and had tabled 158 amendments.

Brown also predicted the Scottish Parliament would become an 'economic powerhouse' and change the face of Scotland, and sought to allay Unionist worries:

'The plans we put forward strengthen the United Kingdom. Scotland does not want to cut itself off from the United Kingdom. We will never retreat into narrow-minded 19th century nationalism. We are leading the way in constitutional reform for a new century.'

Anne Begg, the newly-elected MP for Aberdeen South, shrewdly predicted that the Tories, of all people, might do best out of devolution. It was 'a supreme irony' that they might be saved from political oblivion in Scotland by the proportional voting system for the new Parliament. Donald Dewar saw it as an unhappy side-effect: 'This sort of charitable work by the Labour Party is, of course admirable, but perhaps we could go about it quietly.'

The Campaign

By coincidence, the date set for the referendum was the 700th anniversary of the Battle of Stirling Bridge at which the Scots, led by William Wallace, defeated the English. Despite its historical symbolism, 11 September 1997 was chosen because of the timetable required to produce a White Paper and organise the referendum. Remarkably, the backdrop of history might influence the forthcoming Independence referendum which is likely to be held in 2014, the 700th Anniversary of the Battle of Bannockburn!

On 19 August 1997, despite the animosity of the general election four months previously, a truce was declared by Labour, the SNP and Liberal Democrats as they united to campaign for a Scottish Parliament. The three Scottish party leaders declared their determination to raise the debate from what, the political editor of the *Daily Record*, described as 'the grime' of Scottish politics. He was not only referring to the bitterly-fought (certainly in Scotland) election, but also to the scandal caused by the suicide of the popular Paisley South Labour MP Gordon McMaster.

Donald Dewar, conveniently forgetting the previous devolution referendum, described it as 'an opportunity the like of which we have never seen', while Alex Salmond contributed his sound-bite to the oratory of optimism: 'It's a platform of hope and a platform of opportunity for Scotland.'

Menzies Campbell, perhaps more in hope than expectation, added a warning and a prophecy. He declared that a new kind of politics was on the way: 'We must decide to put away the bad habits of Westminster.' Pointing out that a Scots Parliament elected by proportional representation would not be dominated by any one party, he foreshadowed the eventual Labour–Lib-Dem coalition by saying: 'Where parties agree, they must have the courage to say so.'

The SNP's participation had been cleared by their 300-strong national council at a special meeting on 4 August, despite stiff opposition from the party's fundamentalist 'Independence or nothing' wing. In fact, the motion for the SNP to join in the Scotland Forward campaign, while running their own 'distinctive' campaign, was carried overwhelmingly and three members of the SNP leadership – Alex Neil, George Reid and Kay Ullrich – were authorised to join the executive of the 'Yes, Yes' campaign.

The Independence-or-nothing diehards' attempt to persuade the party not to cooperate in the referendum was defeated by 300 votes to six. Opposition was led by the former SNP leader Gordon Wilson, who angrily denounced his colleagues 'trading principles for power' and vowed: 'I will not be voting 'Yes, Yes'. I will be writing in 'Yes to Independence'.'

The pro-devolution Nationalists were welcomed aboard by the Scotland Forward group and board member Bill Speirs of the Scottish Trades Union Congress (STUC) hailed it as 'the essential popular coalition which will help drive us towards an overwhelming "Yes! Yes!" vote.'

SNP leader Alex Salmond explained: 'Devolution is a step to Independence. It's a step in the right direction.' In view of what has subsequently happened, it is ironic that he refused to contemplate the prospect of himself as First Minister in a devolved parliament: 'There are larger issues at stake than the future of Alex Salmond.'

Former deputy leader and veteran home rule campaigner Jim Sillars accused Salmond of having no strategy for full Independence and called for Scots to abstain. He said: 'The referendum must be a fraud since the SNP say it is a stepping-stone to Independence and Donald Dewar says it will strengthen the Union. Abstention is the best form of contempt.'

Strangely, the same argument came from the Tories, who were left as the only anti-devolution party, repeating their warning that the SNP saw devolution as the 'fastest way to destroy the Union'. Ancram went even further and caused great offence by claiming that devolution was as big a threat to Britain as Hitler.

Lord Fraser of Carmylie, the former Lord Advocate who was director of 'Think Twice', said: 'Donald Dewar claims a Scottish parliament will save the United Kingdom. Alex Salmond believes it will destroy it. Both cannot be right.'

This provided ammunition for George Robertson, who described the Tory Party as 'kissing cousins of the Separatists, adding paraffin to the flames of Separatism by their arrogant defiance of the sensible middle way, the way most Scottish people choose.'

A group led by Edinburgh councillor Brian Meek and Arthur Bell, head of the Scottish Tory Reform Group, called for a breakaway Scottish Conservative Party 'with its own leaders and own distinctive voice, and its own funding.' At the first Scottish Tory conference after their general election wipe-out, leader William Hague appealed for an end to internal faction fighting, saying: 'Scotland needs its Conservatives more than ever'.

The confusion in the Conservative camp, which effectively stifled their opposition to devolution, became obvious 10 days before the referendum, when Hague reversed his previous position by declaring that a future Tory government might hold a referendum to scrap a Scottish Parliament if it did not work out. Scottish chairman Raymond Robertson justified Hague's U-turn by saying: 'Anything that is created with the will of the Scottish people can be un-created with the will of the Scottish people.'

Meanwhile, on 15 August, Donald Dewar launched the posting of 2.2 million leaflets to every Scottish home, titled 'Scotland's Parliament – Your Choice' and outlining how the parliament would work, with the slogan 'It's time to deliver'.

The government had to defend itself against the charge that public funds were being used for propaganda for a 'Yes, Yes' vote. The Tories said it was 'an appalling abuse of the taxpayers' money' and the anti-devolution Think Twice organisation said it should also have a free delivery across Scotland.

Throughout devolution, the position of Scottish business and industry leaders has been a sensitive issue. In the referendum campaign, the Scottish Office was accused of forcing the suppression of a CBI Scotland document that appeared to oppose the principle of devolution.

It was confirmed that Dewar had approached senior business figures expressing his surprise that such a view should be attributed to the organisation. CBI Scotland stated that it was not opposed in principle.

In particular, Sir Bruce Pattullo, governor of the Bank of Scotland, was ferociously attacked for warning that the tax-varying powers of the Scottish Assembly could increase income tax by £6 a week. John Prescott, the Deputy Prime Minister, told him to 'go back to counting banknotes and leave politics to those who know better.'

On 31 August 1997, the referendum was brought to a sudden and complete halt by the death of Princess Diana. The national mood of shock and the unprecedented outpouring of universal grief were such that to continue with campaigning was unthinkable. It was agreed that all parties should suspend activities as a mark of respect until after the funeral of the Princess of Wales, a week later.

It was suggested that the 11 September poll might be postponed, but this would have required the recall of parliament to change the date, which had been set down in statute. Instead, it was decided to concentrate the campaign in a 100-hour 'blitz' leading up to the vote, involving all the UK party leaders and a £132,000 TV and radio campaign. Even in that emotional atmosphere, there were those who calculated the political effect; Tam Dalyell complained there would be no time left for real debate, while a Think Twice campaigner hazarded a guess that they might benefit from a surge in Unionist feelings following the funeral.

The Prime Minister commented: 'This has been an extraordinary outpouring of national and personal grief and it will continue. But I think people still understand that life has to go on and decisions have to be taken – and this is a very important decision for the future of Scotland.'

The 'Yes, Yes' campaign resumed with a high-profile boost from Sean Connery, who joined cross-party leaders for the relaunch. With Chancellor Gordon Brown, he sailed across the Firth of Forth for a highly symbolic photo-call with the Saltire flapping in the stiff breeze from the stern of the *Maid of the Forth*. In fact, despite Connery's support for the SNP, the two men got on so well that Brown had hopes of securing the film star's long-term cooperation.

Later, at a rally in the old Royal High School on Calton Hill in Edinburgh – once suggested as the home of the new Parliament – Connery reverted to basic nationalism by quoting the 1320 Declaration of Arbroath: 'It is not for glory, it is not for riches, but it is for liberty alone that we fight.'

On polling day, the *Daily Record* carried a picture of young children on its front cover and urged its readers: 'Vote for tomorrow's Scots.' More prosaically, it also warned: 'We don't want to wake up tomorrow with a national hangover and a sense of shame.'

That scenario was triumphantly avoided by a four to one majority, far better than the government and the 'Yes, Yes' campaigners had hoped for. 74 per cent of voters backed the parliament and support for tax-varying powers outstripped all expectations at 63 per cent.

Voters in all 32 council areas backed devolution and 30 supported tax powers, with only Orkney and Dumfries and Galloway voting against. In contrast, the 1979 majority for the Scottish Parliament had been a narrow 52 per cent to 48 per cent.

It was clear that, despite the curtailed campaign, most of Scotland had made its mind up months before, and in the last few days of campaigning had swung from 'Yes, No' on the two questions to 'Yes, Yes'.

Former Prime Minister Margaret Thatcher, on a lucrative speechmaking engagement at a convention of US travel agents in Glasgow, sensed what was happening but stubbornly insisted: 'A majority vote will not make right something that is fundamentally wrong. It will not turn something that is true into that which is not true.'

By contrast, Wales voted for a 60-member assembly in Cardiff by the narrowest of margins. Ministers were shaken by the 50.3 per cent support and a relieved Prime Minister, while vowing to press ahead, promised to learn lessons from the dramatic split in Welsh opinion. He said there would be a major drive to win over the critics but, as subsequent events have shown, the Welsh Assembly has proved even less secure than the Scottish Parliament.

Before the final figures were in, the 'No, No' coordinator Brian Monteith (later to become MSP in the Parliament he so bitterly opposed) sent out for a case of champagne, in reality to drown his compatriots' sorrows. Donald Findlay QC, chairman of the Think Twice campaign, took a more realistic view than many disgruntled Tories: 'We have been thumped in a General Election and thumped in referendum. I think it does behove us to learn.'

On the morning the result was declared, Prime Minister Tony Blair flew back to Edinburgh, where he was mobbed by an enthusiastic crowd in Parliament Square. 'Well done!' he told them. 'This is a good day for Scotland and a good day for the United Kingdom.'

However, Alex Salmond spelled out the strategy that the SNP have followed ever since, and have amplified now they are in power at Holyrood: 'Making a success of running some of our affairs is the best grounding for people wanting to run all our affairs.'

There were other signs of the mood of jubilant expectation which swept Scotland. The vigil cabin opposite the Scottish Office building in Regent Road, Edinburgh, which for five years had been the symbol of the fight for the Scottish Parliament, was loaded onto a truck and driven away. It had been set up in protest after the Tories' fourth general election win in 1992 and a flame had burned continuously for 1,980 days until the 'Yes, Yes' vote.

Even as far north as the devo-sceptic Orkneys there was joy. Farmer Eion Scott in the remote community of Firth exulted: 'I have had the Saltire in my cupboard for years but I'll fly it from my house today. No one else will see it but I want my cattle to know how I feel!'

Thirteen years later, the jubilation has faded and many of the expectations may not have been realised – but Scotland has its parliament and would not be without it. The narrative of 1997, the preparation of the White Paper, the referendum campaign and the 'yes, yes' outcome represented a turning point in the evolution of Scottish and UK politics. Looking back over this period there seems little doubt that party positions and perspectives on devolution have not changed to any extent and that the tensions and concerns of September 1997 still exist. What has changed, is the political dynamic and the fact that in such a short space of political time the Parliament has become such an important and enduring feature of our politics and our democracy. Westminster though has not changed to any great extent and viewed through the prism of sovereignty, exceptionalism and centralism it is unlikely to do so.

The impact of 1997 has been felt in the devolved areas of Northern Ireland, Wales and Scotland but the attitude and prevailing mood at Westminster remains grudging, unsympathetic and some-times threatening. There is no real sense that Westminster is in learning mode. It seems unable to see constitutional change as strengthening the Union, not weakening it, and modernising the Union, not dismantling it. Unless the Union can change and adapt and show some confidence in the constituent parts of the Union, then the path to Independence could be made easier. Without that, the paradox is that the impetus for the break-up of the Union may be created at the very heart of Unionism itself. The mere reality of the Union in 2012 is not of itself a justification for its continuing existence; being fit for purpose requires vigilance, scrutiny and ultimately the ability to reform.

CHAPTER 4

Scotland's Political Parties: The Lessons

IN THE NEW EMERGING political order in Scotland there is now a fault-line, not yet seismic, but certainly perceptible, running through the party system. Within the electorate, constitutional issues such as Unionism and nationalism, sovereignty and devolution, identity and nationality, diversity and difference, Separatism and federalism, Independence and integration, have become more important. The parties – with the exception of the Nationalists, whose position is unequivocal – have fumbled their response to this mood of uncertainty about national identity.

Devolution has changed the political landscape and created new, previously unthinkable, alliances. Encrusted political traditions have been discarded along with the attitudes and ideas that underpin the Unionist model.

What do we make of all of this? Is a new political order emerging or is this just a temporary aberration in our political behaviour? This was the question in 2007. Today, 2012, there is more than a hint that political business-as-usual will not return and the face of Scottish politics is forever changed. The split personality of Scottish politics will ensure that Westminster and Holyrood continue to diverge, the mind-set of the voters will be more and more influenced by nationality and identity issues, traditional party allegiances and affiliations will break down and the electors' growing disenchantment and disillusionment with politics – especially at Westminster – will continue. There was also the hope, post 1999, that PR would help bring a new politics to Holyrood. The result of the 2011 election, where the SNP defied the laws of electoral arithmetic, may have put paid to that aspiration. Overall majorities do not help the cause of bi-partisanship, consensus or the breaking down of tribalism.

Greater openness to coalition politics did create opportunities for all parties to participate in government and influence the legislative programme. Indeed, in 2007 a minority Government attempted to reach out and engage other parties. This was also illustrated in Wales, where the result of the assembly elections in 2007 forced the parties to break new ground.

Labour and Plaid Cymru created a historic coalition, despite their mutual bitterness and enmity, which had been a dominant feature of Welsh politics for generations. But with the SNP now in a majority government, this type of opportunity will not arise again in Scotland until at least 2016.

Post-2007 developments in Northern Ireland have shown clearly and in a much more dramatic way how the new political order rips up the traditional rules of the game and delivers the unimaginable – Ian Paisley and Martin McGuinness, the Democratic Unionist Party and Sinn Fein, Right and Left, Unionist and Nationalist, Protestant and Catholic, working together.

This extraordinary cooperation was born out of decades of destruction, bloodshed and conflict. It is the product of new political structures in Ireland, which just 80 years earlier witnessed the Home Rule Bill for Ireland and Independence from the Union. No one can know how long this will last or whether this power-sharing executive will fall apart, but after five years, despite tensions, the immediate achievements are real.

The Scottish Nationalists, with an overall majority in the 2011 Scottish Parliament, have provided another remarkable first in devolved politics.

Since 1999 the Parliament has witnessed the range of parliamentary possibilities, coalition government, minority government and now majority government. The idea of minority government had been a live issue for Labour in the first eight years of devolution, but it was felt that it would not be workable or viable so early in the life of the new parliament. Inexperience, lack of maturity and tribal enmities would lead to instability and uncertainty when issues were being debated. After the upheaval of devolution and the introduction of a new voting system, the last thing anyone wanted was controversial government. The willingness of the Liberal Democrats to join in coalition meant the question of minority government was never fully explored or taken further as a practical proposition.

At least in the early days of the 2007 Parliament, the SNP showed that minority government could work and the difficulties Labour considered might have been overstated. This raises the question of whether Labour ever felt confident enough to try and run Scotland on its own.

The arrival of an SNP majority Government in 2011 has changed all of this. Following the Holyrood elections in 2016 there is scope for a return to other forms of Government, but this will be dependent on what happens in the 2014 referendum, as well as the outcome of the General Election in 2015. There are some tough and testing times ahead for all of the Scottish parties. We are, as a consequence, on the edge of an unprecedented period of change which is likely to throw up some remarkable outcomes for both Scotland and the Union. It is fascinating to recall that from 1999 to 2011 the idea of a new politics was just beginning to take shape with a variety of political permutations possible in the Parliament. The new realities of SNP majority power see us take a step back, once again visiting the tribalism and partisanship of Westminster.

What no one at Westminster in 1999 envisaged was the total domination of the constitutional debate by the SNP and the success of a three-pronged strategy that would lead them to their current position: the delivery of a competent and populist policy agenda; a strident but sophisticated embrace of Independence; and the use of every election and political opportunity to drive home their message and ideas. They have carried their cause and determination into every aspect of Scottish life in a manner which is professional and focused. Political parties at Westminster after 1997 and Scottish parties after 2003 seriously underestimated the capacity and potential of the SNP to learn on the job and to shape a different kind of Scotland. The spirit of the new politics, before the SNP started to rewrite the narrative in 2011, should still be part of our thinking. Westminster-style politics is discredited and people are seriously concerned about how the institution operates. Regardless of the political structures at Holyrood or the form of Government, there has to be an emphasis on doing things better and civilising our ways of working and thinking.

After 13 years, the Holyrood Parliament is becoming older and wiser, and there is a maturity which did not exist in 1999. This allows the real prospect of a new culture and will generate a new understanding of the true potential of devolved government. It will also provide a more credible base for arguing for further changes and more powers. The experiences of Wales and Northern Ireland only serve to illustrate the real potential of breaking the Westminster mould.

All of this challenges Westminster and the idea of Union.

Yet, if the Union is being recast, it is *despite* the efforts of Westminster and the main political parties, who continue to marginalise the importance of devolution, denying its challenges and ignoring the ground-breaking changes to policies and ways of working. Political lessons are there to be learned but the current attitude at Westminster is to make as few concessions as possible and indeed, especially in relation to Scotland, to be often scathing and dismissive. That was the prevailing view under a Labour Government until 2010.

During the May 2007 Scottish Parliament election campaign, as indicated by the Prime Minister, there was a firm rejection of any further powers being devolved; nor did there appear to be any appetite for further progress in relation to England. Short-sightedness has been the hall mark of all the UK parties and Governments over the devolved years. Only recently has the conservative Prime Minister woken up to the fact that, despite 13 years of practical achievement and the emergence of this new political order, devolution was not on the Westminster agenda. It is now. As a new response to the success of the SNP, David Cameron has offered the prospect of new powers for the Scottish Parliament sometime in the future but, of course, only if Scots reject Independence first.

The Scottish Nationalists

The political fortunes of nationalism have changed spectacularly since the handful of Independence campaigners in the early part of the 20th century and the formation of the SNP in 1934 by a mixture of diehard activists, disaffected ILP members, journalists and intellectuals. In hard political terms, the SNP's fortunes ebbed and flowed amid the development of British politics in the second half of the 20th century. A declining Scottish economy, disenchantment with the established UK parties and North Sea oil proved the springboard the Nationalists needed and in the 1970s they doubled their vote, winning 11 seats and compelling Labour to embrace devolution and hold the ill-fated home rule referendum in March 1979.

The Nationalists' high point at Westminster was in the two elections of 1974, when they increased the number of SNP MPs, taking first seven and then 11 seats. When an unpopular Conservative government lost the election in 1974, it was replaced by a Labour government, which quickly ran into major problems. After the Scottish devolution referendum debacle, it was removed from office – helped by a decisive intervention by the SNP on the vote of no-confidence (famously, the SNP 'turkeys voting for Christmas') which led to the Thatcher government in 1979.

Devolution – and, it could be said, the present SNP government in Scotland – was in part due to the long-term legacy of the 18-year Thatcher and Major era. Deeply unpopular Tory policies, anti-Scottish sentiment and insensitivity, the divergence of political cultures and mass unemployment, combined with hard-line inflexible Unionism, began to create doubts in the minds of many Scots about the role of Westminster. Thatcher accelerated the Tory slide in Scotland and helped shape the idea of Scotland being insulated from Tory excesses. This, in turn, helped build more enthusiastic support for devolution, which was eventually delivered by the Blair government in 1999.

While support for the SNP fluctuated throughout the '70s, '80s and '90s, a significant vote for Independence remained visible in elections and opinion polls.

From the party of sentiment to the party of protest, the SNP grew and graduated to a party of power for the first time in its history, albeit running Scotland first as a minority government and now a majority government. Even factoring in the eventual unpopularity of the Blair-led Labour government, the Iraq war, proportional representation and the shambles surrounding spoiled papers in the 2007 Scottish election, leading to nearly five per cent of the electorate being disenfranchised, the SNP victory still remains a remarkable achievement.

Back in 2007, after the SNP victory, *Scotland: The Road Divides* posed a number of important questions. Is this a sign of things to come or a one-off success for the SNP? Is it more a commentary on the new Scottish politics than a statement about the performance of the SNP? Does it provide more of an insight into the Westminster–Holyrood dilemma facing the Labour Party than a reflection of the popularity of the Nationalists? Does it illustrate the growing importance of nationalism or reflect the emerging problems of the Union? Does it suggest a new political order is evolving or is it the product of our troubled democracy, in which nearly half of the electorate do not vote? Is the issue of Scottishness now a potent one in Scottish politics or is the electorate changing in terms of party loyalties, interest and relevance to their lives? There is no doubt that, five years on, the answer to these questions is overwhelmingly in favour of the SNP and the impact they have made in Scotland, the success of which is confirmed by the seismic victory in 2011 and the fact that they are now running the country. The difficulties of Labour are also evident as are the deepening problems of the Conservatives and the Lib-Dems. There is a mood of change and Scots are increasingly turning to a Party that offers identity and nationality politics as well as populism and leadership. In the absence of an effective opposition and the reluctance of the Unionist parties to engage in any meaningful debate about the future governance of Scotland, the drift to the SNP is likely to accelerate rather than diminish

What is of particular significance is the fact that an electorate that – if opinion polls are to believed – is overwhelmingly Unionist has a Parliament now being run by a majority SNP government committed to Independence. Put in simple terms, what is this all about and why has it happened?

The SNP does not continuously have to look over its shoulder to Westminster and this makes life as the Scottish government much easier. The First Minister Alex Salmond has brought stature (and political guile) to the office, creating a new sense of urgency and seriousness about politics and the defence of Scottish interests (even when they are not seriously threatened). Manufactured or not, it is effective and there is now a sense that devolution has a new momentum, with a glimpse of a future in which Scotland can have an expanded role in the Union, in Europe and internationally.

In the short term, the Unionist majority in the 2007 Scottish Parliament ensured that an Independence referendum, which was a key part of the SNP manifesto, would not be implemented. This was in a curious way helpful to the SNP. Only popular measures were put forward and the SNP was forced to avoid proposals which might have been rejected or defeated in parliament by the combined opposition. Paradoxically, this was a 'win-win' situation for the SNP, with the bonus of fewer pieces of legislation coming out of Holyrood. What was surprising was the fact in the four years of this minority government a vote of confidence, which could have resulted in the defeat of the SNP and an early election, was never moved. The failure of the Unionist parties to do this reflected their weak electoral position, their lack of confidence and the growing credibility of the SNP Government in the country. History may show that allowing this new minority Government to find their political feet and build their own strength and confidence as a party, opened the door to a majority Government in 2011 and who knows what might happen in the future? To be fair to the Unionist parties, being in opposition is tough and the obvious often cannot be undertaken. The longer the minority government survived, however, the more time it had to show competence in government, change the nature of Scottish government and politics and position the country for more radical change. The party in government can take advantage of every event, every issue, every contingency and present them as cases of 'defending the nation and Scottish interests'. The SNP have proved to be masters of playing the Scottish card.

'Standing up for Scotland' is an attractive line to sell to the electorate. In contrast, Labour's dilemma, as the party seeking to regain power, has been their instinctive unwillingness to play the Scottish card and as a consequence be seen as disconnected from the Saltire agenda. The SNP government has progressively moved the political ground from under the feet of the opposition. The SNP lost little sleep over its inability to put an Independence referendum to the Scottish Parliament in 2007, since it was making political progress in the medium term and this was more important than losing a referendum vote in the short term.

Currently, there is discipline and unity within both the party and the parliamentary group at Holyrood, but the SNP is not without its internal divisions. Differences over ideology, structures, direction and the tactics to be deployed in the pursuit of Independence are live issues which are unlikely to go away since they reflect the splits which have been with the SNP from its earliest days.

The fundamentalists, now checked because of the responsibilities of government remain uncomfortable with devolution as a concept and are suspicious of the step-by-step process towards Independence. This group – with its *Braveheart* mentality, single-minded sense of purpose in its obsession with Independence, and an intense dislike of England and the English – have a strong but dwindling core support within the party. Its demand for Independence is an all-consuming passion which it sees as a matter of destiny, but is divorced from the new politics and the Scotland that most people want to see.

The more pragmatic wing of the SNP is aware of the real-world challenges that Independence would bring and have some understandable doubts about Scotland's role in the 21st century world. Members of this group struggle to come to terms with a new world order that is increasingly international and interdependent. European integration and globalisation do not recognise geography or national boundaries and transcend nation-states, ancient realms and sub-national governments. The explosion of communications, information technology and travel opportunities is shrinking the world and the global agenda of shared interests throws into sharp focus the anachronism of separation and Independence. The global banking, financial and economic crises have stretched the credibility of some of the SNP claims in relation to compa-rator countries such as Iceland and Ireland whose economies have been so badly hit. The nature of these global events has also served to under-line the interdependency of the global economy and raise questions of what Independence means in the 21st century. The SNP has also been reluctant to make comparisons with the Nordic countries whose standard of living, high-quality services, productive economies and a much more civilized and enlightened view of social issues, are more appropriate countries to use as role models for an independent, devo-plus or 'devo-max' country.

We should not forget that the SNP remains a complex and diverse political grouping which manages to represent views across the ideolog-ical and political spectrum. This is mirrored in the profile of those who vote for the party, including extremes of Left and Right, and it has managed to be chameleon-like in what it offers different parts of the country at elections. More recently, the party has focused on its populism, not necessarily to be confused with popularity. Both a strength and a weakness, appealing to a extremely wide base of potential support is hard work and requires an exceptionally skilful juggling act. It also exposes the SNP in a country like Scotland to charges that it is not Left enough and ignores issues like inequality, material deprivation and social mobility and all the redistributive policies that entails. But, so far, their Scottishness, competent management, financial credibility, and an ability to please most of the people all of the time, serves them well.

However, the SNP's essential characteristic is its Scottishness and its 'Scotland first' approach. What was previously seen as narrow nation-alism (once dismissed by Donald Dewar, when he was Shadow Scottish Secretary, as 'the politics of Brigadoon') has become important for an increasing number of Scots.

At a time when national identities are more evident, the Union is more defensive, Europe is increasingly encroaching, and people have higher expectations and a changing perspective of their country and where it should be going, the SNP rejects some of the old-fashioned arguments used by political parties. Politicians who overstate the Unionist case, adopting scare tactics about separation, run the danger of appearing to diminish pride in Scotland.

All of this makes the SNP a much more difficult target for the other parties. Much of the Scottishness debate is about 'Scotland as a state of mind'. The mood and morale of Scotland are important in this respect, although these are difficult to assess at any point in time. The more the SNP government creates the belief that the people of Scotland have nothing to fear from nationalism, and the extent to which this normalises its brand of politics, the greater the difficulties the other parties will face in mounting credible alternatives and convincing the electorate that Unionism is the only answer.

This also produces a challenge for Westminster, where politicians of all parties have to recognise that there is a fine dividing line between defending the Union and patronising the Scottish electorate. They will have to find a new narrative and new language when discussing devolution and they must frame ideas in a modern context. There is increasing sensitivity to the type of unthinkingly critical comments which all-too-easily alienate Scottish people; the case for the Union can be made, but in less apocalyptic terms. In this regard, there is a growing divide between Scottish Labour and Westminster Labour.

There is also the question of whether we have one Union or many – social, economic, political and constitutional unions, the European Union and the global union. This question of Union is complicated and we do the electorate no favours by ignoring this self-evident truth: Scotland cannot isolate itself from worldwide trends and developments, and the next two years may be a watershed for reinforcing this type of thinking.

The political geography of Scotland remains an important factor. In the 2007 Holyrood elections, as discussed earlier, the SNP won seats north and south of the central belt in both the constituency and list systems and encroached on Labour heartlands. The onward advance of the SNP continued in 2011 when labour strongholds were simply swept away in this nationalist tsunami. Since 2003 the electoral map has been completely transformed. The introduction of PR to local government in

2007 left Labour with control of only two of the 32 councils including Glasgow. Doing significantly better in the local elections in 2012, with overall control of four councils, Labour held on to Glasgow and stopped the onward march of the SNP in the city. For the first time though, the SNP had the largest number of councillors, the largest number of MSPs in the parliament and the largest share of the popular vote in both the constituency and list sections of the parliamentary vote.

The 2007 elections expanded the political base of the SNP in seats, geography and votes so that the platforms for advocating nationalism and Independence have grown in number and will provide the party's enthusiastic membership more opportunities to push the cause. The 2011 elections vastly improved on this and reinforced the success of a strategy which combined a cause, a campaign and credible government. The SNP is now outspending the Labour party , and morale and mood within the party are in better shape than the opposition parties. As a campaigning party, it has a powerful but simple message and the electorate are in no doubt what the SNP stands for. The corollary is that the other parties, especially Labour, are forced to face doubts and uncertainties about their political identities and what their message is.

A number of important and popular measures were introduced between 2007 and 2011. More substance and stature were linked to the First Minister's role – not just because of Alex Salmond's dominance of his party but because of his ability to outshine the leaders of the other parties. The Scottish cabinet was slimmed down to a more manageable size. Removing the Lord Advocate from a potential clash of interests was a bold move and reinforced the Independence of the office, as well as removing the possibility of political interference in the execution of responsibilities. Clearly, this move was effected to avoid the embarrassments experienced in London, where the Attorney General had been involved in a number of high-profile and often controversial political cases.

The call for a louder and larger voice for devolution was pursued in the early days of the new government. This has caused a stir in Labour circles but these tactics should come as no surprise. Frustrated at not having the opportunity to move on the Independence referendum at that point, the SNP government embarked on a strategy which widened out the assault on the Union. It used every leverage possible to change the nature of Scottish politics and, at the same time, build the Independence case brick by brick. An integral part of this strategy sought to obtain popular support for measures that made sense and cannot be cataclysmically represented by the opposition as 'bringing about the end of civilisation as we know it'.

The early meetings with the leaders of the Northern Ireland Assembly and the contacts with parties forming a coalition in Wales dovetailed with this strategic thinking. Again, we saw practical measures of closer cooperation and a stronger voice for devolved government being cloaked in the higher politics of further constitutional change.

Europe was also put high on the political agenda. *Scotland: The Road Divides* asked,

> How long will the new government last or, more importantly, how long will the opposition let it last? The honeymoon period could be short. On the other hand, the parties forming the Unionist majority at Holyrood are divided and are showing little enthusiasm for either cooperation or opposition to the new government. They seem reluctant to engage but, however shell-shocked they are after the election, there is danger in them taking too long to lick their wounds before they start to present some serious but constructive opposition in the parliament.

Again, the opposition drifted for far too long and only the advent of the Calman Commission interrupted this period of enforced lethargy and breathed some new life into the constitutional question and the Unionist parties.

For nearly five years the SNP leader has been allowed to hold court and is under very little pressure. This was a legacy from the time the SNP were a minority Government. There was an understandable concern on the part of the opposition that, at such an early stage, the people of Scotland did not want the new government to be facing votes of 'no confidence', plunging the SNP administration and the parliament into disarray. There is no doubt that the early reaction of the public to the first 100 days of the 2007 Government was positive, with the general opinion being that the new government should be given a fair chance. This deference, plus the FM's performances at the dispatch box, linked to the opposition's failure to learn lessons from their crushing defeat, only added to a sense of the opposition being out of touch.

The problem for Labour and the other parties was how to strike a balance between giving effect to that public feeling and giving the SNP too long a period of tolerance, in which they could settle down and increase their popularity at the expense of the opposition. Appearing to defend Scottish interests, in a more robust and high-profile manner, on carefully selected topics, could prove a vote-winner for the SNP despite the electorate's rejection of the party's basic platform. This is undoubtedly what happened and it has become part of the wasted five years.

To mark the first 100 days of the new Scottish government in 2007, the SNP issued a progress report on 24 August claiming 'significant progress' in making Scotland a more successful country. It asserted there had been 'measurable progress' in delivering a smarter, greener, healthier, wealthier, fairer, safer and stronger Scotland and 'a solid platform of success for four years of government'.

While most of the 'achievements' listed were more speculative than real – with proposals, promises, future commitments and planned legislation outnumbering measurable attainments – it would be churlish not to acknowledge the Salmond administration's immediately favourable impact on the general mood in Scotland, which has continued to this day. Mainly due to the First Minister's unerring feel for populist politics, the SNP-in-government quickly gained the approval of the general public for its fresh approach to long-standing problems, wrong-footed its critics and the parliamentary opposition and even won over most of the usually virulently critical Scottish media.

The SNP administration has shown competence in running national affairs, made devolution work and proved itself effective and efficient on particular and popular issues. It has sought and won consensus on specific issues and displayed sensitivity to the public and a professionalism which put the Scotland Office in a poorer light. The unexpected ease with which the Nationalists, especially Alex Salmond, gave new status to the office of First Minister and made Scottish politics more exciting has resulted in success in both the opinion polls and actual polls culminating in the rout of the opposition in 2011. This was in sharp contrast to Labour's impressive result in the General Election result in 2010 with a remarkable 42% of the Scottish vote; these two contrasting results merely confirmed the continuing divergence of Scottish and British politics.

Scotland now has a split political personality. The absence of effective opposition for a variety of reasons, including the resignation of the Scottish Labour leader Jack McConnell, had helped to make the SNP's early successes in 2007 more visible. Writing then, the authors said, 'This should change as the other parties recover from the election and renew their thinking and energy, but the Unionist parties will have to be more comfortable with the constitutional question and not leave it to the SNP to drive the news agenda or change the debate.' This didn't happen. Five years on, Labour, in particular, is finding it difficult to gain any traction and remains very uncertain and uncomfortable with the constitutional question.

The SNP has already managed to move the Unionist parties into accepting the need for more powers for the parliament and there is now an unambiguous distinction between Scottish and UK politics, which could lead to the electorate in Scotland viewing elections in new and different ways. The strategic positioning of the SNP government should not be ignored; the Unionist parties in Scotland and Westminster have to be careful that they do not actually help promote the kind of change they most fear.

Reflecting back in 2007 we said,

Despite the striking appearance of a flurry of activity, combining commonsense politics with defending and promoting Scottish interests, these are still early days and the SNP will find governing the country takes more than political wiles and presentational skill. The 'phoney war' at Holyrood will not last for much longer and the opposition, especially Labour with new leadership, will revive, regroup and re-engage. The SNP administration will have to produce and attempt to see through a legislative programme; and a budget and financial statement will be needed. In addition, decisions will have to be taken on a number of important policy issues. As a Prime Minister famously said, it is 'events, dear boy, events' that can make or break a government. The new SNP government in Edinburgh will be no exception to this long-accepted political rule.

Very little of this happened and five years on many people are still wondering whatever happened to Labour and the expected revival of the opposition. A week is a long time in politics, five years is an eternity.

The Labour Party

Labour remains a powerful force for economic, social and political change in Scotland, but it is losing traction in the new terrain of Scottish devolution and seems to have lost any sense of direction as it moves further away from its original base and fails to realise the enormity of the constitutional future of the country.

Four big questions dominate the debate about the future of Labour. What does Scottish Labour stand for? What is its Big Idea, its vision for Scotland? How can it renew itself? And why can't Labour be comfortable with Scottishness?

Unlike the other opposition parties, Labour cannot afford to indulge in short-term political fixes. Instead, it needs to look for long-term solutions which are firmly rooted in serious constitutional ideas. There is a need to address the gaps between Labour thinking north and south of the border, between Labour and the other political parties in Scotland and, more surprisingly, within Labour itself.

Labour's record on home rule and devolution is a very mixed one, where feelings and commitment have ebbed and flowed for nearly a century. Even today, despite delivering a significant devolution package in 1999 and dominating the first eight years of the new parliament, Labour still feels uncomfortable and ill-at-ease with itself. There is still much soul-searching within the Labour party about where they are and whether the devolution journey should continue and, if so, in what direction. Labour's dilemma is how to reconcile traditional political views and values with the new Scottish perspective. This issue has deep roots and reflects the difficulties of a party trying to match its history, principles, values, traditional voting intentions and essentially centralist and Unionist structure shaped over a century with the new paradigm of devolution, Scottishness, new electoral systems, partnership thinking, small 'n' nationality not large 'N' Nationalism, difference and diversity, identity not Independence and a more volatile electorate. These are big issues which require new thinking, bold leadership and vision. Labour has to be a progressive centre-left party that embraces justice, fairness and the common good. It doesn't have the luxury of the SNP whose populist platform can appeal to who-ever is listening. Labour must have a deeper moral and ethical base from which, certainly in Scotland, it can win popular support and become the party of Government. But a start has to be made soon. The wake-up calls have become deafening and many Scots are desperate for an alternative to the SNP which combines a passionate embrace of Scottish identity, a clear vision of a fairer society, a new role for Scotland within a transformed Union and a commitment to rebuild our politics and democracy and tackle inequality.

The Labour Party has also to rationalise and come to terms with all of this as Scotland becomes part of not just one Union, but many, and a different world situation impacts on Scotland's view of itself and helps to reshape Scots' perceptions of what the country's role should be. Among the issues they have to address are how the devolution settlement has impacted on Scotland and to what extent it has shifted the views of Scots about their place in the Union.

Labour needs to re-examine its modus operandi since 1997, its struggle with Scottishness and whether the implications of 'one country, many systems' has been understood by the UK Labour party.

In particular, the results of the 2007 and 2011 Scottish elections should be scrutinised with a view to seeking explanations, not excuses. It would be a pity if the 'it could have been worse' attitude prevailed over the learning of deeper and more significant lessons. Labour still has an overwhelming sense of entitlement which makes little sense in a world of rapidly changing affiliations and allegiances. The Scottish electorate have moved on in a variety of complex ways and reflect the new drivers of change in Scottish politics. The fact that only half the electorate wants to vote is a depressing reminder that our democracy is in transition, with dramatic shifts in party affiliation and loyalties. The deepening cynicism about politicians and the political process, a largely hostile media, changing views about Scottish identity and the dominance of global environmental issues and single issues, particularly in the minds of young people, are not solely questions for Labour – but the party has to evolve its own answers to them.

Rather than simply reacting to the situation created by the SNP's electoral success and responding to an SNP-led agenda, Labour must create a new debate which makes sense to modern Scotland and, in the process, provides real choices for Scots. Labour must once again be a party with a cause, be a campaigning party, be self confident and have something positive and relevant to say to the electors: a renewed sense of purpose is needed which doesn't have the SNP as its obsession!

Despite delivering the new constitutional settlement for Scotland, there are still divisions within the Labour Party about devolution in action. Possibly because of an intense hatred of the SNP, there has been over-concentration on snuffing out Separatism and not enough emphasis on more positive policies. There has been a failure to develop a post-devolution strategy and a deeper understanding of the true meaning and potential of devolved government. A strange lack of confidence has resulted in a deteriorating central party apparatus in Scotland, with the focus shifting to the Holyrood Parliament, and a failure to bring MSPs and MPs together in a coherent way to hammer out a working message about devolution.

Labour is not alone in being slow to develop new thinking and intellectually rigorous ideas about the future of Scotland, but probably the key feature of the first 13 years of devolution has been Labour's failure to accept a different political identity and a new political culture. This would never have been easy with the pressure from London to conform, remain wary about the enduring fears of the threats to the Union and do nothing to rock the boat. Of necessity this has constrained the debate and allowed Labour, often unfairly, to be branded a London-based party and not entirely sympathetic to Scotland.

Also unhelpful has been the constant drip-drip of negative briefing from Labour MPs at Westminster, undermining the Scottish Parliament and putting a powerful brake on MSPs and party members who want to think aloud and put forward alternative or dissenting views on devolution and related issues. This has been neither healthy nor conducive to the possibility of a confident and ambitious Scottish party taking control of its future in the brave new world of devolved government. There is no reason why Labour should stop thinking. No reason why Labour should stifle debate. No reason why Holyrood MSPs should be silent on the big issues. No reason for Labour to play second fiddle to the SNP on everything Scottish. But that is the reality of Scottish politics in 2012.

This raises the question of a Scottish Labour Party with far more autonomy and political freedom, remaining loyal to UK Labour but recognising the new realities and the need to be more Scottish, and having the ability to develop new political and constitutional futures for Scotland without having to defer to Westminster influence. Though little progress was made on any of these issues post-2007, some limited progress has been made after the 2011 election. But there is much more work to be done. A great deal of stability has been brought by the new Leader, and a review of Scottish Labour has been undertaken. In addition, a number of speeches have been made by prominent MPs urging a different mind-set in the party as well as suggesting a return to some of the core values. This initial enthusiasm seems to have disappeared. Despite some progress being made, there is a lack of urgency and a feeling that Labour does not really accept how far they have declined in Scotland relative to the rise of the SNP. More importantly, the fear and hesitancy of this position is sapping energy and leaving the party still looking tired and slightly lost in a political world they should be dominating. The party needs to renew itself north of the border, reconnect with the voters and build modern structures and ideas to make members more confident in taking on the SNP. This would also mean arguing and differing with London where necessary, something the Welsh Labour party has managed, and being able in the Scottish Parliament to pursue innovative and distinctively Scottish policies without undue interference from UK Labour or Westminster.

Following the demoralising losses in the May 2007 election, Wendy Alexander, the new Scottish Labour leader, seemed prepared to set just such an agenda. In an interview in *The Times* Scottish edition on 1 September 2007, she indicated a difference of opinion with Gordon Brown, the Prime Minister, on the question of increased financial powers for Holyrood.

This was significant for two reasons: Wendy Alexander, whose brother Douglas was a UK cabinet minister and the Prime Minister's election campaign coordinator, had always been a staunch Brown supporter; and during the May 2007 Scottish election, Brown went on record as saying that the financial powers were already adequate and there was no need to rewrite the Scotland Act. Ms Alexander told *The Times:*

> I have an open mind. It is ten years since the Scotland Act. It was Donald Dewar who said that this was not the last word on the devolution settlement.
>
> We have to be alert to criticism from within Scotland about whether Scottish politicians here are sufficiently accountable.

She also admonished people in England to stop complaining that they would be financially better off if Scotland left the Union and insisted that, contrary to the widespread impression in England, Scotland did not get preferential treatment from the UK Treasury:

> It does not come down to numbers. Every part of the UK outside London is a net beneficiary from the Exchequer and Scotland does not get a uniquely good deal.
>
> That argument, that England would be better off without Scotland, would lead you to declare UDI for London and cast off Newcastle and other parts of England outside London and would lead to California seceding from the rest of the United States.

On English discontent over Scotland's divergent policies on free personal care for the elderly, ending tuition fees and replacing loans with grants for Scottish students, and proposed free prescriptions for the chronically ill, she believed people in England should put aside these differences between the two countries and look to the bigger picture of two countries 'sharing risk, revenue and resources'.

She also pointed out that the argument over more powers cut both ways and said there could also be a case for power over policy areas such as security and climate change to lie entirely with Westminster since these were clearly 'one-island issues' which affected the whole of the UK.

Taking a wider view, she added: 'The bigger issue is what signal it would send to the rest of the world if we [the English and the Scots] said we could not live together.'

The interview produced a predictable reaction from 'Little Englander' readers, one of whom posted the all-too-typical comment, 'The sooner England is free of Scotland and all those Scottish people parachuted in to English constituencies the better. The Scottish Raj is like being ruled by Pol Pot.' This was a remarkably prescient interview in the context of 2007.

At the same time opinion polls were highlighting what has become the central paradox of Scottish politics. Opinion polls have consistently under-scored a meaningful message for the Unionist parties. A poll in the *Scotsman* newspaper revealed that support for the SNP had risen to 48 per cent – 15 per cent more than it achieved at the Holyrood elections three months before – but a Scotland-wide poll also showed support for Independence had fallen from 51 per cent in January to 31 per cent in August. There are completely different trends on two related issues involving the same party.

This is an important finding for the other Unionist parties, suggesting they should be less concerned about Independence and more concerned about a Nationalist party running the country in a very different but apparently popular way. It should be acknowledged that, in Europe, nationalist governments and nationalist coalitions are elected and run the administrations competently, but their populations are not inclined to further embrace separation or Independence. By showing themselves to be happy with the SNP but not comfortable with the idea of separating from the UK, Scots may be showing that they can make devolution work effectively in Scotland's interest, after all. This central weakness of the SNP has never been fully exploited by Labour.

For Labour, being comfortable with the constitutional question presents some difficulties, reviving as it does memories of the divisions within the party at the time of the 1979 referendum and the continuing doubts in 1996. The home rule debate has rumbled on for nearly a century and there are still those in the Labour Party who believe that an embrace of nationalism and identity cuts across their centralist-socialist beliefs; and, as a consequence of this dated and traditional view, they have remained hostile or dismissive towards devolution and the importance of decentralisation and less dependency.

There is, of course, a major obstacle to this strategy: would the UK Labour Party allow this level of autonomy and political freedom in Scotland and still provide the same financial support, especially at elections? It would seem highly unlikely that this would be their response. It will require a new mindset, a radical shake-up in party membership, fund-raising and grassroots activity and a new enthusiasm to be instilled – even among members of the leadership – if this new dawn is ever to break.

The Labour Party's 1945 manifesto did say 'the victory of ideals must be organised'. Labour needs to regain that sense of purpose in Scotland at a time when its political base is shifting and party membership, constituency organisation, trade union support, councillor commitment to political ideals, MP, MEP and MSP relations and traditional working class Labour support are the subject of major change..

The Conservatives

The Tories have paid a high political price for the hard-line Unionism they have believed in and espoused over the last 30 years. For them, change has been difficult, if not impossible, and other parties could learn lessons from their experience.

The Conservative Party failed to see that Scotland was moving inexorably towards some form of self-government and simply did not understand the force of John Smith's dictum that this was 'unfinished business'.

The Tories' future success will depend on their willingness to embrace the idea of coalition and participate in cooperative government. The pain of electoral humiliation in Scotland in 1997 and the collapse of rank-and-file morale could be behind them if they had seized the new agenda and, slowly but surely, revived their political fortunes. For the many traditionalist Tories, this was a process too far. The Tory leadership contest in Scotland in 2012 has all but extinguished any hope of real change. Instead the new Leader, Ruth Davidson, has merely reinforced the mantra of old Unionism. But surely there is a place for a modern right-of-centre party in Scotland if it embraces small 'n' nationalism and distances itself from out-dated attitudes to the Union?

In this, the Tory leader in Scotland may have had more room to manoeuvre and more flexibility than the leaders of other Unionist parties. This will now not happen. David Cameron could have been persuaded to adopt a different strategy if he had been pushed by Annabel Goldie or Ruth Davidson. The Tory high command in London could have exercised less control, the Scottish Tories could have had the political freedom to line up with other parties in formal and informal coalitions or some form of loose 'understanding'. The election of Murdo Fraser could have made a difference.

They are possibly better placed than Labour to break the political mould, since Labour's hostility to and at times hatred of the SNP (feelings that are reciprocated) rule out any coalition with them. The SNP's 'Scotland first' strategy makes life more difficult for the other parties. The more feelings of identity and nationality evolve, the more pressure there will be on the other parties to respond. The Tories may have more to gain and less to lose in the short term if they substitute nationalism for Unionism. The question is: will they ever have the political courage to do? The history of the Conservative party in Scotland is a reminder to every party and political leader that the unthinkable can happen. From a position of dominance in Scottish politics in 1955 where they recorded the highest-ever share of the popular vote in Scotland, 51 per cent, they subsequently slumped to a point in 1997 where they lost every MP with a 17.5 per cent share of the vote. In 2012 the party has 1 MP, 1 MEP and 15 MSPs. There were massive wake up calls at every point of this long decline but no one listened or responded and their condition is now stable but critical. The Tories simply lost the plot, surrendered any sense of Scottishness to Westminster and had the miserable experience of the Thatcher Government contemptuously using Scotland as a test-bed for her alien right-wing ideas. Scots voters simply lost trust and confidence in the party.

The Conservatives have had a difficult decade since 1997, when they lost power to Labour and were humiliated in Scotland, losing the seat of every Conservative MP north of the border. In Westminster terms, Scotland became a 'Tory-free area' and, ironically, it was only PR and the Scottish Parliament they had opposed that gave them a political toe-hold in the new Parliament.

They face an uphill struggle in regaining the trust of the electorate and intense internal policy and personality battles resurfaced at Westminster. Old-fashioned right-wing voices re-emerged and demanded to be heard alongside the radical, modern but superficial reforms of the new Leader, David Cameron. Cameron has acknowledged the desperate electoral plight of the Scottish Tories and gave them more flexibility and autonomy north of the border to seize the opportunities of devolution. 'The Scottish Conservative and Unionist Party' now described itself as the 'Scottish Conservatives', but the truth is that after Cameron became Prime Minister there were warm words for Scotland but not much more.

During the 2007 Scottish election, Scottish Conservative leader Annabel Goldie used the 300th anniversary of the Treaty of Union in a bid to stake her party's claim as 'The Only True Unionists', explaining that the other Unionist parties were 'not doing their job – far from strengthening the Union, they are weakening it.'

She said of the former coalition government partners, Labour's Jack McConnell and Nicol Stephen of the Lib-Dems: 'Their actions, and those of their parties, have sewn the seeds of discontent. Their incompetence in running the country has made Scotland question devolution. Their failure has made Scotland doubt its future. And their lack of vision has led some Scots to wonder whether we should tread a different path.'

She predicted, rightly, inevitably, that support would transfer to the main opposition party, the SNP: 'Not because Scots are impressed with the SNP. It's because they're very unimpressed with the Lib–Lab Pact. It doesn't indicate Scots favouring Independence. It indicates Scots desperate for change. But there's one problem. A change in favour of the SNP carries the ultimate risk.'

She was right on both counts. The 2011 Holyrood elections provided another boost for the SNP as they swept all before them. And, looking ahead, they continue to strengthen their grip on Scottish politics and use every platform possible to build a case for Independence. Paradoxically, for a party which opposed electoral reform of the voting system, proportional representation has given the Tories a life-line in Scotland since their electoral wipe-out in 1997. First-past-the-post gives them one MP at Westminster, an electoral crumb for a party that had a majority of the Scottish seats in the immediate post-war period.

In sharp contrast, PR has provided them with 16 of the 129 seats at Holyrood in 2007(only three of them elected constituency MSPs and the rest on the regional lists) and 15 of the 129 seats in 2011. Given a more attractive policy platform linked to a more modern style of campaigning and achieving more trust from the Scottish electorate, a number of other factors could work in their favour. PR will continue to allow them to have a bigger share of the popular vote and in turn secure more MSPs. The larger the Tory block in the parliament, the greater the opportunity to determine who governs and in the most optimistic scenario – to possibly have a share in government. This is an important consideration if the current rise of the SNP is halted at some point in the future and the Parliament is again left with no overall majority, as was the case in the Holyrood elections in 1999, 2003 and 2007.

As a minimum, the devolved politics in Scotland creates new opportunities. The Tories in Scotland might have a chance of renewal and becoming a party of influence, however limited, again. There is no doubt, though, that the new leader has effectively killed off, at least in the short term, the prospect of the Tories being more distinctively Scottish and pro-devolution. Despite this, the Tories in Scotland have to deal with another challenge from within: their English colleagues' indulgence in anti-Scottish sentiment, coupled with the call for 'English votes for English laws'. Apart from being an unattractive new form of 'grudge and grievance' politics, it fuels resentment of Scotland's new thinking and of policies such as free personal care, scrapping the graduate endowment and the Barnett formula. This is a powerful reminder that Tories at Westminster remain suspicious of devolution and are disinclined to be sympathetic to future demands for more powers to be given to the Scottish Parliament.

This is the hard reality: despite David Cameron's comments on more powers, the passing of the new Scotland Act incorporating the Calman Commission proposals, and the drubbing they received in Scotland at Labour's hands in the 2010 General Election, the Tories are not for turning on the issue that will dominate Scottish politics over the next two years. There is, however, likely to be growing unrest within the Scottish party as the supporters of Murdo Fraser regroup and possibly plot a different path.

Faced with the state of his party north of the border and the self-destruct button the Conservatives have been pressing for nearly two decades and despite rhetoric in response to the Independence question, David Cameron has to decide whether he genuinely wants Scotland to remain within the Union and, if so, on what terms, as the status quo is no longer an option. Or, as some of his party at Westminster are now beginning to think, is he willing to let Scotland go with all the benefits that would provide for the Conservatives in England.

The strategic decisions taken by the PM could have significant implications for the referendum campaign itself as well as the outcome in 2014. Does he think Scotland is worth saving for the Tories and, if so, can he deliver the conditions within the UK to achieve this? Or is this simply a step too far for any Tory leader? The situation might have been completely transformed if the Leadership election in Scotland had resulted in a different outcome. The Scottish Tories could have gone their own way, turning necessity into a political virtue and realigning their future ambitions in a more distinctively Scottish direction? Tories north and south of the border may have a great deal to gain by creating more distance between each other. The Scottish Tories could look at the Bavarian Lander as a model for their future

Any Tory transformation in Scotland will be difficult and painful. The 2012 Scottish council elections are a grim reminder of this continuing decline.

The Liberal Democrats

The 2007 and 2011 Holyrood elections were in their different ways disastrous for the Lib-Dems, but the Scottish council elections in May 2012 were even worse. These elections and their aftermath revealed the Liberal Democrats in a new and unexpected light, particularly in Scotland. Prior to the elections in 2007, the party of partnership, coalition and proportional representation – and, until recently, the sole occupants of the centre-ground of politics – acted in complete rejection of these principles and made it quite clear they were distancing themselves from Labour as far as being potential coalition partners was concerned.

After the election, they also rejected the SNP, who had the largest number of seats. After the 2010 Westminster general election and emergence of the Coalition government with the Conservatives, their popularity in the UK declined rapidly, and with Scotland's intense 'hatred' of the Conservatives, the Lib-Dems took even more of a battering north of the border. There was little surprise, then, when the 2011 elections at Holyrood delivered a devastating indictment of the Lib-Dems' selling out to the Tories. Both their share of the vote and the number of MSPs collapsed. This was followed by a dismal showing in the Scottish council elections and the loss of 80 seats.

They are also sending out confused messages about their role in devolution politics, what they really stand for and what their purpose is in the political order.

They opted out of coalition in Scotland, without even sitting down to talk with the SNP, and they walked away from coalition in Wales. Their image of inclusiveness was dented as they dismissed out of hand an offer to join the new government being formed by Prime Minister Gordon Brown in 2010.

Ostensibly, this was justified by a growing concern within their party in Scotland at that time about appearing to be too close to Labour and the damage this may do to their electoral prospects in the coming UK general election, hence the evident involvement of their Westminster leader in all of this. They had every right to be genuinely fearful that the centre ground of politics is increasingly congested. Both Labour and the Conservatives are now competing in the same political market place, raising doubts about whether the Liberal Democratic product is as attractive as it used to be.

In Scotland, the Lib-Dems were increasingly seen as a fractious party with real tensions and strains bubbling below the surface and doubts about the Scottish leadership being openly voiced. After their slide in 2011 they elected a new leader, Willie Rennie. In the multi-party environment of Scottish politics, their identity is becoming less distinctive and subsumed by others on issues such as energy, the environment, human rights and Europe. More importantly, the punishment being meted out to them by the electors north and south of the border is casting real doubts about their electoral survival. They are fast moving to levels of lack of electoral credibility where the possibility of political realignment and mass losses of supporters, members and elected representatives could become a reality. There is no doubt that in Scotland the centre-left position of many Liberals is being tested to destruction and as a result the disconnect between what Scottish Liberals stand for and the posturing and shallowness of Clegg's defence of the Coalition, is too wide to be bridged. The Lib-Dems are trapped and for now seem unable or unwilling to extricate themselves from the unpopular coalition. After the May 2012 elections in England, Conservatives want Cameron to be more right wing and the Lib-Dems want Clegg to be more Liberal. This is not practical politics and the tensions and bad feeling are likely to deepen. The decision by Nick Clegg to oppose new boundary changes, in response to the Conservatives abandoning Lords reform, only serves to illustrate the fragility of the coalition. Accepting the plausibility of joining the Coalition to save Britain from the evils of debts, austerity, deficits and the so-called 'Brown legacy' being promoted in the national interest, we have surely reached a point where this is no longer tenable with the strategy itself under fire and the Tories behaving in a wildly incompetent and ideological fashion. The Deputy Prime Minister is not in a position to save both his party and his country, even if we accept his posture.

But it is in Scotland on the issue of the constitution that there is much confusion and disappointment. The Liberal Democrats have been conspicuously silent on one of their radical policies: a federal structure for the UK. Federalism is only second to Independence in terms of radical alternatives for the future of the Union. Good work in Scotland such as the Steele Commission have highlighted new thinking on a way forward for Scotland between the extremes of status quo Unionism and Independence, but the UK party and leadership remain silent and are happy to play along with Labour and the Conservatives on the one-question ballot paper and the promises of 'jam tomorrow', but only if the Scots defeat Independence first. An opportunity is being squandered to put a federalist solution at the heart of the debate and provide Scots with a viable and attractive alternative which the majority of Scots might support. There needs to be some joint working between the Lib-Dems and Labour in Scotland to flesh out such a position. The medium term could see a realignment, in Scotland, of both Labour and the Lib-Dems around a federalist solution to the constitutional question and a progressive centre left agenda. Saying 'NO' for two and a half years without a credible alternative, will be a waste of time and intellectual energy.

The party that was dominated by home rule in the first quarter of the 20th century seems to have been content, in the 15 years since the devolution referendum, to stay quiet on this crucial issue. At the present time, devolution comes courtesy of legislation from the sovereign parliament of Westminster. It is not part of any written constitution and there are no safeguards built into the legislation, in terms of either a referendum of the Scottish people, consultation with the Scottish Parliament or conditional majorities at Westminster, to protect against the Scotland Act being changed or abolished. The sovereign parliament of Westminster could abolish the Scotland Act with a one-line Bill in the House of Commons. A federalist solution, similar to Germany or the USA, would remove that uncertainty and provide the framework for an English solution to emerge and move towards genuine power-sharing.

Federalism is a tried and tested system of government yet the Liberal Democrats, its long-time advocates, appear reluctant to talk about it. Outwith the constraints of the now-defunct coalition with Labour between 1999 and 2007, they should now be more willing to talk about federalism. Again, we may have a situation where Westminster politics, having effectively removed devolution from the agenda, intervenes and frustrates the Liberal Democrats by forcing them to accept that it would not be a popular topic for discussion in the eyes of the English press or the public. If there is a difference of opinion between Liberal Democrats north and south of the border, this has not been made clear.

Europe is another issue where the Scottish Liberal Democrats have made little contribution. Their pro-European and pro-federalist background should put them at the forefront of the debate on political and constitutional change, but this is not evident in politics on the ground. The Liberal Democrats are well placed to contribute to the debate about Scotland in the Union and Scotland in the European Union and to remind us of the lessons to be learned from federalist experiences elsewhere in the EU.

In Germany, for example, the states (or Länder) have more powers in relation to the EU than Scotland currently has, and also have more opportunity for consultation on policy formulation with the federal government.

The Liberal Democrats' positive advocacy of Europe and federalism should give an attractive and modern edge to their constitutional and political voice in Scotland. Their failure to find one does not only create the impression that they have lost direction, it is a considerable loss to Scottish politics.

Their self-imposed isolation from the front line of Scottish politics after the May 2007 elections was linked to the strains of their relationship with Labour and the insistence of the SNP that a referendum on Independence was part and parcel of any coalition deal. Their problems with Labour are understandable, but it is difficult to comprehend why they refused even to start talks with the SNP.

Although the Liberal Democrats are opposed to Independence, they could have raised the political stakes and won popular support by agreeing to meet with the SNP and forcing them to abandon the idea of a referendum for the next four years. The probability is that the SNP would have agreed to gain the added security of coalition and, in any case, the Unionist majority in the parliament made the issue of a referendum redundant. The Lib-Dems share a broad policy platform with the SNP on issues such as nuclear energy, the environment, council tax, Europe and radical constitutional change, and their interests on rural affairs were also similar.

The questions for the Liberal Democrats are: where are they heading in the new political order in Scotland? Do they have it in them to make a more meaningful contribution to the debate about the constitutional and political future of our country? This is one area of policy which could help them rebuild their crumbling credibility. Home Rule Lib-

Dems and the Labour Party have much common ground. Labour should be reaching out to those Lib-Dems, but leaving the Coalition Government at Westminster may be a condition for that to happen.

Other Parties

Proportional representation, by its very nature, opens the way for a genuine multi-party system to develop. The first eight years of the Scottish Parliament saw the election of MSPs from a variety of new parties, such as the Scottish Socialists, Independents and the Scottish Senior Citizens Unity Party, and it also provided a platform for the Greens. It seemed that PR had helped deliver a multi-party parliament. In this regard, the 2007 Scottish Parliamentary elections must be seen as a setback, with the Socialists being wiped out, the Greens reduced to two MSPs, along with the lone Independent, Margo MacDonald. Whether or not this is a temporary setback for the smaller parties remains to be seen. The 2011 Holyrood elections and the 2012 Council elections have reinforced these trends. The List System was supposed to help achieve a plurality of partners but this is not happening to any great extent. The fact that the SNP are now a majority government and six Scottish councils have single-party control suggests that either our political bodies are defying the laws of PR electoral politics, or we need to revisit the method we have adopted and look in more detail at other systems used in Europe.

The minority parties are clearly being squeezed as the SNP and Labour fight very tight contests for lead-party status in Scottish politics. The Scottish Socialists were always likely to be heading for meltdown as their stock undoubtedly suffered when their leader became embroiled in a series of scandals and they were doomed by the disintegration of the party into two unelectable factions. The harsh truth was that the electorate saw through what was little more than a ragbag of gimmicks, stunts and North Korea-type communism, led by a charismatic but deeply-flawed leader.

As a party of side-shows and protests against the establishment, they received more attention from the media than their amateurish politics deserved. It can be said that this was one political squeeze that worked to the benefit of the parliament and its wider credibility in Scotland and the UK. The SSP induced a considerable number of poor and disadvantaged voters back to the ballot box, some for the first time. In 2007, a number of these returned to Labour or the SNP but the rest simply drifted away. There is probably scope for a radical left-of-centre party in Scottish politics, but surely one with closer links to the real world.

The Scottish Greens, the closest allies of the SNP minority government in 2007, were the other significant losers, as their numbers fell from six to two; this despite green issues becoming far more important to the electorate as global warming, carbon footprints, renewable energy and sustainable policies assumed more immediacy.

As the mainstream political parties increase their embrace of the green agenda, it remains to be seen whether the Green Party is sustainable in the future as a significant group in the parliament. There should, however, be some role for the Green Party in Scotland; they are successful in Europe, particularly in Germany, but it may be more likely to continue as a pressure group in this vital area of policy but as less of a party political force.

It was hoped that the 2007 election was a temporary setback and the more the public got used to a multi-party regime, the more electoral success would flow their way. This hasn't happened with recent elections merely confirming the two-party squeeze. While the Greens add little weight to coalitions in terms of number of MSPs, they broaden the legitimacy of the coalition and have the potential to add thousands of electors to the new politics of Scotland. Indeed, there was a dramatic increase in the support for minority parties in Scottish elections between 1999 and 2007.

Although it is still early days for the parliament, the single-issue campaign and the single-issue MSP should not be underestimated. Both in Scotland and in England, health and pensioner issues have already helped to elect MSPs – and one MP – campaigning on these high-profile areas of public interest. As the nature of politics changes and the base of party politics shifts in Scotland, an increasing number of 'driven' individuals will run with an issue and either win a seat outright or damage the incumbent candidate. Proportional representation does encourage multi-party involvement but it also encourages single-issue campaigns.

Over the next decade, we are likely to see narrow-band politics develop further as more young people involve themselves in global issues and seek a local outlet for their concerns. Similarly, the dramatic increase in the 'silver' or 'grey' vote over the next 20 years will create a powerful voice in Scottish politics. Over that time, it is expected that one in three of the electorate will be over retirement age – a significant political clout overall, but even more so if they are persuaded to unite around single issues.

This type of thinking will be encouraged by the level of cynicism, scepticism and general disenchantment which now surrounds politics and politicians. Disaffection, even despair, about the perceived inability of the political process to solve some problems could result in the loosening of ties with political orthodoxy and more interest in protest politics.

Another factor driving this will be the scope and intensity of 24/7, wall-to-wall news coverage and internet access to global events and issues at the click of a mouse. This communication revolution in publishing, broadcasting and the printed media will help shape the thinking and the voting intentions of the new political consumer. Social media is in its infancy and this is likely to have a dramatic impact on our political debate, in particular mobilizing the activity and thinking of a new generation of young people who can either be won over to traditional politics or take politics in a very different direction.

CHAPTER 5

Making Sense of our Politics, Democracy and Government

WHILE CONCENTRATING ON the Scottish Parliament and the 129 MSPs, we should not underestimate the role and importance of our MPs, MEPs, and councillors. These are the people who have a key role in making our democracy work, being at the heart of representative democracy, ensuring the views of five million people are heard in the elected forums of parliaments and councils and ensuring through a process of dialogue and debate that collective decisions are made which are in the best interests of the people; this is our democracy where the confidence and trust of the electors are vested in a few people and key institutions. This chapter looks at our politics, government and democracy.

Despite the often corrosive cynicism levelled at what happens in the delivery of all of this, we should never underestimate the importance of our democracy which remains the only fair, rational and peaceful way of organizing our society. We ignore this at our peril as we line up to condemn a great deal of what takes place in our name. But it is clear that our democracy and our politics are gripped by a crisis which needs to be addressed.

Of particular concern is the growing disconnect between the people and the processes and institutions of democracy. The public attitude is challenging as low election turnouts, falling membership of political parties and anger at issues such as the banking and financial crisis, recession, austerity, the Westminster expenses crisis, and the Murdoch media hacking scandal, demonstrate that the public are becoming disillusioned and dissatisfied with politics, politicians and political parties.

Austerity has generated an atmosphere of fear and apprehension about the future as politics and government seem unable to tackle problems and serve the interests of the public. Many people feel threatened by globalization and an economic order which rewards the rich and powerful at the expense of ordinary people. Citizens feel angry and let down. Our politics are on a downward spiral and only the intervention of the SNP in the last decade has, at least for the moment, created excitement and a sense of purpose, which partly accounts for their success against the Unionist parties.

There is a sense in which Westminster attitudes are taking on some of the tone and character of the pre-devolution debate of the mid 1990s. The referendum by no means ended the argument; hearts and minds were not completely won over and for many, the dynamic of devolution was neither embraced nor understood. This was inevitable but political leaders appear to have ignored the necessity of continuously making the case for the new form of devolved government. There have been very few powerful advocates of the Parliament and Government in Scotland and the achievements and successes gained in such a short period of time. This has allowed the SNP in particular to make advances while political critics of Holyrood, often aided by certain sections of the media, continue to snipe and undermine public perceptions of this new form of politics and government.

For many of our Westminster representatives, devolution remains an uncomfortable fact of life and is only seen in terms of the need for Unionism to confront and overcome Nationalism. For them, devolution should go no further and they reject the suggestion that it is unfinished business that must be completed if the United Kingdom is to evolve and be modernised.

In 2007, years of Labour-led power ended and the SNP took control of the Government and Parliament, a position reinforced by their Holyrood victory in 2011. This has ensured a different approach and a whole new outlook as devolution is viewed by the SNP as a step towards Independence. The whole dynamic has changed, with consequences and challenges for the Unionist parties. We are now in a new reality which will demand more from our political leaders. What seems remarkable at times is the total failure of parties and politicians to recognise what is happening and why the electors have responded differently over the past five years to the arrival of the SNP in Government.

At the heart of this confusion are five important issues. First, our democracy is under threat as people become disconnected and dissatisfied with what is on offer from our politicians; this is a UK wide issue of which Scotland is part. Second, there is a major constitutional transformation taking place which is not going to disappear and which is interacting with and influencing every aspect of Scottish politics. Third, there is a struggle taking place, barely recognised by the Unionist parties, between the populism of the SNP and any effort to create some form of progressive centre-left agenda involving Labour, the Lib-Dems and the Greens. At the heart of this is the fairness, justice and equality agenda. Fourth, there is a debate around identity and nationality where the issue of Scottishness is being hijacked by the SNP to the detriment of the other parties. More worryingly, the Unionist parties, especially Labour, fight against the importance of this and see it as a threat to their embrace of the Union and their 'socialism'. Fifth, because of the intense hatred and rivalry between Labour and the SNP, reinforced by the squeeze on the other parties, many of the ideals and aspirations behind devolution and the creation of a new politics are fast disappearing and tribalism and partisanship are all too evident in our public discourse and parliamentary debates.

An inexorable transfer of power is taking place, both nationally and globally, and centres of authority can either compete or cooperate. Local and central government are moving to competition and privatisation – increasingly, government functions are carried out by private and commercial operators – there is less dependency on the state and meanwhile, ordinary people are less knowledgeable and often confused about what different levels of government or institutions do for them.

The revolution in communications and information technology, especially the internet, along with globalisation, European integration and the changing shape of the Union are influencing how people understand and relate to their political environment. There is more concern with single issues – from the environment, global terrorism and human rights to local hospital closures – than with party politics; people are still interested in political issues but not traditional politics.

For politicians at all levels and all parliaments, the challenge is to sustain a debate that is not about 'turf wars', clinging to the powers they have or seeking more power for power's sake, but about building a practical modern democracy that satisfies the aspirations and demands of the people.

MPs

The strains between Westminster and Holyrood are self-evident but they are not necessary. Under devolution, Scottish MPs at Westminster have suffered a curtailment of their powers, with demands for them to cede still more responsibilities – yet at the same time they are under constant attack from 'Little Englander' factions in the 'Mother of Parliaments' who resent their continuing capacity to vote on English issues. Tensions have also arisen as Scottish MPs are excluded from much of the political media coverage, and this has resulted in much internal party and inter-parliament bickering. Often expressed in off-the-record briefings and a simmering resentment and contempt for the new parliament and an undermining of its status.

With the Scottish media spotlight now firmly on Holyrood, the MPs – who are always understandably preoccupied with their public profile – are losing ground to the MSPs. The Scottish Parliament is now the focus of attention and this is where the media can find, or create, political drama which is immediate and easily covered. Setting aside the national coverage given to prominent Scots in the UK cabinet, there is little coverage of backbench activity at Westminster. This is a source of real aggravation for Scottish MPs and often leads to disputes at constituency level about local issues that are worthy of press coverage and at parliamentary level, where 'turf war' tensions can emerge.

This is the main source of dismissive comments about the 'second class, second division, second-rate nature' of the Scottish Parliament and doubts about devolution. It creates a powerful negative psychology about the parliament. It is no exaggeration to say this has a corrosive effect on the morale of Scottish Labour at Holyrood.

This is not helpful for two reasons. First, the vitally important reserved powers at Westminster deserve more coverage in Scotland because of their obvious impact on people and country. But the MPs have to work harder to secure coverage. Second, ironically, the failure to give adequate coverage to Westminster business reinforces the view that the Edinburgh parliament is the one that really matters. The Scottish press is overwhelmingly Unionist and at times hypercritical of the Scottish Parliament and Government; yet its lack of coverage of Westminster (at least in the popular press) only serves to give more prominence and more credibility to Holyrood. A by-product of this ambivalent media attitude is that it helps the SNP talk up the importance of the Scottish Parliament and by definition undermine the credibility of Westminster.

The centralist Westminster preoccupation with viewing devolution as a very Scottish affair creates a sense of Unionism which is inflexible and unwilling to absorb the changes that are taking place. This is the basis for the argument that Westminster – the parliament, the government and the UK parties – may form the real threat to the future of the Union.

The fact that Holyrood can – and does – discuss reserved matters despite having no legislative or executive competence to do so merely serves to reinforce this overall perception and increase irritation among MPs.

The Westminster MPs themselves could take certain steps to counter their current difficulties. Central to their thinking should be the political fact of life that Holyrood will, for a variety of reasons, grow in importance and Europe will continue to take further powers and responsibilities from Westminster. Westminster has to come to terms with the changing realities of Europe and Devolution. That being the case, a more flexible Union will be essential, as will their ability to demonstrate a much clearer link between their work at Westminster and the interests of Scotland.

Continuing with the 'turf wars' mentality will only further isolate them at their workplace as anti-Scottish sentiment takes hold at Westminster. Defending devolution should become a regular feature of their work – and more visibility in Scotland would also help. A new understanding between Westminster and Holyrood is long overdue.

MEPs

The European Union, with further political and economic integration and enlargement, will continue to impact on both the UK and Scotland. The European Parliament is growing in importance as it gains more powers and will be further strengthened despite the anti-European sentiment being encouraged by the Conservative party in Westminster and throughout England. The growing consequence of the EU is not reflected in the coverage given to MEPs or the issues they discuss, debate and legislate on in Brussels and Strasbourg. In the UK, there is not a great deal of positive advocacy of the EU by the Westminster government – and Europhiles are not expecting too much support from Prime Minister David Cameron.

It would be easy to reach the conclusion that the last Labour government lost control of the European agenda in the UK. Early tactical decisions taken by the Labour government on the Euro, in particular, served a useful political purpose but, as a consequence of this, the European idea has suffered some setbacks in the UK. Euro sceptics, anti-European media sentiment and a growing number of hard-line anti-European interests have won control of the agenda in Britain. This of course was not helped by the return of the Conservative party to Westminster in 2010.

Scotland is different and new alliances need to be forged with our MEPs across party lines to embrace Europeanism and build a more positive view of the EU and its importance to Scotland. The EU now consists of 27 member countries with a population of nearly 500 million people. In view of the growing importance of their work, we should be doing a great deal more to increase our influence and understand Europe's part in Scotland's future, becoming more European and more outward-looking as a consequence. Clearly, the Euro-zone crisis has been a major setback for the European project, but new discussions about a political and banking union for the 17 members of the Euro-zone could create new momentum and a revived sense of purpose.

Scottish politics suffers from a two-tier or second-class mentality. In sharp contrast to much of Western Europe, there is no parity of esteem between membership of our political institutions – Westminster, Holyrood, Brussels and local government. Little regard is paid to the fact that these are representative institutions, each in its different way having an impact across local community, Scottish, UK and European jurisdictions. It is commonplace in Europe for politicians to move freely between institutions, rather than seeing themselves as elected to one place for life, and the value of their experience in each forum is recognised. This may not be the British or Scottish way but it makes more sense and reflects a more mature attitude towards political representation.

Local Government

Local government remains an important part of Scotland's governance and has experienced a great deal of change as a result of the May 2012 elections. The introduction of proportional representation – intensely disliked by councillors, especially Labour caucuses who had been in long-term power across a broad swathe of Central Scotland – has altered the power structure of local government and the composition of every council in Scotland.

Labour's influence in local government has diminished and, as a result of PR and the improved performance of the SNP, Labour's domination of many parts of Scotland remains under serious threat. Of the 32 councils, Labour now controls 4. The SNP has the largest number of councillors and there are more coalitions running Scottish councils than ever before.

There is a certain irony in all of this in that the Conservatives in 1996 tried to destroy the power of Labour in local government by dismantling the regional councils, with Strathclyde the main target, and gerrymandering the boundaries of the 32 newly-created unitary councils. The real aim of destroying the Labour hegemony failed and it was left to proportional representation, a measure spurned by the Tories, to do that job in 2007. Paradoxically, PR has also allowed the Tories to remain a limited political force in both the Scottish Parliament and the councils.

The SNP is in many ways a stronger and better-organised political party than Labour at the present time. It seems to be able to use its power to draw together central command, its membership, local government councillors, MSPs and key figures throughout Scotland in a much more coordinated, enthusiastic, determined and disciplined approach to its overall strategic aims. In mid-2012, the morale of the SNP remains high and the mood is positive. In sharp contrast, Labour still seems to lack self-belief and a positive narrative. Labour's hold of Glasgow City council in the 2012 council elections was a boost for them, while exposing some of the weaknesses of the SNP.

Setting aside the battle between Labour and the SNP for control of local government, there is another potential conflict ahead. This time, it is likely to revolve around the future of local government itself as its identity and Independence seem under threat as the Scottish government pursues a highly centralised agenda. There is a danger that low turn-out in local elections encourages the government to think that local control and local democracy are not valued by the public. Over the past five years, local government has been drawn closer to the centre as a number of policy developments, such as unitary police and fire authorities, the freezing of the council tax and the putting in place of a number of concordats and agreements, have fundamentally altered the balance between central and local government and undermined even further the already weak financial accountability of local councils. We are fast approaching the point where nearly 90 per cent of local government finance will come from Central Government. This is bad enough, but the longer the freeze on council tax remains, a larger proportion of finance will come from central government and remove the ability of councils to link spend with local need and remove any semblance of local accountability.

The freeze on council tax is a political measure which has three unfortunate consequences; it benefits the well off, it damages local accountability and wastes large sums of public funds which would be better earmarked for more deserving items of expenditure. The shift in the balance of power after the local council elections may result in more resistance to the Government's agenda. Local Government faces some real challenges in financial freedom, democratic accountability and their ability to act as independent brokers with a distinct identity out with the ever growing control of central government.

The renewal of local government is long overdue. Far too much effort has gone into management processes, cost effectiveness, contracting out and commercialisation and the question of privatisation. Too little thought has gone into purpose and direction, a more credible financial structure, policy innovation and new systems of service delivery, which need not include forms of privatisation. Local government does not take itself seriously enough. It leaves too much of the strategic thinking to central Government and then, in a top-down process, is told what to do. This is why the centralisation process has continued apace. Local government has to become more attractive, interesting, independent and engaging to the people it serves while at the same time politicians, national and local, will have to find the courage to reform local government finance.

The plight of local government is similar to the Scottish Parliament; it receives virtually all of its money in a hand-down, raises a small amount of its cash direct but it is responsible for spending all of the money. This is not sustainable.

There are demands for the Scottish government to be responsible for the raising of its finance and being accountable for the spend. Surely, local government deserves a similar debate. One thing is clear: for the benefit of democracy, local councils should not be so close to central government.

Patronage in Scotland

The wider political landscape has changed with the new government at Holyrood. Alongside elected government there is also an extensive system of patronage which reaches out to every aspect of Scottish life. Never obvious and rarely controversial, day in and day out, a wide network of boards, commissions, committees and assorted quangos play an important role in the country's life. Neither elected nor fully accountable, these bodies and their membership are in the 'gift' of the government of Scotland and now in the hands of the SNP. The significance of this should not be underestimated. As part of its strategic plan to take Scotland towards Independence, the face of the patronage state in Scotland will change. At the present time there is also a danger that reward for public service and deserving causes are being relegated in importance as the influence of business and the powerful ring more loudly in the corridors of power. For the public, this is an alienating process which elevates power and wealth to extremes.

CHAPTER 6

The State of the Union

THE CONTINUED EXISTENCE of the Union between Scotland and England after 305 years is no reason to assume that it can survive without changing. Inertia or resistance to the need to adapt are not options if the United Kingdom is to be sustained and have relevance in the 21st century. This notion may be critical to retaining a role of Scotland in that Union. The Union of the UK is an explicitly multinational state, as indicated in its very name, created in the succession of England and Wales in 1536, with Scotland in 1707 and with Ireland in 1801.

Devolution, with the creation of parliaments and assemblies in Scotland, Wales and Northern Ireland, has transformed the relationships within the UK, but its purpose was to preserve and strengthen the Union, not to transform it. In the 1997 referendum campaign, Shadow Scottish Secretary George Robertson said devolution would 'kill Independence stone dead'.

The debate is now moving to the concept of the ancient Union in the contemporary context and the events of 2007 renewed the examination of the state of the Union and Anglo–Scottish interaction. The accession of the minority Nationalist government in Scotland and the participation of nationalists in the administrations in Wales and Northern Ireland may have been unprecedented, leading some to doubt the ability of the Union to endure – but there was at that point no credible sign that it would prove to be the 'stepping stone to Independence'. The election of the majority SNP Government in 2011 may have changed all the calculations.

The different nations and regions in the British Isles have widely varying views and attitudes towards the Union. It is one of a number of unions which directly affect our lives, including the European Union and globalism. In this new way of thinking about politics, there are not one but many unions.

To make sense of the Union in the modern context, the debate has to move beyond the constitutional limits and look at different models. This approach will help the Union to be seen in a looser, more flexible and modern perspective and in turn allow the issues at the heart of devolution – sovereignty, identity, difference, diversity, democracy and nationality – to be better understood and made more relevant to Scotland, Wales, Northern Ireland and England in this new millennium.

The immediate post-devolution period was not as traumatic as it might have been, with very few dramatic conflicts or major upheavals. This was helped by Labour being in power in all parts of Britain, an unprecedented period of growth in public expenditure, steady and stable economic progress and a period in which the SNP in Scotland, in the early years of devolution, did not make the electoral advances they hoped for and had difficulty in adjusting to a devolved parliament. All of that has changed as the SNP has continued to transform and dominate Scottish politics in the last five years.

This 'steady state' political environment in Scotland is now changing, with potentially dramatic consequences. Change is also evident in England, where criticism is growing and attitudes are less benign towards devolution; but it remains to be seen whether this results in a positive embrace of devolution for England and Westminster or a hardening of Unionism and anti-Scottish sentiment. The Conservative-Lib-Dem Coalition has only worsened this overall sense of frustration at Westminster with Scotland and the Scots. In addition, the debate outwith the Parliament, generated by a London-centric media, has only made the debate more anti-Scottish and pro status quo Unionism.

Paradoxically, it would appear that the main threat to the Union will not be the advance of Nationalism, but failures at the heart of Unionism and misjudgements by the Unionist parties. These could include:

- Failure to address long standing post-devolution anomalies such as the Barnett formula and the West Lothian question.

- The Conservative Party and Government at Westminster struggling to renew itself and pursuing political opportunism on devolved matters, in the process encouraging the crude 'Little Englander' mentality and a new strain of 'grudge and grievance' politics.

- The London-based media operating within the 'Westminster bubble', trivialising the achievements of devolution and at the same time trumpeting the threats to centralism and the Union.

- A failure of the Labour Party and Westminster to defend the constitutional settlement while allowing ill-informed and partisan criticism to go unchecked and as a consequence allowing fiction to masquerade as political fact.

- Inability by government ministers to see devolution politics as anything other than a battlefield to settle old political scores and confront the demon of Nationalism in Scotland and Wales. Devolution was one of the big policy success stories of the Labour government on its return to power after 18 years in the wilderness and, along with some other major innovations, changed the political and constitutional landscape of the UK forever. It could be asked where it is now on the political agenda and why the lessons of 13 years have not been understood.

Sadly, in all of this debate, one factor remains constant, UK exceptionalism. Devolution or sub-national politics is still seen as an issue for the peripheral territories, only to be legislated for, only to be administered, only to be tolerated, never to be part of the transformation of the Union, never to be about the search for a role for England, never to be a process that could give the Union renewed purpose or a modern outlook in the 21st century. The current approach of Westminster will threaten the Union if it is not checked by reality and just a glimmer of imagination and inspiration. There is a refusal to accept that old Unionism is dead and must now renew, and this is a process that now has its own momentum. What matters is who will lead the debate and who will be dragged along in its wake.

Much of this is about party politics but there are broader concerns about the condition of the relationship between Scotland and England. A YouGov poll in 2006, a few months before the 300th anniversary of the Union, found 56 per cent of English people thought Scottish MPs should not be able to vote on issues affecting only England and Wales and 46 per cent of Scots agreed, but 70 per cent of the English thought it wrong to continue the Barnett formula 'as the rest of the UK subsidises Scotland', compared to just 12 per cent of Scots.

Further evidence of rising English nationalism was provided by an ICM poll in November 2006, showing 59 per cent of English voters approved of full Scottish Independence. Support for the establishment of an English parliament had reached 'an historic high' of 68 per cent amongst English voters. Somewhat questionable was the finding that almost half – 48 per cent – also wanted complete Independence for England and 58 per cent of Scottish voters also backed an English breakaway with its own parliament with similar powers to Holyrood.

Higher levels of public spending per head of population in Scotland were 'unjustified' according to 60 per cent of English voters and 36 per cent of Scots said the system was unfair, with only 51 per cent supporting the Barnett formula.

The West Lothian question, the ability of Scottish MPs at Westminster to vote on solely English matters while devolved Scottish issues are decided in Edinburgh, met with strong resentment. 62 per cent of English voters wanted Scottish MPs stripped of this right and 46 per cent of Scots agreed.

The poll showed that the English are more likely to think of themselves as British: only 16 per cent of English people said they were 'English, not British', compared to 26 per cent of Scots who said they were 'Scottish, not British'.

The English sense of 'Britishness' (not to mention 'fair play') compared to Scottish patriotism is thrown into even stronger contrast in the sporting arena. While 70 per cent of English people said they would support a Scottish team playing football or rugby against a nation other than England, only 48 per cent of Scots said they would back England – and 34 per cent said they would support England's opponent, no matter which country it was. Outwith party politics, there remains a great deal of confusion about the nature of devolution and its impact on the cultural and social thinking of the public. Three issues, however, stand out. First, Scots have a greater feel for identity than the English. Second, the idea that the English subsidise the Scots remains strong. Third, grudge and grievance sum up the views of the English. None of these have changed very much over the period since 1999. What is also apparent is the indifference of Westminster and the genuine ignorance of the English as to what is happening in Scotland and Wales in the post devolution period.

Scottishness and Britishness

In trying to explain the complex thinking underpinning, Scottish politics the issues of identity, nationality and diversity are absolutely crucial. Any attempt to chart the political and constitutional future cannot avoid the question of 'Scottishness'. This has been the major influence and the driving force of devolution. Throughout the 20th century, from the 1914 Liberal government's Home Rule Bill, which was so nearly successful, through the 1979 referendum, to the 1998 Scotland Act, UK governments sought to respond to the demands created by the Scottish sense of identity.

Difficult to define or categorise, it could be said that there are as many types of Scottishness as there are Scots! The author has no difficulty in defining himself as a Fifer, a Scot and a Brit in that order – being European also matters. Indeed, when Gordon Brown was Prime Minister, his nationality became a political focus for those who were obsessed by the West Lothian question and resented Scots in the UK government whose ministries include English affairs. As a result, Gordon Brown found it necessary to emphasise his undeniable 'Britishness', something no previous Prime Minister has had to do.

The most impressive attempt to define Scottishness and assess the impact of 'birth, blood and belonging' on politics and constitutional developments has been the Nations and Regions research programme of the Institute of Governance at Edinburgh University. Between 1999 and 2004, the programme investigated the importance of national identity at a time of far-reaching constitutional change in the UK.

In their summary of the project's findings, Ross Bond and Michael Rosie said the trend since the 1970s showed an increase in Scottishness and a decrease in Britishness and, given a 'multiple choice' of national identities, the vast majority (86 per cent) of those questioned chose 'Scottish'. This sense of identity manifested itself in a number of ways, including national flags – the Scottish Saltire being regarded with pride and the Union flag with indifference.

Of greater significance was the conclusion that, even among those who identified most strongly as Scottish, around half supported neither the SNP nor Scottish Independence. Irrespective of an individual's choice of national identity, devolution proved the most popular means of government.

The 2003 Scottish Social Attitudes Survey found that English birth is 'a significant barrier to a successful claim to be Scottish'. Yet 70 per cent of Scots are more inclusive when it comes to regarding 'non-white' Scottish residents as Scottish.

In 2004, around three-quarters of Scots felt 'exclusively' or 'mainly' Scottish, a significantly higher proportion than the equivalent measures in England and Wales, but that awareness need not mean that a demand for political Independence is inevitable. More likely, it is yet another manifestation of the Union's historic capacity not only for flexibility but for giving full and easy scope for the Welsh, English and Scots to express their cultural and ethnic identities within a UK framework.

Perhaps inevitably, however, most recent comment both in the media and among academic analysts has been about the reasons for the decline of 'Britishness' over the past half-century. The Institute of Public Policy Research (IPPR) suggests that an obvious checklist might include:

the waning of Protestantism (a key ideological British resource for earlier generations); the end of the empire and Britain's subsequent fall for a time to the status of a second-rate power; the huge and increasing importance of Europe and the parallel decline in the authority of the British state; and, not least, the ebbing of respect for the institution of monarchy.

Moreover, since the end of the Second World War and the collapse of the Soviet threat, there is the loss of a clear 'Other', or an external enemy, which can help to sustain British national solidarity against a common foe.

Whether all this means that a political divorce in the short term is likely is less certain. The IPPR says:

300 years of Union have resulted in multiple familial, personal, economic and cultural connections between the two nations. Many hundreds of thousands of Scots have long migrated to England. Less well known is the continuous movement in modern times from England to Scotland. Between 1841 and 1911 a quarter of a million English and Welsh men, women and children apparently came north. At the time of the 2001 census, more than 400,000 English-born people were resident in Scotland, by far the nation's largest immigrant group. Not so long ago, it was possible to speak with concern about the 'Englishing' of Scotland. More common nowadays is reference to the 'Scottish Raj' in English politics and media and in London's financial institutions.

The question of 'Britishness' and how it can be reinforced has recently exercised politicians and think-tanks, but their suggested solutions have shown muddled (and, it has to be said, Anglo-centric) thinking on national identity. In August 2007, the IPPR published a report calling on the Prime Minister to establish 'a British national day' as an extra bank holiday. It said:

> Gordon Brown's attempts to build a British national identity would be boosted by having a new bank holiday which would act as a national 'thank you' for community heroes and as a national 'ask' for people to give back to their communities.

The day would be the single focus of awarding honours and those should be on ordinary people who have made a significant contribution to their communities, such as:

> the baggage handler who intervened in the Glasgow airport attack, the traffic warden who spotted the London car bomb and other ordinary people who showed bravery and vigilance during those attacks in July; emergency service workers who helped people stranded by July's flooding; and people nominated by their local communities for their tireless contribution to community life.

Somehow, it is hard to imagine even pro-Unionists – perhaps in Gordon Brown's own Fife constituency or the Glasgow baggage handler's neighbourhood – taking advantage of their extra day's holiday to raise a glass in their local pub to toast 'Britishness'.

The Scottish sense of identity has been constant over the generations, while there has been a loosening of party political and class loyalties, affiliations and allegiances. People do not regard the Union as a formal entity, in the same way as politicians and academics, but have a greater sense of it as being social, economic and cultural.

As a result, they do not necessarily respond to perceived threats to the Union in the way politicians expect. The younger generation is more adaptable and combines the need to express its nationalism and identity with a more idealistic global agenda.

The cultural renaissance, the IPPR argues:

> 'has seen a flowering of internationally-recognised writers, artists, musicians and performers, has also contributed to pride in Scottishness.

There is a tendency in political circles to underestimate these feelings, since they do not fit neatly into the accepted view of the political order. The new order in the 21st century is likely to leave 'pigeon-hole politics', rigid party lines and institutional loyalties behind.

If Britain is facing an identity crisis, this is not necessarily a bad thing if it results in an examination of the meaning of Britishness and of whether a Union with different national identities continues to be workable. For this to happen, it is necessary to recognise that the 'Union' is multi-faceted'.

The IPPR has provided a useful summary of the main aspects of what it defines as this multi-faceted union; these arguments are designed to reinforce the case for the union. In view of how close the IPPR is to the Labour Government at Westminster, it is worthwhile outlining in detail its concerns about the Economic and Commercial Union and the Social and Cultural Union.

The Economic and Commercial Union

From the Scottish side, economic advantage was the prime motive for the Treaty of Union in 1707, and by the late 18th century the benefits of prosperity and thriving trade began to flow. In modern times, attention has concentrated on public expenditure, the Barnett formula and the size of the block grant – and that has resulted in the demand for greater fiscal autonomy for the Scottish Parliament.

As long as the UK budget and public spending have been on a rising curve during the first decade of devolution, Scottish public opinion has largely been satisfied with the arrangement. However, cuts which appeared under a tighter fiscal regime of the Brown Government and were embraced by the austerity package of the Cameron Government seriously affect Scotland and will have political repercussions.

Reductions in the Scottish financial settlement by the UK government, to tackle deficits and debt reduction risk reaping a political whirlwind in Scotland. The SNP Government would interpret any Westminster-imposed cut in the Scottish budget, with resulting economies in Scottish policies and programmes, as re-imposing control of the devolved powers by another means.

More important, however, is the case for preserving the economic and commercial Union, on which there appears to be conflicting views. Unionists may have thought in the past that the case was self-evident but the Scottish National Party has been able to recruit business, enterprise and banking leaders who support the case for separation, while others are prepared only to support the debate, without declaring themselves for Independence.

If the UK government wishes to lead this debate more work requires to be done in establishing the interdependence of Scotland and England, not only in terms of exchequer and benefits, but more as a closely-integrated trading area for goods, services, capital and labour. What we have instead is very little rational debate but the use of the 'fear factor' approach to frighten Scots into believing that the worst of all worlds will visit Scotland if we don't stick close to the Union. Closer integration with Europe is a core argument of the Scottish Nationalists, since they see 'Independence in Europe' as the alternative to membership of the United Kingdom. Their policy states:

> The SNP supports a confederal Europe, a voluntary coming-together of states in a union that collectively exercises certain sovereign rights pooled by its members. But, in order to get the most out of Europe, we must be able to make political decisions on our own behalf, rather than letting London decide for us.
>
> We must be free to pursue our national interests, just as the other nations of Europe pursue theirs. That is what Independence is all about.

To answer this argument, the case must be made that, in an age of increased economic interdependence, Scotland and England have greater mutual interests with each other than with European countries – and the effect of the European Union on the economic and other links between England and Scotland must be examined.

The Social and Cultural Union

Even stronger than economic links are the historic ties of kinship, joint citizenship, values and shared sacrifice. It has been said, with justification, that Scots earned and have continued to justify their equal partnership in the Union through their contribution in blood and heroism over the centuries. The stability of the Union was assured as Scotland prospered as an industrial and trading powerhouse in the 19th century and the two world wars reinforced the sense of British togetherness throughout the 20th century.

Until now, it has been possible – almost unquestioned – for Scots to proclaim their intense loyalty to Scotland while remaining and feeling British. Gordon Brown and Douglas Alexander in their tract *New Scotland, New Britain* (The Smith Institute, 1999), a powerful anti-Nationalist polemic produced for the first Scottish Parliament election campaign, said: 'Feelings of Scottishness have never required the eradication of Britishness.' They also called in evidence George Galloway (surely something that would not happen now!) for his reference to the Anglo–Scottish bonds of 'intermarriage, intermingling and immigration'.

Although some of the suggestions in *New Scotland, New Britain* about the effects of Separatism, such as customs and immigration posts and changing currencies at the border, were exaggerated, and vehemently denied by the SNP, their basic argument about identity remains valid. With the SNP now in power, Scottish Labour, Conservative and Liberal Democrat parties have been ineffectual in opposition to First Minister Alex Salmond's gradualist initiatives to create the climate for Separatism, not least his White Paper on an Independence referendum in 2007.

A sense of the peoples of Scotland and England drifting apart has been created by London-based media and opportunist English politicians who give the impression of, not only not caring about Scotland, but actively resenting Scotland's rightful place in the Union. And, it has to be said, the disconnection is not helped by leading Scottish politicians who say they will support 'anyone but England' or 'whoever is playing England' in international competitions for which Scotland has not qualified.

It is surprising that 305 years after the Treaty of the Union, there has been little effort made by the defenders of the existing Union to articulate in a more sophisticated way the components of the Union and their importance in the ongoing debate.

Despite devolution, the choice facing Scotland has continued to be presented in stark terms: unchanging Unionism or uncompromising Independence. Yet the first is not really an option and the second is unacceptable to the majority of Scots.

Traditionalists who now regard devolution as a finished product and do not see the need for further examination of the powers of the Scottish Parliament and the Welsh and Northern Irish assemblies are ignoring the pressing political realities.

Until now, the customary response of straightforward Unionist confrontation with the SNP has worked. The 2007 and 2012 election results show the Scottish electorate have a more subtle understanding of the issues and practicalities of devolution than the politicians. With three full terms of the Scottish Parliament behind them and dramatic changes in Scotland's communal life, votes have been used to send multiple messages: disillusion with the Blair government, objection to the Iraq invasion, impatience with the lacklustre performance of the Lab–Lib-Dem administration in Edinburgh, concern about the Conservative-Lib-Dem Coalition at Westminster and resentment at being 'taken for granted' in the former Labour heartlands. Traditional loyalties, class barriers and national identity are no longer guarantees of voting patterns. Scots have a new forum in which to comment on matters of importance north and south of the border.

The Scottish voters showed a degree of political sophistication, unrealised by the Unionist parties, by showing that they are prepared to vote for one party for Holyrood and a different party for Westminster. In voting for the SNP in Scotland, they can send a strong reminder to the party in power in the UK; competence in government and capability in representing Scotland's best interests will be the criteria. Meanwhile, the UK government is put on notice that, although Scotland rejects separation, the option remains on the table.

The task for Westminster is to respond positively to the changes in Scottish society and the new political realities in Wales and Northern Ireland. That way, it can ensure that the Union is not merely a political bone to be fought over at elections, but that it is seen as a living entity which is constantly relevant to the lives of all – whether they call themselves 'Scottish' or 'British' or both.

CHAPTER 7

Date with destiny, 2014

THIS BOOK ARGUES FOR a new and more enlightened debate about Scotland's constitutional and political future. The urgency of this argument has been dramatically underlined by recent events in Westminster and Holyrood with the publication of consultation papers on a referendum, probably to be held in the autumn of 2014. This hectic level of activity in the early part of 2012 was the result of the seismic victory of the SNP in the Holyrood elections in 2011. The phoney war has ended and the prospect of a real referendum on Independence will ensure the most dramatic and intense debates ever seen in Scotland since the referendum on the Blair White Paper in 1997. There is no guarantee that such a fevered level of debate will be taking place in either England or Westminster. Based on the devolution narrative so far, this will not be surprising. Before considering recent consultation papers and the launch of the SNP's campaign for Independence in May 2012 it will provide useful context to look back at two other Green and White Papers produced by the SNP and Labour Governments in 2007. The publication of a Green Paper by the UK government and a White Paper by the Scottish government which took diametrically opposed views and visions of the future of Scotland. This demonstrates, more than anything else, the dilemma at the heart of constitutional politics in Scotland and the UK and the challenge now facing all of us as our date with destiny looms.

The Green Paper, 'The Governance of Britain', sets out in stark terms a Unionist line which seeks to reinforce and strengthen Westminster, limiting the powers of the executive in relation to parliament, transferring powers to parliament, preferring nine regional select committees and rejecting regional assemblies for England, reshaping the administration of the English regions, providing more powers for local government and ensuring a more effective listening and consulting role for the recently-appointed ministers for the English regions.

In a foreword to the paper, the UK government says: 'We want to forge a new relationship between government and citizen, and begin the journey towards a new constitutional settlement – a settlement that entrusts Parliament and people with more power...The paper does not seek to set out a final blueprint for our constitutional settlement. It is the first step in a national conversation.'

What is striking is the complete lack of any mention of political and constitutional devolution for England and the fact that, in a 62-page paper, only five paragraphs – two-thirds of one page – are given over to devolution. And even then it is defensive and dismissive.

By accident or design, it is hard to escape the conclusion that this Green Paper puts a freeze on political devolution being extended to England and at the same time seems to close the door on further changes, especially the transfer of more powers, to Scotland, Northern Ireland and Wales. For the UK Labour Government devolution seemed to be off the Westminster agenda. Instead Unionism, Britishness and strengthening the role of Westminster were the priorities.

In sharp contrast, the SNP government in Scotland published a White Paper on 'A Referendum on Independence', which delivered a manifesto commitment to produce the paper in its first 100 days in power. This document is the complete antithesis of the Westminster position. Despite the Unionist majority in the Scottish parliament guaranteeing defeat for any legislation on a referendum, the publication of the White Paper broke new political ground, provided the minority government with a campaigning tool and sharpened and deepened the concern at Westminster about the threat to the Union and how the SNP would use this to create some tactical advantage over the next four years.

The publication of the White Paper was an audacious, dramatic and remarkable development in Scottish politics and much more than the realisation of a manifesto commitment to be delivered in the first 100 days of the SNP government. Its significance is less about Independence (a Unionist majority in the parliament and declining support among the Scottish people for this option means that Independence or a referendum on it will not be going anywhere in the foreseeable future) but more about the impact the SNP is already having in motivating the other parties to engage and at the same time boosting their confidence and capacity to build a campaign that some day would lead to the battle for Scotland. Five years on and we can see that their strategy has worked so far and the Nation is being prepared for an unprecedented event.

English Labour MP and former minister Frank Field, a provocative but always progressive thinker, commented in the *Daily Telegraph* on 14 August 2007:

> What Gordon Brown must know is that the debate on Britishness will not end with Mr Salmond's White Paper. The Scottish First Minister has an agenda for Independence and, on his performance so far, he also has the political skill to engage with voters well beyond the SNP tribe. He will therefore be highly pragmatic in developing a 'softly, softly, catchee monkey' approach. No single action will be seen as extreme, but each action will help push Scotland inexorably towards his desired goal.

Field predicted:

> Scottish Independence is now one of the big questions that the English, who make up more than four fifths of the electorate to Westminster, will have to face. They can only sensibly do so by developing, in response, a clear statement on what it means to be English as distinct from simply British.
>
> The Brown Government therefore must engage with the Scottish question while, at the same time, ceding yet more British sovereignty to the European Union – which will most affect the English. And it is here that the interests of the English and the other nationalities of the United Kingdom divide.

Summary of the White Paper

There is no doubting the accuracy of Frank Field's analysis and in particular his assessment of Alex Salmond's political cunning and the manner in which he will sell Independence as nothing more than the introduction of some new politics while the role of Scotland in the Union will hardly change at all. Unfortunately, the Field view of the future was not shared by his Labour colleagues at Westminster. It is worth quoting in full the summary of the Holyrood White Paper as it says a great deal about the SNP strategy and reveals insights into their short and long-term thinking. This is a party with a plan for government, despite the fact there is little prospect of progressing an Independence referendum in the short to medium term. This is also a party with a political plan for the whole of Scotland.

Of particular significance is the call for a clear and distinctive option that builds well beyond Westminster and current Union thinking but stops short of Independence. The 'national conversation', regardless of party political persuasion or particular constitutional position, should have been taken seriously... it wasn't, and should have been part of a bigger conversation throughout the United Kingdom... It didn't happen!

The establishment of the Scottish Parliament under the Scotland Act 1998 gave the people of Scotland a direct democratic voice in decisions across a wide range of government activities already administered in Scotland. The devolution settlement explicitly recognised that the responsibilities given to the Scottish Parliament and Scottish Government in 1999 could be changed, and important mechanisms were included in the Act to allow for further devolution.

Significant powers are currently reserved to the United Kingdom Parliament and the United Kingdom Government. Further devolution in these important areas would allow the Scottish Parliament and Scottish Government to take their own decisions on these issues in the interests of Scotland and reflecting the views of the people of Scotland. In some areas, further devolution could also provide greater coherence in decision making and democratic accountability for delivery of policy.

To go beyond enhanced devolution to Independence would involve bringing to an end the United Kingdom Parliament's power to legislate for Scotland, and the competence of United Kingdom Ministers to exercise executive powers in respect of Scotland. All of the remaining reservations in the Scotland Act would cease to have effect, and the Scottish Parliament and Scottish Government would acquire responsibility for all domestic and international policy, similar to independent states everywhere, subject to the provisions of the European Union Treaties and other inherited treaty obligations.

The nature of the constitution of the United Kingdom is changing. There have been historic developments in Wales and Northern Ireland, and the United Kingdom Government has published proposals to develop further the Governance of the United Kingdom. Scotland, whether in the United Kingdom or independent should continue to play a leading role with our neighbours, taking the opportunity to improve the mechanisms for joint working arrangements between governments across the current United Kingdom and with the Republic of Ireland.

Enhanced devolution or Independence would require legislation, probably at both Westminster and Holyrood. Substantially enhanced devolution would arguably, and Independence would certainly, require the consent of the Scottish people through a referendum. Such a vote, while not constitutionally binding, has been accepted as the correct way of determining Scotland's constitutional future. There must, therefore, be due consideration of appropriate forms of legislation for such a vote, and of the question of how a referendum could be initiated by the Scottish Parliament.

In the Scottish Government's view there are three realistic choices. First, retention of the devolution scheme defined by the Scotland Act 1998, with the possibility of further evolution in powers, extending these individually as occasion arises. Second, redesigning devolution by adopting a specific range of extensions to the current powers of the Scottish Parliament and Scottish Government, possibly involving fiscal autonomy, but short of progress to full Independence. Third, which the Scottish Government favours, extending the powers of the Scottish Parliament and Scottish Government to the point of Independence. These possibilities are described more fully in the paper.

This paper is the first step in a wide ranging national conversation about the future of Scotland. This conversation will allow the people of Scotland to consider all the options for the future of the country and make informed decisions. This paper invites the people of Scotland to sign up for the national conversation and to suggest how the conversation should be designed to ensure the greatest possible participation'.

The Labour Response

For Scottish Labour, the SNP White Paper opened up the prospect of a real clash with Westminster and confirmed for those who were still sceptical that devolution *is* a process, not an event. The response from the Scottish Secretary Des Browne and the Scotland Office to the White Paper, after the SNP victory in 2007, showed how out of touch Westminster was with the prevailing mood of Scotland.

First, the Scotland Office issued a press release pointing out that the White Paper had failed to mention 'that reserved powers could be added to the Scotland Act, thereby transferring the functions of Holyrood Ministers to their Westminster counterparts.' Such a statement – which reads to sensitive Scots like a veiled threat – was a major own-goal for the government. Second, the Secretary of State for Defence (and Scotland) again demonstrated Unionist inflexibility by reaffirming the view that devolution was 'an event *not* a process' and insisted there was no need for more powers to be devolved to the Scottish Parliament. 'I am a Scot who supports the Union. I am a representative of a substantial majority in Scotland... who believe our future lies in the shared partnership of the Union, not in an isolated Scotland where we become strangers to ourselves.' It was difficult for anyone to make sense of the phrase 'an isolated Scotland where we become strangers to ourselves' – which seems symptomatic of the woolly thinking about devolution by those who put such words in the mouths of UK ministers.

He may have had in mind the Andrew Neil quote, quickly ridiculed by the late Donald Dewar in 1998, in which the fervently-Unionist and Scottish expatriate Neil mourned: 'Those of us who are proud to be Scottish and British have become strangers in our own land.'

Neil also complained: 'The foul-mouthed, anti-English rant of an Edinburgh heroin crackhead in *Trainspotting* has been made into Scotland's Gettysburg Address by fashionable bletherers.' In a typically dry put-down, Dewar commented: 'No case ever knowingly understated...'

Third, the Secretary of State suggested that Donald Dewar never said devolution was 'a process and not an event' and has issued a challenge to validate the quotation. The provenance of the quote hardly matters and is not a substitute for serious constitutional debate. In fact, the phrase may have been originated by Ron Davies, the former First Minister of Wales, but in any case Donald Dewar clearly supported the concept when he titled his Spectator Lecture, delivered on 18 November 1998, the day after the passing of the Scotland Act: 'Towards a Modern and Flexible Constitution'.

Dewar insisted:

Clearly, the debate should not stop when the doors of the Scottish Parliament open. What we have done in Scotland may be a catalyst for further change.

But there is a need for proper consideration. What is right for Scotland is not necessarily right for England. Scottish circumstances are different to English circumstances. There is already innovation in recognising the regional diversity here in England: there are ideas to be assessed, options to be explored. There is time to get it right'.

'He was also adamant that devolution would not separate Scotland from the rest of the United Kingdom because of 'that sense of tolerance which makes our political system work' and added:

> It would be absurd to think that the UK is so fragile that any change to the constitutional settlement is bound to result in the fracturing of the whole. It would be even more absurd to believe that the UK can saunter on into the future with precisely the same set of arrangements that have served it in the past'.

In his memorable and far-seeing speech at the opening of the Scottish Parliament on 1 July 1999, Dewar was even more explicit in predicting that devolution would be a process:

> For any Scot, today is a proud moment; a new stage on a journey begun long ago and which has no end. A Scottish Parliament. Not an end; a means to greater ends.

Against all that, the Whitehall response to the White Paper on an Independence referendum, delivered via the Scottish Secretary's office at Dover House, ignored the reality of the new politics in Scotland. Certainly, its dismissive attitude was in sharp contrast to the interest generated in Scotland by its publication and the launch speech by First Minister Alex Salmond.

In fairness, it should be pointed out that there are authoritative figures who argue that devolution was an adequate end in itself, that the basic legislation is sound and that change would create unnecessary stress. Lord Sewel, the former Scottish Office Minister at the time of the Scotland Act, has described those who view devolution as a process rather than a settlement as 'insidious' (*Towards A New Constitutional Settlement*, The Smith Institute, 2007) and warned:

> With a process there is a likelihood of ending up at some unforeseen and unwelcome destination. Indeed, until recently there have been too few politicians in Scotland who have confidently argued that devolution has secured for Scotland the best of all possible worlds. By this failure of confidence there has been created the impression that somehow the settlement is incomplete and that something more and better lies beyond.

However, Lord Sewel did admit:

Given that devolution constituted a unique legislative challenge, it is unlikely that every last detail of the settlement was 'got right' at the first attempt. Indeed, the ability of the settlement to develop organically has been one of its strengths...

What is essential is that, in resolving any tensions, those who value the Union should do so in ways that enable the different voices and interests within the Union to be heard and, even more importantly, that any adjustments are recognised as being fair to the constituent elements of the Union.

In other words, change is possible if it is made sensitively. We would argue that adjustments on powers are not only possible – but necessary.

The 'National Conversation'

Before the White Paper was published in Edinburgh, the opposition parties had issued a press release denouncing Independence, attacking the idea of a referendum and generally reiterating their hostility to any debate that had Independence as a possible outcome. However, of particular interest was the idea that there could be a review of the powers of the parliament.

This was the first time that all parties, especially the Unionist parties, had conceded that the debate was moving on. For the SNP government, the desired effect had been achieved in that they welcomed a debate beyond the substance of the Scotland Act – a process that would also create a split between Labour north and south of the border. Political and constitutional progress was now giving the 'national conversation' immediate legitimacy.

For Labour, in particular, their response was significant. A firm commitment to look at the powers of the parliament was linked to a joint statement of the main opposition parties; and by involving themselves in this with the Tories, Labour were breaking new ground.

This development was reinforced by opinion polls which suggested there was little enthusiasm for Independence but more support for new powers for the Scottish Parliament – a decisive rebuff to the 'status quo' devolution position of Westminster. Labour in Scotland have little to lose by adopting a tougher stand against inflexible Unionism at Westminster but a great deal to gain by parading their 'Scottishness' and being identified with an uncompromising approach to Scotland's interests.

On 28 August 2007, the three main Unionist parties in Scotland went a step further and held talks to agree a framework for their own 'national conversation', in rivalry with that launched by First Minister Alex Salmond on his Independence referendum plan. In what was described by the media as 'an historic alliance', the interim leader of Scottish Labour Cathy Jamieson, former Scottish Tory leader David McLetchie, and Scottish Lib-Dem leader Nicol Stephen committed their parties to a joint bid for more powers for the Scottish Parliament.

Significantly, among the issues discussed was the transfer of more tax powers to Holyrood and the party representatives agreed to take their initiative to the Scottish public and the Westminster Parliament. Their joint communiqué affirmed: 'We reject Independence. The real conversation, and the one in which the overwhelming majority of Scots wish to participate, is about how devolution can develop to best serve the people of Scotland.'

Mr Stephen said possibilities included a new Scottish Constitutional Convention to look into the devolution settlement, the setting up of a commission, or a special committee of the Holyrood Parliament.

A spokesman for Mr Salmond said the First Minister was 'delighted', adding: 'The national conversation train has left the station – it's a matter for the London-based parties which compartment they want to get on.' Alex Salmond had always argued for a broad debate. The SNP had nothing to lose as any step beyond the Scotland Act 1998 would take them closer to their ultimate goal of Independence. Of course, this was also the same reason why many Unionists, especially Labour were so concerned about making any further concessions to Nationalism and moving further down this slippery slope. There has never been a period in recent Labour history when this major mental block has given way to more progressive thinking. For Labour this has always been about stopping the Nationalists never about promoting the interests of Scotland.

The party representatives were emphatic that their initiative would not provide a pattern for any 'alternative executive', in which the opposition parties would cooperate on proposals and render the SNP government ineffective. They stressed that the meeting was designed purely to deal with the issue of the devolution settlement.

Mr McLetchie sounded a note of caution and said each of the parties had to work out their 'red, blue and yellow lines', the markers beyond which each party would refuse to go. For instance, Labour and the Tories would stop short of the Liberal Democrat call for a wide range of new powers, including control of tax and revenue-raising.

In effect, by signalling their willingness to consider reforms short of an Independence referendum, the Unionist parties were attempting to retrieve the initiative and isolate the SNP. This expectation may be ambitious but it provided some hopeful signs that the Unionist parties do not fear the constitutional issue and were willing to engage and be confident about their own ideas.

Whether UK politicians like it or not, the next stage of devolution was an all-party issue, not a single-party campaign. In the coming debate, the Scottish parties had to maintain their show of confidence and, if necessary, create clear blue-and-white water between Westminster and Holyrood. The fact could no longer be disguised that the constitutional debate was underway, reinforcing the now-distinctive politics of Scotland and giving some slight encouragement to the efforts of those who want a middle way between the hard-line positions of 'no more devolution' and 'no more Unionism'.

First Minister Alex Salmond maintained 'no change is no longer an option', but in opinion polls the Scottish people have said repeatedly that Independence is not a favoured choice. It is ironic that it took a White Paper on Independence produced by an SNP government to bring the other parties to their senses, move the debate forward and at the same time make everyone accept that devolution is unfinished business. The Calman Commission was the outcome of this latest twist on the devolution path. Further reflection suggested that this all Unionist party initiative did not really herald new thinking or an acceptance that further change was essential. At a time when the SNP were dominating the Constitutional debate and riding high in the opinion polls the Unionist parties viewed Calman as providing the least they could do, addressing critics of their apparent paralysis in the face of the SNP and ensuring the heat would be off them until the Commission reported. The Calman proposals, at least some of them, now form the new Scotland Act 2012. Some progress was made with new tax proposals and some policy transfer, but overall the Act has now been overtaken by recent events and is unlikely to make much impact in Scotland where the debate is further down the devolution road. Calman and the Scotland

Act will be best remembered for the political opportunity that brought the Unionist parties together to create some momentum to counter the surge of the SNP.

A Third Way

This search for a third way on the constitutional question has been around for a long time as an idea with a compelling logic between two extremes as well as satisfying the desire of many Scots who do not wish to be independent but want Scotland to go much further than Unionism allows. The perverse nature of our politics seems content with extremes, confrontation, drama and tribal affiliations to out dated ideas and arguments. On this issue we are selling the public short and not giving them either sensible leadership or sound ideas for a better future for our nation. There is little wonder that the public are increasingly disenchanted with the performance of our politics as their wishes expressed in opinion polls and in other ways are simply ignored to preserve the uninspiring politics that are destroying any prospect of real change. Describing anything as 'third way' clearly concerns the political classes because it smacks of common sense and consensus and, remarkably, responding to public opinion. Scots feel they are caught between a constitutional rock and a political hard place. The 2007 White Paper sets out the three main realistic choices for Scots – the present devolved set-up; redesigning devolution by extending the powers of the Scottish Parliament in specific areas; or full Independence. There are however a significant number of variations around the middle option which go beyond powers and seek a more European, modern and ambitious view of Scotland's future.

The debate in Scotland cannot be removed from the wider UK debate about the constitutional future of the Union. Scots must be able to assess and involve themselves in discussion of the significance of England, Wales and Northern Ireland and ensure the UK government and parliament do not regard devolution as a distinctive (and often tiresome) Scottish issue. One effect of the 'new politics' of Scotland should be to stimulate the debate in England. The current gaping disconnect between London and Edinburgh is harmful, and lack of a more flexible and informed approach which will allow Scotland to become more autonomous could be a serious threat to the future of the Union. Constant reference to 'Britishness', appearing to ignore the diversity of the constituent parts of the UK, actually undermines the broader reality it seeks to reflect. Diversity and pluralism are strengths and, if dealt with intelligently, could shape a different kind of Union which harnesses more effectively the energy, enterprise and decency of the people. Those same people will embrace bigger ideas and will not be shackled with outdated notions of sovereignty and Britishness. New political realities are competing for the loyalty and trust of our citizens. The devolution/Independence debate tends to focus on past history, where we are and where we have come from, instead of being concerned with what we can achieve and where we are going.

CHAPTER 8

The Battle for Scotland

THE SCOTTISH WHITE PAPER and the UK Green Paper, both 2007, and the Scottish Government and UK Consultation papers 2012, have clearly defined the context of Scotland's date with destiny and have drawn the battle lines in a way that identifies two diametrically opposed options for Scotland's political and constitutional future and the rigid thinking that lies behind them. The stable-state politics needed by Scotland will not be delivered by either approach.

The White Paper of 2007 may have a fully independent Scotland as its aim, but its overwhelming significance was that it opened the debate that may result in the less extreme 'third way' solution.

In his foreword, Alex Salmond rightly says: 'Whatever the differences between the political parties, the message of the [May 2007] election was obvious – the constitutional position of Scotland must move forward.'

He proposed 'that we have a national conversation on our future to allow the people of Scotland to debate, reflect and then decide on the type of government which best equips us for the future... this paper is intended as the starting point and inspiration for that conversation'.

He is also at pains to point out: 'The political debate in Scotland concerns the 1707 political union, the amendment or repeal of which would still leave the Union of the Crowns intact.'

The White Paper captures the wider significance of the devolution debate: 'There have also been recent, historic constitutional developments in Northern Ireland and Wales, with new parties coming to government and new responsibilities being devolved. The United Kingdom government has now published a discussion paper on the governance of Britain.'

Among the areas in which the White Paper suggests Scotland could take on further responsibilities are 'employment, our national finances, or legislation on public safety such as firearms – as well as the concept of Independence, and wider constitutional developments in Britain.'

Of course, the White Paper leaves us in no doubt as to the long-term intentions of the SNP and its new government: 'I [the First Minister] lead the first Scottish National Party Government to be elected in a devolved

Scotland, so I will put the case for Independence, its benefits and opportunities.'

Mr Salmond heightens the drama by saying: 'I believe it is now time for us, the people of Scotland, to consider and choose our own future in the modern world.' The use of the words 'us' and 'our' builds on the SNP's embrace of a distinctly inclusive and Scottish approach and tends to emphasise more constitutional change as matter-of-fact and common sense given the start already made and the achievements gained in ten years of devolution.

There is little to which even the most bitter opponents of Independence could take exception, in view of the fact that this is merely the SNP delivering a manifesto commitment in the first 100 days. It is no surprise that the document is part of a long-term strategy to win Independence for Scotland.

The key question was whether the other parties can turn this into a genuine national conversation about the political and constitutional future of Scotland and have the courage and confidence to take ownership of the debate and be comfortable with the issues. The majority of the Scottish people and the majority of the political parties in the parliament do not support Independence; but on the other hand the public seemed to be giving more political support to the new SNP minority government in 2007 because they liked what was on offer, especially in relation to defending Scotland's interests.

All roads may not lead to Independence and Scotland's departure from the political Union but, if the opposition parties and Westminster do not urgently embrace the new debate and new thinking, then all options will remain open. The people of Scotland will decide, but that decision should be made with a clear choice of political futures. Scotland is in transition and 2007 was only the start of the political transformation which has shown the emergence of a new politics. The SNP's domination of the constitutional debate has continued unchecked and in the 2011 Holyrood elections they achieved majority government status. As never before, politics north of the border is distinctive and volatile and it has always provided an opportunity for the opposition parties to seize the opportunity to lead the debate, present alternatives to Independence and not be left in the SNP's slipstream. To date, this has never happened and, while Scots remain opposed to Independence, there is a danger that, over time, a number of political and economic factors will change the context of the debate and Scots will become less opposed to taking their country out of the Union.

The Meaning of Independence

The summary of the White Paper sets out a way forward for the national conversation and, in doing so, provides more than a hint of what a future Scotland could look like. This raises a number of questions:

- What does Independence actually mean in a world of dramatic and continuing change in which interdependence and internationalism, global and European issues transcend borders and boundaries?;
- The narrative contains references to the continuance of the Union of the Crowns, even if the Treaty of Union is repealed; this does raise some doubts about whether Britain as a whole would be broken up or only certain dimensions of it. If so, what would remain?
- If we are talking about the political union, what about the social union, the cultural union, the economic union and the constitutional union? Would they remain in their present form or would repealing the Treaty of Union affect them too?
- The Union of the UK is not the only union in which we participate; others include the European Union and the global union. The shifting political power balance between the three unions again raises doubts about the nature of Independence and the extent to which it has any significant meaning: recent events thrown up by the global economic, financial and banking crisis have cast doubt over whether any country, with the exception of the USA, could be conceived as having economic Independence.
- Are we in danger of creating 'virtual Independence', where everything changes but everything remains the same? This will certainly be the style adopted by the First Minister to convince Scots that there is nothing to fear about Independence, especially when the Union of the UK does not seem fit for purpose.
- Does all of this ambiguity about Independence not strengthen the idea of a constitutional option which provides Scotland with the

best of all worlds? A Scotland which remains part of a dramatically changed or transformed Union and has the maximum level of fiscal and financial autonomy consistent with this and a range of powers which stops short of Defence, certain key treasury and currency matters and certain aspects of Foreign affairs. This would provide Scotland with the best platform for realising its potential. What the SNP want for Scotland may not be what Scotland needs! The domination of the constitutional debate by the SNP is bad for Scotland but only if there are political parties exploiting the obvious weaknesses of the SNP's concern with Independence. Unionism is equally out of touch with much of what is happening in Europe and internationally. Scotland deserves better than a Union which is not fit for purpose, an Independence argument which does not make sense in an interdependent world, and the dangers of big 'N' nationalism. The case for an alternative grows ever stronger.

- The fact that our debates are so narrowly focused within the UK means we are ignoring alternatives to Independence which work well for other countries and ancient nations in other parts of Europe. Respecting the desire to be independent as a nation state at the end of the 30 years' War and the post Peace of Westphalia in 1648 mode of thinking, there are other definitions of 'Independence' which may be more modern and relevant to the kind of Scotland that we want to be. This is where current language has been constraining and maybe we need not only new thinking, but new language which better suits the issues that we face and the solutions we seek.

- There is a distinction to be drawn between 'hard and 'soft' politics. In international affairs, these terms are often used to describe different approaches and their objectives. We should not under-estimate Alex Salmond's ability to use the softer side of constitutional politics to persuade Scots to accept the much harder elements of Independence.

- Independence, by its focus on sentiment, identity and nationality and pride and patriotism, tugs at the very being of most Scots. We should not under-estimate the impact of this when the only alternative is an uncaring and uncompromising Unionism which doesn't touch any part of being a Scot. This poses the question of what the Union stands for and what it will mean to Scots in 2014. Salmond understands the subtlety and sophistication of these issues.

All of these questions raise an important issue: is Independence a state of mind, an aspiration wholly divorced from, or at least lacking real impact on, the real lives of the Scottish people? Would it be meaningless in tomorrow's world or would it add any value to Scotland or its people? An evidence-based debate which acknowledges the interdependence of the world in which we live might produce answers the SNP would not wish to contemplate, and would focus on issues which are not based on materialism and the economy.

Much of the constitutional debate so far, and certainly over the last ten years, has been short on facts and evidence and shallow at the expense of substance. It has often been abstract and off the radar of most people. As a result, the dialogue has been emotional and ideological with party political exchanges crowding out any deeper meaningful insights. The debate about the nation's constitutional future has been of a very low order and the 2007 and 2011 Scottish elections only served to underline this, with Labour and the SNP heatedly disputing an agenda barely understood by the electorate.

It is trite to say that Scottish politics has to raise its game, but the projected 'national conversation' (irrespective of which party initiates it) provides the opportunity for this to happen. The White Paper post-2007 provided the opposition parties with the best of reasons for contesting and rejecting the notion that we are already on a slippery slope to Independence. It also brings to the fore issues and ideas not often seen in the constitutional debate and provides the basis for serious argument and reflection about the doubts, confusions and contradictions at the heart of Independence, its relevance and its meaning to a nation and its people.

The historic debates in Wales and Northern Ireland over the past five years also adds significant meaning to the debate in Scotland, and signposts ideas to strengthen our links, build new structures and create a louder and more vigorous voice for devolution and the new politics. A new dynamic is at work and it cannot be avoided. Wales is likely to demand more powers from Westminster in the future as its Assembly gains in stature and confidence; the new coalition of Plaid Cymru and Labour in 2007 has signed an agreement which seems likely to see more demands. Some primary legislative powers have recently been added and these will continue to weaken the links with Westminster. After the 2011 elections, where the Welsh Labour Party did remarkably well, there have been significant new developments. The remarkable performance over the last five years of the Welsh Labour party is in sharp contrast to what has happened in Scotland. There are lessons to be learned from Wales in regard to a party getting closer to its national roots, taking on Plaid Cymru and putting forward more progressive political values.

The remarkable developments in Northern Ireland may create the conditions for more dramatic change in the future. Overcoming sectarian violence and confirming the primacy of the ballot box opens up a new future for the Province and there are many different options for further development within Northern Ireland itself, on the island of Ireland, between the six counties of the North and the 26 counties of the Republic, between the Province and Westminster and within the devolved nations and regions of the Union. The politics and practicalities of all this may as yet be difficult to comprehend – but what happens to our neighbours will inevitably impact on Scotland.

When the changes taking place in the devolved areas (including London) are considered, it is hard to escape the conclusion that they are likely to continue in the future. The question is whether the Union, as embodied by the Westminster government and parliament, will be a willing partner or whether change will have to be rung out of it on a 'grudge and grievance' basis. The role of Westminster over the next few years will be crucial if devolution and constitutional change are to proceed and Independence for Scotland is to remain an aspiration for some – but never a reality for the nation as a whole.

Strategy – or Fantasy?

The danger of the SNP strategy for the opposition parties in Scotland is that the national conversation is sold as an effortless debate about the future of Scotland where we are all on a journey and the road could take one of three directions, each of which has its merits. No matter which route is taken, everyone is a neighbour and the UK government and parliament act as cheerleaders, waving encouragement from the side of the road as Scotland drives further and further away from the political Union.

Of course, for some this is in the realm of Nationalist fantasy – but more and more electors could buy into what is presented as a painless and trouble-free future. The less compelling the case for devolution and the Union, the more compelling will be the case for Independence and separation. The national conversation offers the Unionist parties an opportunity to prevent that from happening, but they should guard against their own tribal feuds, which are based on polarised positions. The SNP is a formidable force in Scottish politics and should never be underestimated, as complacent Unionist politicians and commentators have done in the past.

For the SNP in 2007, their inability to get the referendum legislation through the Scottish Parliament was tactically useful. They needed time to prove that they can govern with competence, build popular support in the country for practical policies and exploit the perceived anti-Scottish sentiment at Westminster, at the same time showing that the apocalyptic fears of an SNP government are misplaced and that 'standing up for Scotland' is a workable approach. While the wrangling over a referendum continues, they can constantly use the mantra that at least they are willing to consult the Scottish people and allow them to have their say. The election of a majority Government in 2011 has changed everything. The worst nightmare of the Unionist parties, in Scotland and Westminster, has become a reality and five wasted years later Labour, the Lib-Dems and the Conservatives are only now engaging.

For the opposition parties in Scotland, this represents both a threat and an opportunity. The longer the SNP's Holyrood honeymoon lasted, the more chance this strategy had of working. The SNP-inspired idea of a Speaker's (or Presiding Officer's) conference to look at new powers on a cross-party basis was both clever and helpful. It sought to build on the obvious consensus that exists for more powers and at the same time acknowledged the fact that the legislation path, at least for now, was blocked. This didn't happen and control of the agenda for political and constitutional change remained in the SNP's hands and under their direction and leadership. The other parties in the aftermath of the 2007 election ignored the compelling logic that they must start to think strategically and afresh about the future and not be left following the debate rather than leading it. Five wasted years have intervened and little if no progress was made. The SNP as a result continued to dominate Scottish politics, not just the constitutional question

This is where Scottishness and strategic thinking can pay dividends. It should not be forgotten that being the party of government gives credibility and legitimacy to the SNP, putting enormous pressure on the opposition parties in Scotland, and also the Coalition government at Westminster, to be smarter in their response to developments north of the border. They have to accept the fact that the constitution is a live issue and will not go away.

Of deeper significance is the idea that Scots might start to warm to a party that is distinctively Scottish, especially if the Westminster government appears more rigidly Unionist. There are obvious dividends for a party that is seen to defend Scottish interests while managing to provide efficient and modern government – especially if the other parties in Scotland cannot shrug off their overriding allegiances to Westminster.

A Split Personality

Paradoxically, an SNP government could continue to be elected at the same time as Scots continue to vote against Independence in a referendum. This is the Québécois scenario of the 'neverendum', which could be replicated in Scotland: the voters park their ideology and values at the elections to the Holyrood Parliament and elect an SNP or SNP coalition government, but vote differently at Westminster elections. These are issues which have emerged elsewhere in the world but which we simply have not mastered. The impressive success of Scottish Labour's campaign in the General Election in 2010 was a telling reminder of Scotland's hatred of the Conservative party, but also evidence that Scots are voting and thinking differently in this post-devolution era. Scotland has a political split-personality and we ignore this fact of political life at our peril.

This is the new Scottish politics and there are critical dangers for the other political parties if they fail to appreciate the opportunities and threats. The Scottish people might buy the view that the SNP is an 'insurance policy' against the UK government. They might also use the SNP as a threat to Westminster, in the same way the Westminster parties currently try to present the SNP as a threat. For that reason, Scots might maintain the SNP in government, although they would never vote for Independence. The Scottish electorate are exercising more critical and strategic thinking than they have been given credit for and this could have a major impact on the politics of Scotland in the longer term. This new mindset could be influenced by other arguments for constitutional change, vital to this would be the approach of Westminster and whether or not there is a willingness to be more relaxed and flexible about the future of the Union. What is remarkable is that, since the rise of the SNP from the 2003 Holyrood election, the Unionist parties have simply ignored this unfolding nightmare, being guided by their complacency and their sense of entitlement; and have failed to understand what is going on. Whatever the reason, there are now traps being laid by the SNP and the First Minister and if they are not careful, Scotland could be slipping from their grasp sometime in the future.

From the setting up of the Scottish Parliament to the present time, there has been much discussion about whether any new form of politics was taking shape. Looking at this from the narrow and traditional view of the political parties, it would be reasonable to conclude that there has been little change. If, however, we adopt a more critical and less superficial analysis, then a different understanding emerges.

Rather than surface appearances, deeper analysis would show that there have been significant changes in the mood and mindset of Scottish voters and that these have gained momentum since the May 2007 and May 2011 elections. This is made more complex by the myriad other changes that are taking place in society and the economy, at the various levels of political activity from the global to the local and in terms of individual aspirations, ambitions and lifestyles.

A quiet revolution has been taking place which does not ensure any specific political outcome but certainly does guarantee political change and uncertainty. The politics of change were not recognised to any perceptible degree – until mid-2007, when the recognition was forced upon Scotland's political class. This transformation is now complete and the political fortunes of all the political parties have been shaken up.

Scottish voters may be accepting the line from Westminster factions, including some Labour MPs, seeking to downplay the importance of devolution and the Scottish Parliament. As a consequence, these voters resort to voting in a different way from the Westminster elections. A parallel is the apparently more sophisticated attitude being adopted to the second vote, the list vote, in the Scottish Parliament elections.

Many voters may be identifying more with their Scottishness and less with their traditional party affiliation, class loyalty and generational allegiances. This was certainly evident in the May 2007 and May 2011 elections where a number of complex factors were at work. The lessons of 2007 and 2011 are quite different. With only a marginal increase in turn-out, the SNP gained dramatically in seats but not in popular vote, while Labour did not do too badly overall on either count in 2007. But in 2011, the SNP dramatically increased their number of seats and increased their share of the vote and Labour did disastrously on both. The rise of the SNP makes uncomfortable reading for Labour in particular. While providing credible, competent and confident Government at Holyrood, the SNP is also deploying a well-organized strategic campaign throughout the country, election by election, and they are building capacity and organizational strength. This was evident in the 2012 Council elections, where Labour may have captured some headlines by their powerful showing in Glasgow and in some other areas, but overall the SNP just kept building their base and extending their political reach, essential if they are to fight a successful Independence campaign. If the Unionist parties were interested, lessons could be learned.

When the same party (i.e. Labour) is in power at Westminster and Holyrood, Scotland may not be seen as having a distinct political culture and identity and as a result, a vote in the Scottish election may be used as a protest against the ruling party.

The role of the media becomes decisive in setting the national mood. The degree of trivialisation of the work of the Scottish Parliament and the opportunity taken to use its openness and transparency to focus on personalities, not policies, can undermine the confidence of the legislators and create negativity among the electorate. This will not help the parliament to be more inclusive nor help attract the 'brightest and best' from outwith the narrow recruiting grounds of the public sector, trade unions and local government. There are consequences in this for the quality of our new democracy in Scotland.

The voting habits and the breaking down of allegiances, affiliations and alliances in the election to the Scottish Parliament could in the future spill over into the Westminster elections. This again would be Labour's worst nightmare if the elections for Westminster started to follow the pattern of Holyrood. The possibility of proportional representation being introduced for these elections would have dire consequences for the established political order and the Unionist parties. The defeat of the Alternative Vote system (AV) in the referendum removed that immediate threat. It could also be the case that, if Scotland moves on and develops a distinctive political culture and identity, voting SNP in Westminster elections becomes less attractive and increasingly irrelevant to the extent that the SNP contemplate withdrawing from London and concentrate on Scotland.

The attitude of the Union in this changed political environment becomes more important. The political parties in Scotland, in particular the SNP and Labour, will continue to be the main players but the role of Westminster cannot be overstated. UK politicians need to recognise that, in a time of change and uncertainty, a split political personality is developing in Scotland.

Thus, the battle for Scotland is underway, with Unionism and Separatism head-to-head, and much of it is already happening below the surface of mainstream politics.

CHAPTER 9

Powers and the People

THERE HAS BEEN MUCH discussion about how the constitutional debate should be taken forward and the issue of more powers for the Scottish Parliament has led the agenda. Westminster is not enthusiastic and would like to see a review of the effectiveness of existing powers before countenancing any talk about additional powers. It stands to reason that any consideration of powers would certainly have to include an examination of the use and efficacy of existing powers. Since 1997, the Calman Commission was set up to undertake such a review but for many, the work of the Commission was limited and was constrained by the Unionist parties who remained concerned about what might emerge. The Calman report was published and their findings found expression in the Scotland Act 2012.

There is an important point to be made about powers. In an ideal world, consensus provides a sound basis upon which to build change and move forward. The SNP are happy to endorse any change that helps to move them towards their ultimate goal. For the Unionist parties, deeply suspicious of anything the SNP say, this has the opposite effect, and makes them extremely wary of even talking about further powers. This allows the SNP to criticise them. The SNP are always in a 'win, win' situation because of the lack of tactical nous on the part of the Unionist parties.

When the White Paper 'Scotland's Parliament' was published in 1997 and the Scotland Act was delivered in 1999, there was broad agreement about the powers. Across party lines, there was a positive acceptance of how substantial the powers were, even support (albeit grudging) from the SNP. The quality of the 1997 White Paper influenced every other step in the devolution process. This was largely the result of Donald Dewar's skilful defence of the proposed powers and his unwillingness to make any concessions which would weaken the settlement during the gruelling sessions of the constitutional sub-committee at Westminster that was overseeing the contents of the White Paper.

Over the first two terms of the Scottish Parliament, these substantial powers were used to good effect in creating often ground-breaking legislation, as well as in providing the basis for effective executive decision-making.

A number of things have changed since the framing of the original White Paper. The Scottish Parliament and MSPs now have 13 years of experience of the devolved powers and are in a position to reflect and, if appropriate, seek changes to the settlement – including deciding whether new powers are needed.

Fiscal Responsibility

Taxation is the most obvious power for discussion, but there are others just as far-reaching. It is highly unlikely that the tax-raising powers in the 1998 Act could ever be used. On reflection, the inclusion of tax-raising powers in the legislation had more to do with reinforcing the credibility of the settlement than providing a practical financial option for any Scottish government.

This raises the possibility of revisiting the fiscal powers available to Holyrood and, in turn, the Scottish Parliament's financial relationship with Westminster. These are complex and politically-sensitive matters that strike at the heart of the constitutional question and challenge Westminster on how flexible it wants to be.

The issue of Scotland's relative tax competitiveness with other parts of the UK cannot be ignored. The block grant from Westminster, based on English spend subject to the Barnett formula, does not create fiscal responsibility and leaves the Scottish Parliament entirely dependent on Westminster for all of its cash. The idea of Holyrood being responsible for all its spending but having no responsibility for raising any of its funds doesn't make sense and will continue to eat away at the credibility of the Scottish Parliament. Any substantial change in this will have profound consequences for Holyrood and more importantly for its relationship with Westminster. Westminster likes to control the purse strings although it remains concerned about what we spend it on and the impact this has on English voters. The Fiscal issue is the key to substantial further change to devolution, it is, however, the issue that most worries the Unionist parties north and south of the border. A grudging and resentful mentality has developed on these issues among MPs at Westminster, especially the Conservative led Coalition and English Tories, and is regularly nurtured by some London-based newspapers. Scotland's Parliament needs to take more responsibility for tax and spend and be accountable to Scots for their actions

The devolution settlement largely excludes foreign affairs, international development and international relations. These matters are reserved to Westminster but, again, the parliament and Scottish government find this restrictive. There is a genuine interest in expanding Scotland's role on the world stage and being able to raise significantly its international profile in line with the remarkable worldwide impact Scots have made over the centuries. The size of Scotland's diaspora and expatriate networks and the contribution the Scottish Enlightenment played in developing the modern world have meant Scotland's influence has been utterly disproportionate to the size of its population.

With the supranational agenda sweeping aside barriers, making national boundaries less relevant and breaking down traditional rules for global engagement, a devolved Scotland understandably sees its role and its international aspirations changing.

Faced with these changes, it is unsurprising that there should be a growing movement in Scotland for powers to be on the agenda, and the response of Westminster will be decisive. That being the case, Scotland's approach should be thorough and show how effectively existing powers have been used. The theme should be powers with a purpose, not just for politics. In April of 2012, some of Scotland's Trade Union leaders made a telling intervention in the debate by arguing that much of the constitutional debate was abstract and divorced from the needs of ordinary people, making the point that we should decide on what kind of Scotland we want and then debate more thoroughly the kind of powers and fiscal responsibilities we need. There is a great deal of truth in this, as we continually talk about structures and process but rarely discuss anything else. This is about to change as the referendum campaign begins and the Unionist parties start to take seriously ideas of fiscal federalism, fiscal autonomy and fiscal responsibility.

A working agenda should cover improving on the current settlement as well as looking at more radical ideas which capture more fiscal responsibility, such as devo-plus or devo-max or some hybrid of the two. This acknowledges the new Scotland Act 2012, but has to be more ambitious as the political temperature rises and the referendum approaches.

- The need to entrench the devolution settlement with safeguards that provide some protection against unreasonable or ill-judged changes being made at Westminster. Powers are devolved and not shared as they would be in a federal structure. It should also rectify the technical position which hangs like a Sword of Damocles over devolution: the fact that a one-line, one-clause Bill to abolish the Scottish Parliament could be passed in the House of Commons. A referendum of the Scottish people requiring assent to two questions was necessary before the Scotland Act was processed at Westminster – but there is no equivalent provision for its abolition. Clearly, nothing so dramatic will happen but the possibility exists that governments in the future could amend the Scotland Act to the detriment of Scotland, without the need for consultation or agreement. The sovereignty of the Westminster Parliament makes little sense in this context; in federal systems, safeguards are built into the constitution which demand stringent levels of consent before any changes can be made. Of course, the United Kingdom does not have a written constitution and, as yet, we do not have multiple sources of sovereignty.
- What new powers are needed and why: consideration could be given to the broad areas of Europe, taxes, finance, immigration, environment, employment and the economy, social security, governance... and of course, oil and gas, and energy generally. Within these areas, reserved to Westminster, there are specific concerns which need to be addressed. An important idea could be the 'opt-out' much used by the Westminster government in the European Union, which would allow Scotland more variation on key issues where Scottish needs, priorities or wishes were different from the rest of the UK. There is a powerful analogy to be made between the union of the UK and the EU and this may help Scotland find a way forward on seeking derogations or opt-outs from UK legislation.
- Areas which do not require a shift in powers but where more

effective consultation, cooperation and involvement in policy-making and implementation are needed: the EU, immigration and justice are obvious examples. The 'memorandum of understandings' covers these matters but may now need to be renegotiated.

- Important issues such as the Barnett formula, which are not in the Scotland Act, but are now the focus of criticism and debate. There is much talk of a new needs assessment: what role, if any, would the Scottish government or the parliament have if such a review took place?

- Democracy, governance and elections: the distribution of powers should be a subject of a review. After the Scottish Parliamentary election shambles in 2007, where over 140,000 Scots electors (3.5per cent of the total electorate) were disenfranchised and then not included in the turn-out figure, raised serious doubts about who should be held to account. The matter was reported to MPs on the floor of the House of Commons by the Secretary of State for Scotland because it was a reserved matter. Scots felt someone should be held to account for this, but that did not happen.

The referendum campaign should ensure all areas of reserved matters to Westminster are debated and in particular the level of fiscal responsibility Scotland should aspire to.

A Missed Opportunity

Underpinning all of this is an urgent need for more original thinking, ideas and innovation in Scotland in terms of the contributions from universities, think-tanks and other centres of knowledge. It is surprising that in the aftermath of the remarkable political and constitutional changes that took place in the UK after 1997, especially in Scotland, we have not become an important international focus of excellence for debate and expertise on devolved governments and legislatures. Scotland seems to have missed an opportunity, since there is enormous interest overseas; yet, with some notable exceptions, there is a failure to take advantage of the body of knowledge and experience that has been built up.

Scots have also developed the mindset that, in some way, devolution is unique to them and Scotland is exceptional in terms of developments over the last ten years. This has resulted in failure to learn from the experiences of others overseas and isolation from ideas, trends and changes which are part and parcel of everyday devolution experience elsewhere in the world. There is still time to change this.

Of most significance is the lack of modern and inspired thinking from the Unionist parties, especially Labour. While the SNP talks about Independence, there is often little substance to their vision for the future of the country and surprisingly little work on nation-building and what Independence would mean.

Academics, thinkers, political parties, politicians, ministers, civil servants and other policy-makers should lead the drive for more informed and evidence-based material. A better exchange of information and a new language for dialogue – making the direct link between political and constitutional change and the lives of the Scottish people – could create a more informed electorate and inspire, enthuse and enrich our democracy.

The Barnett Formula

The UK failure to come to terms with the new politics in Scotland is aggravated by the two-pronged attack on the relationship between Westminster and the devolved parliaments. In tandem with the 'English votes for English laws' faction, is the continuing campaign against the Barnett formula.

The method of allocating proportionate shares of public expenditure to Scotland, Wales and Northern Ireland – devised in the late 1970s by then Chief Secretary to the Treasury, Joel Barnett – was a settlement of convenience, a solution to the problem of the day, which has survived in the face of on-going criticism. The whole ethos of Barnett is now so divorced from its original concept that the evidence needs to be revisited; from being a mere mechanism of fiscal policy, it has taken on a political life and symbolism far beyond the original intention.

The advent of a Scottish Nationalist government in Edinburgh has rekindled the controversy and Lord Barnett himself has said there is clearly a need for change. In the House of Lords on 5 June 2007, he asked the government: 'Following recent elections to the Scottish

Parliament, what plans do they have for changes in financial policies with regard to Scotland?'

He pinpointed the source of English discontent by citing the latest Treasury figures on public expenditure, showing that in England the figure was £6,949 per head, while in Scotland it was £8,414. This, he said, was 'unacceptable'. (The figures for 2010/11 were England £8,588 and Scotland £10,212) Lord Barnett thought the least the government could concede is the need for a review of the current formula 'to see that we have one based on genuine need', adding: 'I can assure Lord Davies of Oldham, Cabinet Office Minister in the Lords that if such a formula were agreed, I would be happy to see the name continue!'

Unsatisfied by the government reply that it had no plans to change the formula at this stage, he returned a month later – the day after the government Green Paper on 'The Governance of Britain' – with a call for the appointment of a select committee on a review of the formula. This time, he received support from Lord Forsyth of Drumlean (as Michael Forsyth, the former Tory Secretary of State for Scotland), who said:

> It will clearly be untenable for Scotland to continue to receive more expenditure per head while implementing policies such as having free tuition fees for Scottish students when English students have to pay, allowing Lucentis, which prevents blindness, to be prescribed on the NHS in Scotland but not in the UK, and having free care for the elderly north of the Border. I accept that the Scottish Parliament is entitled to take these decisions, but it has to do so in the context of a funding system that is seen to be fair to all parts of the United Kingdom.

Lord Sewel, in his contribution to the Smith Institute pamphlet *Towards a New Constitutional Settlement*, wrote:

> Barnett served the UK well prior to devolution and was important in enabling a smooth transition to be made to devolved government. It has now outlived its usefulness. Its lack of transparency is, at least in part, the reason for it being perceived as a cause of grievance between England and Scotland.
>
> But, more powerfully, fairness demands that the relative expenditure levels of Scotland to the rest of the UK should be based on a new, objective study of relative expenditure needs.

Unlike the responsible approach of Lords Barnett and Sewel, much of the attack on the Barnett formula is ill-informed and often driven by the politics of envy. If Barnett is to be reformed, it can only be done by the UK government and then it should be in consultation with the devolved administrations and peoples.

It must also be a debate untainted by a narrow nationalist perspective on the one extreme and Little Englander, generally anti-Scottish, prejudice on the other. Any reform that smacks of a 'dish the Scots' mentality would be politically disastrous.

The harsh reality is that there is nothing to prevent that, since Barnett is not protected by any constitutional or legal safeguards. A Westminster government of another political complexion could, if so minded, simply say the formula has been changed.

As Chancellor of the Exchequer, Gordon Brown had no reason to want the Barnett formula opened up for discussion or review but, whether he likes it or not, recent events have caused such a discussion to happen. If Northern Ireland wants more money, which may well be a condition of the remarkable settlement achieved there, the Welsh will not be content with a lesser share. Nor would there be any political sense in Scotland apparently losing out to satisfy to satisfy English pettiness.

The solutions to the Barnett problem are possible within one of the following:

1   Independence.
2   Fiscal autonomy of a kind that sees Scots spending their own money and being more accountable for the taxes they raise, while remitting a due amount to Westminster for UK services – which would still require a Barnett-type calculation (devo-max).
3   A more credible modern formula with an objective assessment of the needs of the various constituent parts of the UK, including English regions.
4   Fiscal federalism where the responsibility of raising and spending money is with Holyrood and there is a separate receipt raised for the services that remain with Westminster (devo-plus).

The strong implication of the third solution is that Scotland could lose out and would have to call on the so-called 'Tartan Tax', the Scottish

Parliament's unused power to raise or lower income tax by 3p in the pound. This is one of the main criticisms of the Calman proposals. They are neither one thing nor the other and leave unresolved the long-term fiscal problem and the issues of responsibility and accountability.

Options 2 and 4 are the focus of the devo-diversity debate now taking place in Scotland regarding the alternative to the 'in and out' options and the second question.

Another factor is that 1999–2007 was a purple patch for public investment. From 2008, the financial outlook has been dramatically altered. The referendum will take place against a backdrop of one of the most austere periods in a generation and the debt and deficit reductions will have an enormous impact on Scotland as well as the campaign. That is bound to be less favourable for Scotland's finances under any system of distribution – and the SNP would be able to present this as Scotland being disadvantaged for England's gain. There are powerful reasons why fiscal federalism or fiscal autonomy should be options in our constitutional debate. Without a serious outcome to the financial issues, the UK, England, Westminster and London will be blamed for our misfortunes to no-one's benefit other than the SNP. Public finance is all about politics and lies at the heart of what we do next.

CHAPTER 10

The 'English Question'

IN THE DEVOLUTION DEBATE, the future should be more important than the shibboleths and slogans of the past. But a new and dangerous slogan that has emerged from the Tory benches at Westminster is 'English votes for English laws'.

The catchphrase is simply a reworking of the West Lothian question, but what makes it more perilous for the Union is that it is motivated by political opportunism, in which the Conservatives in particular seek to compensate for their pitiful electoral showing in Scotland by attacking Scottish representation at Westminster. The incongruity of this position has not dawned on them: the self-declared defenders of the Union are endangering it by their ill-conceived campaign, which is a recipe for alienation, division and constitutional chaos. The West Lothian question cannot be resolved until there is a constitutional settlement which establishes a serious and sustainable long term role for Scotland in the Union. For Westminster, Tam Dalyell's remarkable question will remain an irritation until they engage sensibly with the debate instead of using it as a stick with which to beat Scots MPs. There are sound reasons why Scots should not be able to vote on areas of domestic policy that are dealt with in London. Setting aside the constitutional issue, the English people feel that it is unfair that Scots can vote on matters affecting them but they can't vote on the same issues devolved to Scotland.

By concentrating on the restricted issue of whether Scottish MPs should be able to vote on English issues – while, it should be said, unable to vote on the same issues as they affect their own constituencies north of the border – the Tories would undermine the House of Commons and destroy the link between UK parliamentary democracy and the UK government. MPs from Scotland, Wales and Northern Ireland would be down-graded to second-class representatives and an England-only caucus could create havoc for the UK government's legislative programme.

Suggested solutions to the 'English question' have included federalism and a separate English Parliament, some form of reconfigured business at Westminster, assemblies in the English regions and an English Grand Committee at Westminster. Westminster seems to again miss the point. This issue, like many others, requires a political solution and not some short term technical fix. The McKay Commission set up by the Westminster Parliament is currently looking at the matter.

Any attempt to deal with the emerging aspects of the English question requires England and Westminster to take responsibility for their future in the changing politics of the Union. England should become a significant part of the debate, which has concentrated up to now on Scotland, Wales and Northern Ireland. These devolved components of the Union are not out of step with current constitutional politics; England is the anomaly. This has been the folly of regarding devolution as only a matter for the devolved territories.

It is important for Westminster and the English to acknowledge how far the devolution debate has moved on. England is four-fifths of the Union, so it is a distortion to suggest that the Union should be the focus of change without addressing the English question. At the same time, there should be less clamour for that 'dispossessed majority' to be linked to anti-Scottishness. The problems of England and the Union will not be solved by attacking the constitutional settlement for Scotland, Wales and Northern Ireland and their achievements in the last decade. England has identity, diversity, difference and nationality and should not regard Westminster as the final solution to the multiplicity of cultures, needs and problems that exist from Newcastle to Newquay. If Scotland feels the distorting and disproportionate impact of the London metropolis, then other parts of England will undoubtedly be in the same position if not worse!

In a thoughtful contribution, *The Unfinished Business of Devolution – The Challenges Ahead*, published by the Institute of Public Policy Research (IPPR), there is a useful insight into the existing UK devolution settlement, which the authors describe as 'a very British affair'. They argue that the three different devolved situations have been the subject of favourable conditions over the last decade, with Labour in power in all three capitals of mainland Britain and high levels of public expenditure – which are unlikely to be sustained in the long term.

The IPPR argues that 'constitutional reform has unleashed powerful and dynamic forces with anticipated and unanticipated consequences –

legal, political and constitutional', and conclude that 'there is unfinished business in the form of outstanding anomalies and new challenges which need to be addressed at a time when the favourable conditions are unravelling'. These insights have been reinforced by the sharply deteriorating financial situation, the banking crisis and recession, the defeat of the Labour Government and the arrival of the Conservative-Lib-Dem Coalition. Austerity has sharpened divisions between parts of the UK and this resentment is in danger of creating a grudge and grievance agenda, creating discord and looking for scapegoats. The strengthening of the Scottish Parliament and Welsh Assembly by parties opposed to Westminster has also created further tensions as witnessed by the unrest among Tory backbenchers and their colleagues in the Lords who used the recent Lords stages of the Scotland Bill to attack Scotland, the SNP and Alex Salmond.

Of particular significance, the IPPR identifies the 'unfinished business' as being:

- The position of England.
- The West Lothian question.
- Finance and the Barnett formula.
- The end of 'Labour hegemony' and the reality of new political configurations.
- Party-political conflict, especially over funding: the Barnett formula and the end of the spectacular growth in public expenditure, and the growing resentment of funding of new policies in Scotland, intensified by the fact that these public-policy benefits are not available in England.
- 'Devolution' meaning 'difference', as there is now substantial policy divergence, for instance with four health services.
- The centre (Westminster) having turned its back on devolution, regarding it as an event not a process.
- A Union without Britishness and a growth of national identities at the expense of Britishness. In 2003, polls showed how the peoples regard their nationality – Scottish not British, 72 per cent; Welsh not British, 60 per cent; English not British, 38 per cent and growing.

However, following this incisive analysis of the issues facing the Union and the English, the IPPR reveals a real lack of understanding, indeed confusion, about what devolution means and suggests some policy options that make little sense in terms of working relationships between Westminster and devolved governments of a different political make-up.

The IPPR believes that redefining the centre is part of the solution and suggests Westminster 'sets up a Department of the Nations and the localities to manage territorial conflict, to capture innovation and to provide leadership on devolution' and 'that the UK should reinvent itself as a guarantor of the UK wide minimum standards' and provide 'a constitutional statement on the level of divergence on social minimum and fiscal transfers'.

The IPPR concludes it is 'time for the centre to engage with devolution' – though it would appear that it means it is time for the centre to take over devolution! Devolution means difference and there will be divergence on the policy front as different priorities will be pursued. As such, it makes little sense for Westminster to police the settlements to avoid 'post-code lottery provision' of services. The future of Scotland and indeed Wales and Northern Ireland are now well beyond this kind of Westminster response.

Responding to the Green Paper on 'The Governance of Britain' in an article in the *Parliamentary Monitor* in July 2007, two of the researchers from the IPPR said: 'This welcome move will give England a stronger voice in Westminster, but in itself is insufficient. Gordon Brown, Prime Minister at the time, needs a further package of reforms which deal with the anomalies of devolution and improve the way England is governed by taking power away from the centre.'

They urged the government at Westminster to move fast, as the English question was rapidly moving up the political agenda. But their answer to the English question is to address the 'real grievance in England, the curse of overbearing centralism', which they say 'undermines the way England is governed'. Their solutions (remembering that the IPPR is very close to the Labour Party) are very different and reinforce our emerging view that the Union pays lip service to any idea of further political devolution or regionalism in England.

Instead, the IPPR argued that 'England would do better with a new deal in central-local relations with powers being devolved to localities and communities.' Strengthening the powers of local government, not the regions, is seen as the solution.

All of this shows there is a need for a new question for England. The spotlight must shift to the Union, and engagement with negative aspects of devolution should give way to a positive embrace of ideas and policies designed to improve the government of England and help ease the United Kingdom into the 21st century.

A new strand of thinking in Europe is based on the idea of 'adding value' to existing structures of government and territorial politics. This could give another dimension by looking at the United Kingdom and the process of devolution through the prism of 'the competitive region or nation'.

In the post-war period up until the early 1990s, the economy, industry and unemployment were the main drivers of regional policy. Since then, the nature of the debate has changed but social and economic disparities and inequalities between different parts of the United Kingdom remain an important priority for the Westminster government. Its ability to influence events has diminished, however, as a result of international and European economic change, the impact of the global rule book and the new economic order, which gives priority to learning, education, knowledge and the importance of human capital and requires new thinking and new solutions to deep-seated and enduring problems.

Faced with these new challenges and the accelerating pace of change, there is a very positive case for the Union to be more flexible and modern and to look upon the nations and regions of the UK as having more economic potential if only they could be given more responsibility and powers to lessen their dependency on Westminster, search for new solutions to enduring economic problems in their own areas, assume a more direct responsibility for their own future and search for new ideas and innovative solutions for long-term economic and competitive advantage. The regions of England and the Nations of the UK are far too dependent on Westminster and need to take more responsibility for their social and economic futures.

The UK remains one of the most highly-centralised countries in Europe despite devolution. Outwith Northern Ireland, Wales and Scotland, there is only administrative devolution to the English regions. An urgent case can be made for a more enlightened economic approach that would release the energies of each part of the UK and in turn create a new dynamic – an approach that would not only advance the regions but would help boost the productive potential of the UK as a whole. Successive Westminster Governments have done little to embrace this type of thinking. Surely they must accept that one of the reasons the UK is slipping further behind some of our competitors is our failure to decentralise and for the English regions to become less dependent on the Mother of Parliaments. Excessive centralisation shows a lack of confidence at Westminster about handling change and reinforces a mindset and culture which is undoubtedly holding the UK back

For this to happen, we need to shift the mindset and recognise that globalisation and European integration have altered the psychology and practices of economic intervention, subsidies from the centre and top-down initiatives.

The new global order has now altered the economic landscape and, in a world without borders, boundaries and barriers, there is no reason why economic power cannot be devolved downwards from the centre as well as being ceded upwards to the EU. This radical transformation of economic power should lead to new economic structures in the UK. Each part of the UK must take more ownership of its economic future, be more competitive and – in partnership with the UK as a whole – make a bigger contribution to economic inclusion and employment.

This approach is especially relevant to the new economic climate, dramatically accelerated by the communications revolution, in which the development of human capital through learning, education and knowledge is the driver of economic success. The potential for this exists in every part of the Union and requires inspired and enthusiastic leadership to effectively tap the possibilities.

The unlocking of these untapped reserves of energy, enterprise and entrepreneurship can only be done by empowering the regions and nations of the Union through new thinking on economic policy. It requires a belief that there is the capacity and the leadership for these nations to be full partners in tackling enduring problems and new challenges.

This 'competitive' dimension to devolved government is absolutely vital if we are to see any real embrace of change for the English regions. It is frequently argued that the English regions lack the clear-cut cultural and community identities and historical characteristics that help to define Scotland, Wales and Northern Ireland and entitle them to a special status within the Union. The English regions do have many distinct characteristics and differences but, even regardless of this, there is undoubtedly a case to be made for more devolved economic powers and responsibilities being part of a solution to the English question, while at the same time helping to reinvigorate the UK economy.

The UK has to embrace change because the days of centralisation, state intervention, redistribution and subsidies are now over. A wealth of academic work now points the way and there are excellent examples throughout Europe and the USA of progressive approaches to the new economic order and the challenges of the 'knowledge society'.

Backing this up is the overwhelming evidence that, despite a long period of economic growth, stability and high employment levels, the key fundamentals of the UK economy lag behind other countries in Europe and the USA. At the same time, the gap between the income levels of the rich and poor continues to widen, while real problems of social and economic inclusion remain and crucial drivers of change such as demographics, migration, public finance, communications technology, environment and learning are posing urgent challenges for every region of the UK.

The devolution debate is about facing up to new challenges in ways that are distinctively new.

The culture of big and centralised government – always seeking to control and direct and unwilling to let go – is deeply embedded in the UK. Devolution is about more effectively realising the potential of all of the UK and providing the best form of governance to achieve that.

Devolution is the solution, not the problem – and centralist diehards need to realise this. It is the UK that is out of step and holding back the progressive transformation of all of the Union. Devolution runs with the grain of decentralisation, empowerment and decision-making at local level. It is about responsibility, confronting people with change and choice and the consequences of action or inaction. It is about innovation, experimentation and new mindsets.

Devolution should be a way of thinking as well as a way of governing. Although many at Westminster refuse to accept the obvious, it goes without saying that there are inevitable consequences. To work, devolution depends upon the 'new politics' of consensus and must be about seeking more cross-party cooperation on the most pressing issues. It demands recognition of the changing nature of political space and the constantly-shifting distribution of power and responsibility at global, European, UK, national, regional and local levels.

Every part of the Union has to be engaged in the task of tackling more effectively the strategic issues of productivity, growth, competitiveness, workforce participation rates, small business formation and innovation – while at the same time building local confidence and self-belief. Essential to this would be giving the English regions and the devolved nations a more significant role in their own futures and making them less dependent on Westminster.

There are many compelling reasons why England, through the Westminster Parliament, should start to engage with this new thinking. Deepening disenchantment and disillusionment with Westminster politics is helping to create political tensions in England leading to the increase in right wing extremism and a growing disrespect for difference. Other countries in Europe – acknowledging the different cultures and political history – have much more sensible systems of governance. It is a sign of how dated Westminster is that few lessons, if any, have been learned from the experience of sub-national government elsewhere in Europe.

CHAPTER II

The Mood of a Nation: Scotland a Split Personality

Making Politics Make Sense

THE MOOD AND MORALE of the electorate matters in politics. Over the next four years there will be an unprecedented series of tough political tests for the Scottish electors, and the importance of the decisions to be made cannot be overstated. The series of social, economic, financial, institutional and political crises over the last five years have not only changed the political landscape; they have revealed a Scotland with a split personality. On the one hand, there is a divergence of Westminster and Holyrood election results, an electorate increasingly disillusioned and disenchanted with politics and political parties, declining confidence in our institutions and governance, and a sense of deepening pessimism surrounding our democracy. In contrast, the rise of the SNP has captured the imagination of many Scots and has injected some excitement, a sense of purpose and new enthusiasm into what has become a very traditional and uninspiring political landscape north of the border. A combination of credible and populist Government, positive leadership, an embrace of Scottishness and a radical agenda on issues such as justice and alcohol have won over many Scots to a different kind of politics.

The scale of the changes in SNP–Labour politics is dramatically underlined by comparisons of the outcomes of the 2010 General Election results – where Labour were convincing winners – and those of the Holyrood election in 2011, where the SNP defied the laws of PR and won an overall majority at Holyrood. Since 2003, the SNP has steadily expanded its sphere of electoral influence and now dominates the politics of Scotland. In sharp contrast, indeed a mirror image, Labour has declined and even the safest of Labour's seats have turned to the SNP. These maps confirm, if any confirmation was needed, that the SNP are in a commanding position over all other parties in Scotland. This chapter looks at the forthcoming referendum, the state of politics, the political parties

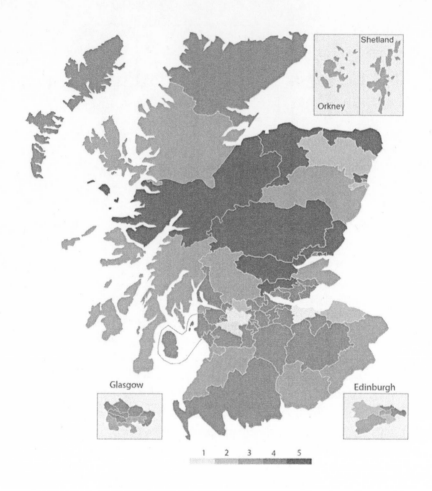

Scotland | SNP 2003

Party rank by constituency

and their prospects, and what this means for our democracy in the run up to the 2014 referendum.

The People's Choice

Election outcomes are decided by the personal choices of nearly four million Scots over the age of 18. There is, within the electorate, a great deal of volatility, uncertainty and fear, with a breaking down of traditional party loyalties and allegiances. What political parties offer on the doorsteps

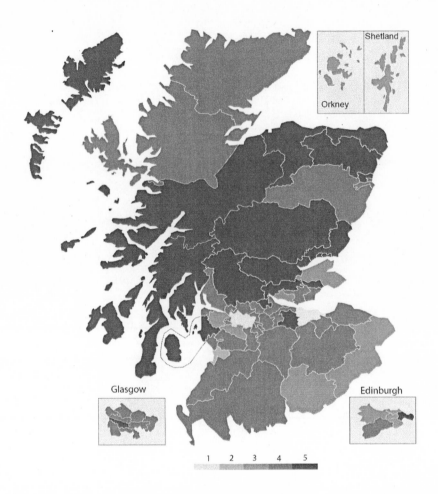

Shetland

Orkney

Glasgow

Edinburgh

1   2   3   4   5

Scotland | SNP 2007

Party rank by constituency

and through the media will influence the choices that people make, but so will a large number of other factors, including events, cultural, social and psychological factors. The referendum on Independence in 2014 is not just another day at the polls. For the first time in recent history, a decision will be made which is all-embracing in terms of its potential impact on the future of Scotland and the lives of every single Scot. This is where the fusion of so many different factors, not just political ones, will have an impact on how people might vote.

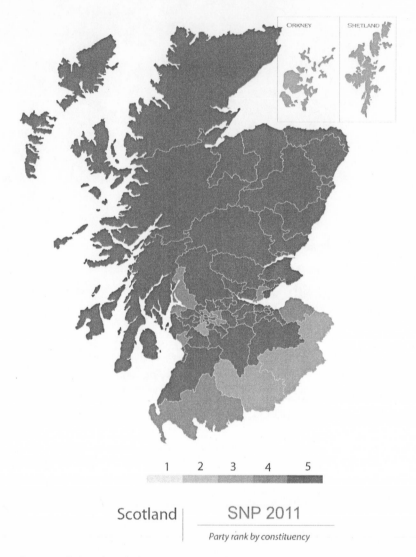

ORKNEY SHETLAND

1 2 3 4 5

Scotland | SNP 2011

Party rank by constituency

So how will Scotland shape up over the next two years? What are the factors which will influence voting intentions? Are our politics broken? Are our political parties up to the challenge of a changing electorate? These are some of the questions this chapter will consider in an attempt to demonstrate whether our politics in 2012 is fit for purpose and, equally important, what this could mean for the Independence referendum.

Our politics and the public attitudes to this are changing and political parties should be alert to the implications of this. Tony Judt, in his remarkable book, *Ill Fares the Land*, published in 2010 just before his death said,

> Something is profoundly wrong with the way we live today. For thirty years we have made a virtue out of the pursuit of material self interest... we know what things cost but have no idea what they are worth... we no longer ask of a judicial ruling or a legislative act: Is it good? Is it just? Is it right? Will it help bring about a better society or better world? Those used to be the political questions, even if they invited no easy answers. **We must learn once again to pose them.**

Capturing the mood after the financial and banking crisis, Tony Judt argued that there is much in society to be angry at – growing inequalities of wealth and opportunity, injustice of class, economic exploitation and corruption, money and privilege damaging democracy. Arguing passionately for change, Judt worried about the age of insecurity we have entered into – physical, economic and political. This insecurity breeds fear, corroding the trust and interdependence on which civil societies rest.

This is the state of Scotland and Britain today. Fear of change and mistrust of politics may be leading to a growing disconnect between electors and traditional politics, declining numbers of people voting and a growing sense of frustration that our political parties can't deliver. In a world where so much power and influence is wielded by unaccountable corporations, global bodies and trans-national entities, Judt highlights the need to dissent from this economically-driven way of thinking and return to an 'ethically informed public conversation'.

Adam Smith in *The Theory of Moral Sentiments* says,

> The disposition to admire, and almost to worship, the rich and the powerful, and to despise, or, at least, to neglect, persons of poor and mean condition... is... the great and most universal cause of the corruption of moral sentiments.

This drive for community, solidarity and the politics of the common good have been severely undermined by a series of national events that have shocked the electorate and cast doubt on the credibility of our political parties and even democracy itself. What has been accepted as part of the trust factor of the post war consensus now lies in ruins.

The Conservative led Coalition at Westminster

Scots are being, and will continue to be, influenced by the politics of the Coalition at Westminster. 'Austerity Britain' and the cuts and deficits agenda are likely to exact a heavy toll from the public, especially those dependent on social welfare and the public sector. No sane person would argue against the idea of balancing our books, but there is anger and resentment about the way this is being done. Recession, austerity, high unemployment and public sector cuts will have a significant impact on Scotland. Scots also resent the alien political culture emerging from the Coalition where the Conservatives, helped by the fast-fading cloak of Lib-Dem respectability, are trying to tear up the post-war consensus on the NHS, Europe, Education and the Welfare state. By putting ideology before the national interest, the Coalition risk wrecking hard-won achievements in these areas of policy.

This is very reminiscent of the Thatcher era when Scots first lost faith in the Conservatives. Scotland is being heavily influenced by an agenda that is not our own. Although devolution gives us a large measure of protection from right wing politics, the fear of Coalitions and Conservative Governments at Westminster may incline many Scots to be wary of remaining within a Union which is capable of such excesses.

Politics Matters

Politics is about the tough process of arriving at collective decisions out of a bewildering array of multiple and competing interests and opinions. Politics matters because we have different views and perspectives in society about public resources and how they should be used. Politics is essentially about judgement at any point in time and is inextricably linked to the powerful idea of coping with change in an uncertain world.

Against the current difficult background, it is little wonder that our politicians and political parties in Scotland find it difficult to anticipate, understand and manage change. Making sense of change and seeking to influence the future rather than constantly reacting to issues and events is now more important than ever as the accelerating pace of social, financial, economic, technological and environmental change threatens to overwhelm us.

Our political culture in Scotland is uneasy with the idea of change: this could be about a lack of confidence, a deep-seated conservatism or a failure to take ourselves seriously in the post-devolution era. It could also be linked to the fact that the political classes in Scotland, our business community, civic institutions and the well-defined constituencies of interest, including the media, are so closely knitted together that there is no political distance between them to enable politicians, parliament and Government to develop the intellectual, inspirational and enlightened approach for a radical and different look at our future. Devolution has certainly failed to let a thousand ideas bloom!

As demographics, globalisation, information technologies and social change crowd in on us, we need a much clearer vision of the future. This can only be achieved if we have a new inspired and informed dialogue.

Gerry Stoker, in his book *Why Politics Matter – Making Democracy Work*, states,

> The weakness of democratic politics and the growing disenchantment of electors have resulted from a number of factors including a profound shift in our society including: the dominance of individualism and consumerism; the increasing complexity of globalisation; the collapse of deference; and the role of the media in fostering cynicism. These have undoubtedly made governance and political leadership much harder.

Further to this, Stoker argues that

> Politics is doomed to disappoint because, like any centralised collective form of decision making, it requires trade -offs between competing interests, is prone to failures in communication and often produces muddled and messy outcomes.

Democracy as an idea is more popular than ever, but citizens in democracies, not only in Britain, appear disenchanted with the political process. It is important to reflect on the fact that as people in North Africa and the Middle East lose their lives in trying to win the vote, we are losing our interest in voting.

Democracy is a demanding way of doing the politics of compromise and reconciliation because it rests on the fundamental idea that all adult citizens have a right to a say in matters that affect them. The future of Scotland is therefore very dependent on retaining our faith and trust in our democracy, particularly as we approach what is likely to be the most challenging period of elections in a generation.

Why has disenchantment grown?

In, *Why Politics Matters,* Gerry Stoker provides an insightful framework of explanations for this growing political disenchantment. He puts forward six explanations, two basically blaming politicians, two looking at the changing nature of society and the attitudes of citizens and two looking at the environment for democratic politics which has become much harder and more out of control:

> Many people believe that the behaviour of politicians or their performance or their economic competence have somehow declined compared to some past 'golden era' and this helps explain their loss of legitimacy.
>
> There are the issues of truth and power. This argument is based on the notion that politicians are more interested in power than in truth. Worldwide, politicians are the least trusted occupation and many people believe that politicians do not tell the truth most of the time. What is clear is that fewer people trust politics and politicians than in the past. Stoker suggests that this may have more to do with the changing role of citizens and less to do with the behaviour of politicians.
>
> People have become harder to govern and more critical and more demanding of government and politicians. As a result, they are more dissatisfied with the performance of their politicians, political parties and other important institutions of representative government.
>
> People are more individual and fragmented. This raises the idea that a lack of social cohesion limits the scope of collective decision making and collective trust. People are becoming better consumers and worse citizens. This results in a different relationship with politics and the political process. The common good seems less attractive as an idea compared to individual benefits.
>
> Issues are moving beyond the control of politics. If Globalisation means the world is beyond our collective control or beyond the control of our political institutions then politics runs the

danger of becoming more and more irrelevant and, in the eyes of the electors, provides more reasons for avoiding the ballot box and engagement in politics. The low level of political or civic literacy in our society also creates tensions and mistrust. The more the public feel these big issues are beyond the control and influence of the political system the more dissatisfaction grows with all aspects of our politics.

Technological impact has a growing influence on politics and how people engage with it. Hugely complex, subject to different scientific interpretations and the basis of public controversy, science and technology issues certainly add to the complexity of politics: but at the same time the media and the public seek simplicity.

Faced with these challenges, politics will become an increasingly tough business, and will face demands for a different and more intelligent kind of politics. If the growing disenchantment and disillusionment are to be reversed, then a radical reappraisal of how politics deals with change is long overdue. Politics has lost its grip and that is why increasing numbers of people think it no longer matters.

This raises the question of whether elections will be much more difficult to predict in the future as a very different set of social, economic and psychological factors fuse with more traditional considerations to influence the electorate.

The great danger of the rise of anti-political sentiment is that it may generate a shift away from collective action towards a more individualised structure that is simply ill-equipped to deal with the major social, economic, and environmental challenges that will shape the 21st century. We will have lost those levers of social trust and social engagement, direction and mutual support that politics delivers.

The lack of political literacy and political understanding, rapidly changing demographics and the increasing influence of the media will all play their part in shaping politics in the years ahead. The battle between the State and the market, between public and private and the struggle between the common good and the individual have helped undermine, and in some cases destroy, the influence of the Church, Trade Unions, the voluntary sector and other institutions as they don't fit neatly into the struggle between extremes. Real social networks have given way to virtual networks. A vacuum has been created into which many of these trusted organisations have disappeared. Civic culture and working class culture have been transformed.

Philip Blond in his book, *Red Tory*, says,

> We are more isolated that at any time in recorded history. Most of us avoid voting at local elections, and little more than half manage to make it to the polls for national ones. We certainly don't join a church or political party and we have fewer friends and social contacts than any British generation for which figures exist.

The atomised society, talked about by Margaret Thatcher in her 'no such thing as society' vision, is fast becoming a reality. Blond continues by arguing that,

> A stronger civic culture would have permitted modernisation and technological development without sacrificing its social foundations. But in Britain we have achieved none of those things; listless and indifferent we slide into a post-democratic culture of passive consumption and political acquiescence.

Consumers versus Citizens

Robert Reich, one of America's foremost economic and political thinkers and former Labour Secretary in the Clinton administration, provides a new analysis of the competitive economy and its effect on democracy. In a book published in 2007, *Super Capitalism: The Transformation of Business, Democracy and Everyday Life* he says:

> A clear separation of politics and capitalism will foster an environment in which both business and government thrive, by putting capitalism in the service of democracy, and not the other way around.

Reich argues that capitalism has become more responsive to what we want as individual purchasers of goods, but democracy has grown less responsive to what we want together as citizens. This has enormous implications for our understanding of the current crisis.

Our role as citizens within the democratic process needs to be strengthened.

We have to think about the bigger picture. British people are losing confidence in democracy, as are many inhabitants of other democracies. There is a pattern of declining trust, respect and confidence in Government. The current financial crisis and recession provides the opportunity for this to change.

Michael J Sandel in his new book, *What Money Can't Buy – The Moral Limit of Markets*, asks,

> Is there something wrong with a world in which everything is for sale? If so, how can we prevent market values reaching into spheres of life where they don't belong? What are the moral limits of markets?

Sandel argues that we have drifted from having a market economy to being a market society and asks 'is this where we want to be?'

The atomisation of society, and the growth of selfishness, not self, pose real challenges to those who want politics to be based on progressive and ethical thinking. There is a move away from collective ways of distributing resources and opportunities and this core idea is at the heart of our changing society and a major threat to our politics and democracy.

Sandel argues,

> The contemporary climate of anti-politics is arguably rooted in a generation that has become complacent. We have created little more than a political market place in which there are few incentives for politicians to be transparent, and too many people who take for granted democratic politics and what it delivers. The currency of politics is being devalued and we have allowed political standards to drop and far too often seem content with the lowest common denominator.

There is a remarkable undermining of our democracy and our politics taking place. Societies are changing and this influences how people think and vote and indeed, whether they vote at all.

The Role of the Media

A certain level of credibility is central to the operation of politics. The role of the media in maintaining that becomes crucial. Bearing in mind the importance of understanding politics and the issues surrounding political and civic literacy, future elections in Scotland will have to be fought with a greater understanding of the citizen and the consequences of change. Politics in the modern era requires a new understanding of the nature of individualism, the spread of market based consumerism and the nature of citizenship.

There should be an emphasis on how the media can support the wider interests of our politics and our democracy. How does the coverage of the media impact on the politics and the involvement of the citizen? There seems to be a view that much of the media hinders both the effective functioning of our politics and the engagement of the public.

First, it can 'dumb down' the coverage of news and political issues, depriving many people of the comprehensive arguments. Second, in the cycle of 24-hour news coverage politics can quickly become a matter of opinion with little resort to evidence or argument. The facts become obscured by opinions, with the conclusion that politics is all a bit pointless. Combine this with a low level of political literacy which allows this kind of material to go unchallenged, and it is evident that there is a problem in the way people are engaging in political issues.

Third, certain sectors of the media have a contempt for politics. This can be based on the ownership issues or the values and ideologies of a particular newspaper or media outlet.

The media, though, has a vital role to play in any free and healthy democracy. Of course, the Murdoch crisis and the on-going examination of the relationships between the press, public, police and politicians being discussed by the Leveson inquiry, have exposed many worrying aspects of the media. What is vital in this exposé is the impact it is likely to have on the mood of the electors in the run-up to the future elections and the 2014 referendum in terms of pessimism, cynicism and lack of interest. We should also be concerned about the manner in which the fear factor steps in and politicians become overcautious and concerned about what they say.

The media should play a significant role in strengthening our democracy and our politics, but there is a need for a fair and balanced approach. There has to be recognition that the media is not always a value free, objective distributor of information and knowledge, standing up for the public interest and the interest of ordinary citizens. Instead, it represents a bewildering mix of news, information entertainment and personal opinion. While it remains a key component of our system of checks and balances in society, the media has, in recent times, been less effective at what it should be doing.

The Murdoch scandal and the Leveson inquiry have now fully exposed the fear among politicians and government that the printed press is a very powerful force which can distort the national debate, influence policy development and change the relationship between the electors and the elected. The forthcoming referendum debate, faced with the current alternatives, is likely to be partisan and tribal, the subject of much fear and scaremongering, reflecting the differences between Scottish and UK perspectives.

Developing political literacy is an essential part of our drive to build a stronger base for our democracy. One thing is certain: progressive politics, informed citizenry, inspired politics and a stronger democracy require a fair and balanced media. This requires more emphasis on political literacy and treating the citizens of our country as grown-ups, rather than subjecting them to dumbed-down versions of political reality.

The State of our politics and democracy

Our democracy is fragile and our politics seem broken. All the evidence suggests an increasingly volatile electorate, the breaking down of traditional loyalties, the weakening of class allegiances and a growing dissatisfaction with politicians and political parties. There are a number of important consequences that flow from this growing distrust of politicians and disenchantment with our politics. People appear to like the idea of democracy, but do not like the politics that goes along with it. There is a real danger that the slide in our politics will continue and we lose faith in the system or our ability to change it. So why should we be concerned? And how will this impact on Scottish Politics and the forthcoming referendum?

Election Turn-out

Overshadowing many of the party performances in recent elections has been the shocking overall turn-out. The local council elections in 2012 were the most recent reminder with a turn-out of only 39 per cent. For

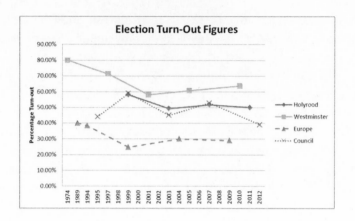

many seats, nearly 70 per cent of electors did not vote and only two councils out of 32 managed to attract more than 50 per cent of the voters. Our forefathers (and foremothers!) campaigned in this country to win the right to vote. Why have we stopped taking advantage of this? Many of us have lost interest in voting.

This is not just an issue for council elections. For all elections the turn-out figures have been decreasing, as shown in the graph above. Holyrood's turn-out figure was 50 per cent in 2011, compared to 51.72 per cent in 2007, 49.2 per cent in 2003 and 58.16 per cent in 1999.

Turn-out figures for Westminster elections were 63.8 per cent in 2010, compared to 60.8 per centin 2005 and 58.2 per cent in 2001. Compare this with 71.3 per cent in 1997 and nearly 80 per cent in 1974.

The high point for General Election turn-out in Scotland was in 1832, the year of the Great Reform Act, when the turnout was 85 per cent and the electorate was only 64,447! The other noteworthy election was 1910 when the turn-out was 84.7 per cent. In more recent times, 75.1 per cent was recorded in 1955 when the Conservative party in Scotland had the highest percentage share of the poll ever of any party in Scotland. How things have changed!

The European election in 2009 had a 29 per cent turn-out compared with 30 per cent in 2004, 24.7 per cent in 1999, 38.3 per cent in 1994 and 40 per cent in 1989.

The Council elections in 2012 had a 39 per cent turn-out (this was the first time the council poll was not held on the same day as the Scottish Parliament elections), compared to 52.8 per cent in 2007, 45 per cent in

2003, 59 per cent in 1999, (held on the same day as the new Scottish Parliament elections) and 44 per cent in 1995. The marked increase in turn-out for council elections when held on the same day as the Holyrood election clearly illustrates the differences in the perceived importance of council elections compared to Scottish Parliament elections.

Averaged out over the years and the different types of elections, at least 1 in 2 of the eligible electors do not see any merit in our system of representative democracy. 4 in 10 stay away in General elections, 5 in 10 stay away in Scottish elections, nearly 7 in 10 stay away in European Elections and 6 in 10 stay away in council elections. These are overall turn-out figures, even more depressing are the figures for 18–25 year olds.

Our lack of interest in the ballot box casts a long shadow over our democracy and our politics. Society is changing, as we have discussed earlier, and there is a growing body of thinking which suggests that, without a major rethink of how our politics serves our democracy, there will be fewer people engaging in elections. If this happens, we devalue both the process and the product.

Inequality Matters

A look at the turn-out in 2011 Holyrood election reveals the true extent of the problem. There was a marked difference in turn-out between Edinburgh (highest) and Glasgow (lowest). As a percentage share of the vote nearly twice as many voted in Eastwood, 62.8 per cent, the highest, than in Glasgow Provan, 34.5 per cent, the lowest. The best seat had nearly 40 per cent not voting, which is depressing in itself, but when measured against the five lowest seats, of Glasgow Kelvin, Pollock, Shettleston, Maryhill/Springburn and Provan we see an even more alarming outcome of between 60 per cent and 65 per cent not bothering to vote!

This level of disenfranchisement, the volatility of electors, the changing nature of society and the low levels of trust and confidence in political parties and politicians, raises real fears about the future of our politics and the impact this will have on the outcome of elections in next few years. If our politics are broken we need to fix them. Any lack of concern on the part of all the political parties could have consequences for the turn-out at the Referendum and the outcome

A Lack of Trust

Trust is another area where politicians and politics are losing the confidence of the public. The 'Survey of public attitudes towards conduct in public life in 2010' was conducted about 18 months after the height of the MPs expenses scandal, nearly 10 months after the 2010 General election. The evidence collected shows a long term decline in public confidence in those holding public office between 2004 and 2010.

On many issues, the 2010 results show a steeper decline than in the previous period. It was not possible to identify with certainty the cause of the electorate's declining confidence but it is possible that the expenses scandal has had an impact on people's views and appears to have fed into and exacerbated the long-run trend of increasingly negative evaluations of politicians.

The key findings included people rating standards of conduct less positively in 2010 than in previous years. In 2004–2008, at least four in ten (44 per cent) people rated standards as very high or quite high, but by 2010 only about three in ten (33 per cent) people rated them as such. In addition, 15 per cent of respondents rated standards as very low, compared to only 5 per cent in 2004. Public satisfaction with the conduct of MPs has declined on every measure since the last survey was conducted.

Most worryingly, between 2008 and 2010 the proportion of respondents who thought that most MPs are dedicated to doing a good job for the public fell by twenty percentage points (from 46 to 26 per cent). The proportion thinking that most MPs are competent at their jobs fell by ten percentage points (from 36 to 26 per cent). There was a drop of 14 per cent in the proportion thinking that most MPs are in touch with what the public thinks is important (from 29 per cent to only 15 per cent). There were also large drops in the proportion thinking that most MPs set a good example in their private lives (from 36 per cent to 22 per cent), make sure money is used wisely (from 28 per cent to 18 per cent) and that they all tell the truth (from 26 per cent to 20 per cent).

The state of politics in Scotland and the UK has consequences. Turnout is dramatically down. Trust in politicians, and political parties, is at a low point. Party membership has slumped. Political and civic literacy remain at low levels. Young people remain uninspired by our politics and shun the polls. People, especially the young, have embraced issue-based politics at the expense of traditional politics. Inequality in Scotland has pushed the poorest in our communities to be even more dismissive of elections than the rest of the population and where disenfranchisement is at record levels. Inspiration and vision are lacking as austerity undermines confidence and creates resentment and disinterest. Add to all of this a deafening silence from our political parties and politicians. The referendum might ignite interest among those who rarely vote. If this was to happen, then the outcome might be less predictable than seems to be the case today.

Politics is an activity in which the people engage or disengage according to the circumstances confronting them. What they lack at present is any sense of sustained engagement with political institutions and the political system. The picture is one of many citizens alienated from formal politics and trying as best they can to cope with the world of politics and government – but only when they have to because of some pressing need. Maybe the future of their country is such a pressing need.

The public are not to blame. It is politics and politicians that are letting people down. Consequently, the people are disillusioned and increasingly disconnected from a world which seems remote and irrelevant. They now question the relevance of what parties and politicians are supposed to be doing on their behalf. This is a crisis that needs a response.

Our politics once again needs to inspire, enthuse, educate and be relevant to the needs and aspirations of the public. We have to move away from the mindless tribalism and partisanship that too often dominates what passes as political debate.

We have become better consumers but poorer citizens. We get a wake-up call at every election, but no one seems to be listening.

The referendum in 2014 may be a simple single question, or at most two, but how and why people vote will be a much more complex decision, reflecting a confusing mix of factors, influences and considerations. This volatility and unpredictability could create a few shocks in the autumn of 2014. The future of Scotland will be centre-stage, but so will our democracy.

CHAPTER 12

The Soul of the Nation;
Inspiring the Debate

OUR DEBATE ON DEVOLUTION and the wider question of sub-national government has been incredibly narrow and barely informed by events and ideas outside the UK. A wider vision through which political parties in Scotland can develop deeper insights into the constitutional and political debate is taking place throughout Europe. We are sometimes too preoccupied by narrow thinking and the idea that we are exceptional to appreciate that the issues we are dealing with, both in Scotland and the United Kingdom, are being embraced by politicians, policy-makers and academics in Europe as they seek to give meaning to the complex and diverse changes that are taking place in our systems of governance and democracy. The devolution debate in this country gives the impression we invented the idea and have nothing to learn from anyone. Nothing could be further from the truth. Our debate should have been enriched by the experiences of others.

Too often, the debate about Scotland's political future is vitriolic in tone and tribal in nature and rarely rises above rhetoric and meaningless slogans. What is missing, even at this stage, two years before a referendum, is any real engagement with the public, as if they either did not exist or had no real interest in any possible outcomes. The contribution of the academics can often be technical and intellectual but they are also far-seeing and offer practical solutions.

Foremost among these is Michael Keating, Professor of Scottish Politics at the University of Aberdeen. In his book *Plurinational Democracy: Stateless Nations in a Post-Sovereign Era*, (Oxford University Press, 2006) Keating says:

> Trans-national integration [global and European] and other challenges to the nation-state have deprived it of its mystique and broken the automatic link between the state and the nation. This has encouraged the revival of the stateless nationalism – what we are seeing in Scotland today.

This very important book provides the foundation for the development of an alternative to the status quo and Independence. The idea of a third way or a solution which stops short of Independence is what Scotland needs. To date, however, while there have been attempts made to put an alternative on the constitutional agenda, Devo-diversity, in the form of Devo-max or Devo-plus, has had little philosophical context or clear definition or political substance or, party political support. This does not devalue the importance of such an alternative; it merely confirms the ambivalence of the Unionist parties, despite the overwhelming evidence of opinion polls which suggest the public do want a different way forward for their country. Keating's work provides the constitutional, international and philosophical platform for that alternative to be developed and allow Scotland to lead the world on constitutional change instead of playing second best to the best compromise Westminster can provide.

He argues:

> These changes call for a radical rethinking of the nature of sovereignty and of the state itself to meet the twin challenges of recognition of nationality and democracy (and identity).

Drawing on the experiences of what he describes as four 'plurinational' states – the United Kingdom, Spain, Belgium and Canada – and of the European Union, he analyses the challenges of plurinationalism and its recognition:

> We are not moving to a world without states but to a complex political order with multiple sites of sovereignty, authority and asymmetrical constitutional arrangements. This political order is new, but at the same time old, as traditions of diffused authority and shared sovereignty before the rise of the nation-state are rediscovered and rehabilitated.
>
> Democracy can no longer be confined to the framework of the nation-state [the United Kingdom] but must extend to the new political spaces which are emerging above [Europe and globalisation] and below [Scotland].
>
> Political movements and public opinion in the stateless nations are increasingly embracing these ideas and are the harbingers of a post-sovereignty political order.

This is very much the case in Scotland where the public seem to be ahead of the politicians. Social, economic and political changes are recasting the political outlook in Scotland and class attraction has declined. National identity is now increasingly a substitute for social class as the basis for solidarity.

In Scotland this is not based on ethnicity but is about assimilation, inclusiveness and integration. This emerging reality, articulated by Keating, should be the backdrop for the new battle for Scotland in which different views, feelings, aspirations and ideas will compete and political parties will have to acknowledge the drivers of change within the Union of the UK, the European Union and Global union. It is this failure of the political parties to face up to the new realities that is threatening the Union.

This demands a wider, deeper, more informed and inspired debate about Scotland's constitutional future. All roads do not automatically lead to 'Unionism and no more devolution' or 'separation and Independence and no more Unionism'. These polarised positions do not reflect the only options available to Scots, nor do they reflect anything like a serious debate about what Independence and Unionism actually mean in the first decade of the 21st century. There are more choices for Scots to make, which may be more relevant and representative of a new world order, their own modern lifestyles and ambitions and the new and distinctive politics of Scotland.

There are five broad scenarios which capture most of the important elements likely to be included in any possible future constitutional solution for Scotland. The boundaries are not precise nor do they evolve logically one into another. They have no timescales and are not mutually exclusive but are illustrative of the different directions our national debate is taking and could take.

They are not tidy because the debate is not tidy in the sense that you cannot compartmentalise the complex and difficult issues at its heart.

These options will hopefully provide a useful new way of looking at Scotland and its future. They also provide political parties in Scotland with the background to form their own views on where the devolution process is likely to go and allow us to measure their progress in post-devolution Scotland and how well they are adapting to these new realities. Overall there is a pressing need to enrich and inspire our political and constitutional debate with some form of philosophical and ethical framework. There is now a sense of urgency as the First Minister closes in on his preferred date for the referendum in 2014.

Classical Unionism

This comprises a traditional centralist model based on the sovereignty of the Westminster Parliament, which sees devolution to Scotland, Wales and Northern Ireland as complete and in turn does not foresee any significant political and constitutional change for England.

Instead, in this scenario priorities for the 'Governance of Britain' in the last Labour Government were focused on the relationship between the Executive and Parliament, the reform of the House of Lords, further administrative devolution within England, reinforcing a sense of Britishness and providing some further limited responsibilities to local government as part of a drive for localism, not devolution or regionalism.

All of this was served up with the idea of Westminster being more sensitive to England and new measures being introduced to consult, listen and learn. This approach is detailed in the Green Paper 'The Governance of Britain', published by the Prime Minister, Gordon Brown in the summer of 2007. What is important to note about this strategy is the lack of interest in the English question within the Union and the reluctance, at least at that stage, to contemplate any further political and constitutional devolution.

The unfinished business of 1997, expressed through two Scotland Acts, now seems complete 15 years on. The drive to strengthen the Union in this way provides the opportunity for the Westminster government to continue to take an ambivalent view of both Europe and devolution in Scotland, Wales and Northern Ireland. It is worth noting that Westminster's view of both devolution and Europe hold at times a similar level of derision, ambivalence and irritation. There seems to be some truth in the quip, 'lost an empire, but still haven't found a roll'.

What seems to be lacking is any modern idea of what Unionism means and how it can adapt to meet events, issues and challenges. There seems to be no progressive Unionist philosophy, no Unionist strategy and very little sense of what the Union now means. It appears that very little political capital is being invested in redefining the Union at a time when dramatic changes are taking place in Scotland, Wales and Northern Ireland.

There is every indication that a desperate search is underway to come up with a standing definition of the Union instead of getting to grips with issues such as identity, nationalism, sovereignty, diversity, pluralism and democracy and how they should be shaping the political future of the United Kingdom.

There is a preoccupation with issues on the margin, such as 'What is Britishness?', 'English votes for English laws' and public holidays to celebrate giving and goodness. Enmeshed with the Union Jack waving is a developing and distasteful anti-Scottish sentiment at Westminster. This is where some people think we should remain.

'Next Step' Devolution

This view of the future assumes the momentum of devolved government continues with a new agenda of issues and challenges to be addressed, as and when they emerge. It asks whether the Scottish Parliament and government should have new powers and whether existing commitments should be entrenched to give stronger constitutional safeguards for the devolution settlement, and the Scotland Acts of 1998 and 2012. The question is whether new ways of working between the devolved areas and Westminster should be developed, and a larger and louder voice for devolution is likely to be part of this new agenda.

For this to work, there has to be a more flexible Union and a well-thought-out case has to be made for further change. The logic seems compelling: if deep-seated and enduring problems in Scotland require new thinking and new approaches to tackle them, why should more powers for the parliament be a problem for Westminster – especially after 300 years of the Union and more than 13 years of devolution? The Calman Commission, though its setting up was largely based on political expediency, reflected this process and earlier in 2012, Prime Minister David Cameron, faced with the SNP's dominance of Scottish politics, promised some unspecified new powers at some unspecified date in some unspecified future. This was more about opportunism and convenience rather than a contribution to Scotland's devolved future. There have been no attempts to entrench the devolution legislation in order to provide greater protection. Without a written constitution, most of what we do in different forms of governance in the UK is handed down from

Westminster and is entirely based on the sacred sovereignty of that Institution: the history of which is complex and confused.

Devolution and the English Question

This option assumes devolution is still evolving in other nations and regions of the UK. Importantly, in this scenario the English question must now be tackled. The Union recognises the need to be flexible and accepts the case for further devolution either for England or within England. It calls for recognition that long-term political and constitutional change is the only way to tap the potential of enterprise, competitiveness and ambition in every part of the UK. It would also clear away the anomalies and tensions of the 1997 settlement for Scotland and Wales, which have impacted on the workings of Westminster. There are no signs that the future of England is a serious part of mainstream Westminster thinking. Skirmishes on the West Lothian Question and the idea of English votes for English laws surface occasionally but are not part of any joined-up thinking about the role of England in the Union. There is no embrace of the notion that some of the serious social, city, ethnic, Islamic and inequalities issues might be related to an over centralized state which has become remote from the people it is intended to serve and has run out of ides to deal with contemporary problems

Toward Quasi-Federalism

This alternative moves the debate on and assumes, despite the asymmetrical nature of the political and constitutional configuration of the Union, some form of quasi-federalist future for the UK. This would mean power being shared, not power being devolved. It would require some acknowledgement of the new political order and the need for significant safeguards in some form of written constitution. It would recognise the need for new ideas on sovereignty, identity, nationality and democracy. Difference would be both welcomed and protected.

This is the basis of new thinking in Scotland which sees a form of federalism as the best way forward, stopping short of Independence but in addition making some sense of a Union which is not fit for purpose. For this to work, there has to be a radical overhaul of the finance and fiscal powers of the Scottish Parliament and acceptance that there would be the maximum devolution of powers, consistent with agreements about what powers would remain at Westminster. Currently only the Lib-Dems in Scotland would support such a scheme. David Steel, former leader of the Liberal Party, has written a great deal on this and his work could yet be a blueprint for the future of Scotland.

Independence and Political and Constitutional Separation

This is the policy of the Scottish National Party and would lead to Scotland becoming a 'sovereign' nation with representation at the top tables of world and European forums dealing with social, economic, environmental, energy and political affairs.

After 300 years, Scotland would be politically separate from the Union. The Treaty of Union would be repealed but other links with the Union would remain. The SNP has confirmed that in its Independent Scotland the Union of the Crowns would remain.

This policy appears to be supported by around 30 per cent of the electorate in Scotland, reflecting a very diverse group of people. It is a simple and apparently straightforward solution to Scotland's problems and its relationship with England. This, at any rate, is the matter-of-fact view of the SNP.

The reality of this option is, however, far more complex, with considerable uncertainty and short-term instability. It has three immediate attractions to the electorate: it is less complex than defending the Union; it appeals directly to pride, patriotism and sentiment; and it directly embraces Scottishness.

This explains the ebb and flow of the Independence appeal to the electorate and until the 1970s it also acted as a vehicle for protest against either of the two main Unionist parties in Scotland. Were these still the factors behind the success of the SNP in 2007, when it formed a minority government, or in 2011 when it formed a majority government? Or are there other considerations at work which indicate a more substantial shift in the mood of the country and a politics based on identity and nationality and an embrace of some form of nationalism?

It has been too easy in the past to dismiss the SNP. That facile dismissal could now be dangerous, since we are dealing with 'Scotland as a state of mind' in an entirely different context, with 13 years' experience of devolution and a society and economy that are changing at a remarkable rate.

Is the SNP becoming the default position for voters as traditional alliances and loyalties break down and identity and small 'n' nationalism become less threatening? There are deeply complicated factors at work. The other political parties would serve their interests better if they attempted to understand these before offering alternatives. As change permeates society, political culture changes slowly and imperceptibly. There is no political Richter scale to measure change but the outcomes are only too evident. Election after election shows the rise and rise of the SNP. It is comforting to think that people vote for them because they are a credible and competent government with a populist agenda and not because they promote Independence. Is there not a danger that in the public mind the different sides of the SNP eventually fuse together and Alex Salmond's mission would be nearly complete?

It should also be acknowledged that life is far more complex for the UK parties operating in post-devolution Scotland – and, unlike the Unionist parties, the SNP does not constantly have to look over its shoulder to London and Westminster.

For Westminster and the Union, the challenge is an obvious one: how do you bring the Union from a state of atrophy back to vibrant life? The 2007 tercentennial commemoration could in no sense be described as a celebration and seemed more of a memorial than a birthday.

To an increasingly sceptical electorate, whose Scottishness grows and whose Britishness declines, more justification of the Union's meaning for them is required. In this, the concept of a more flexible, modern and more responsive Union could be helpful.

What does the Union offer Scotland and Scots in the early part of this new millennium and is it able to understand and respond to more radical constitutional change if that is the mind of the Scottish people?

It could well be the case that the opposing positions of no-more-devolution Unionism and remove-ourselves-from-the-Union Separatism will start to lose their appeal if the constitutional debate is widened and deepened, reflecting the new trends, ideas and movements in Europe and elsewhere.

New Ideas of Dealing with Sovereignty, Identity, Nationalism and Democracy

New and more imaginative ideas are emerging from leading academics in Europe. They see a future for stateless nations, are re-examining the concepts of identity, nationalism, sovereignty and democracy and envisage alternative structures of government to accommodate them.

This new look at political space takes a far more flexible view of territory and borders and asks why the aspirations of many nations, including Scotland, cannot be met through new concepts and structures which stop short of Independence. Scotland is well placed to be a successful model for this. Their analysis reflects on what is happening in Europe and internationally in terms of social and economic change, the institutional and constitutional structures needed to give expression to the rapidly-changing demands of an increasingly diverse population, and the political culture and democracy which is needed to serve their interests.

They seek to modernise the debate and to work out new perspectives which have less to do with what happens in a physically-defined territory and more to do with people and how their needs and demands can be met. Their thinking acknowledges our inability to see a wider canvas of opportunity but at the same time rejects the polarisation of the currently narrow debate. Their views provide new ways of looking at a problem, not a blueprint for any distinctive solution. By raising the intellectual level of the debate they hope to enable the public to have more choice and a better sense of devolution being not exceptional but commonplace throughout Europe and the rest of the world. In particular they challenge and confront many of the cherished concepts that underpin the ideas of the Union and which in turn are used to dismiss aspirations for further political and constitutional change – the Unionist parties are reluctant to accept or do anything about the weaknesses of Westminster. The academics provide new thinking, new mindsets and new insights into a more enlightened and more relevant debate on the changing relationship between nations and nation-states. While the language may be academic, there is no doubting the rich and relevant ideas they produce.

For Keating and his colleagues, this new approach requires:

- A better understanding of nations and sovereignty. It questions why the United Kingdom is obsessed with the sovereignty of the Westminster Parliament and cannot conceive of shared sovereignty or sovereignty in different sites or territories.
- Giving new meaning in a modern context to issues such as nationality, identity, democracy, diversity and sovereignty the politics of difference given new meaning.
- A more enlightened understanding of history and the needs of the present.
- A clearer view of national aspirations and transnational integration, i.e. the European Union.
- An acceptance of asymmetrical government and the 'plurinational' state (a sophisticated and deeper concept of many nations). Further devolution or a form of autonomous region or quasi-federalism does not require symmetry.
- Looking beyond sovereignty to a political and constitutional settlement for the UK involving shared power, not devolved power.
- Looking to European integration and multi-level governance (global including multilateral and bilateral relationships).
- Building plurinational democracy where there is a recognition of difference.
- Developing a body of political thinking which provides the substance of the argument and a platform for promoting a bigger vision, a wider and deeper debate, a more inspired and informed agenda and greater political and constitutional options for the future of Scotland and the Union – in particular, more choice for the Scottish people.
- Putting the political and constitutional issues at the heart of our politics by making links with achieving national economic and social success; creating the opportunities for individual fulfilment; generating new solutions to deep-seated problems; and providing new ideas to respond to new challenges. Not an issue for the few but for the many and using this as the basis for arguing for more change and more powers.
- A 'New Enlightenment', involving the ideas and participation of the people of Scotland in a new Age of Reason.

The new approach outlined above captures the essence of what a new alternative for Scotland should be aiming for.

The general principles are: respecting difference; suspending belief in the old doctrines of sovereignty; putting the nation-state (United Kingdom) into proper perspective in a world of change; and having different levels of government.

This is not a blueprint for constitutional reform but an evolving political practice in which issues of plurinationality can be worked out through politics. The ideas do not have to be treated as absolutes, as non-negotiable items or as matters to be settled once and for all, but as part of a continual process of adjustment. There is no shortage of ingenious devices to help. What is missing is a philosophy to bind them together and give them democratic rationale. General principles could be an important first step and the basis for developing an alternative to the current ideas for Scotland's political future.

All of this demands a new mindset and a new vision for the Union. In a multi-nation UK, it requires the centre to respond. If not, the strains and tensions remain and the fault lines become more visible, the outcomes perhaps more predictable and Scotland's secession from the Union a stronger possibility.

This new way of thinking does not rule in or out any possibility. If devolution is a journey, then it is hard to pinpoint a destination; what it does do is to make more sense of the current constitutional settlement and the politics that surround it. Independence or status quo Unionism are not inevitable but our failure to see the issues differently could cause one to lead to the other. Is the Union capable of delivering 'stable-state politics' or is it destined to deliver 'big-bang politics'?

For all of the scenarios, except classical Unionism and Independence, there is a need for a flexible Union that can provide asymmetrical patterns of government, a sharing of power, sovereignty in different places, different structures of democracy and new ways of accommodating national aspirations and identity. These are not wholly separate scenarios but are about an attitude, a state of mind and a new way of thinking about Scotland's future and the future of the UK.

In *Culture, Institutions and Economic Development – A Study of Eight European Regions* by Michael Keating, John Loughlin and Kris Deschower (Edward Elgar Publications, 2005) more context is provided about the changing world we live in and the impact it is having on regional policy and sub-national government. In particular, the work relates to the 'new regionalism' in Europe. Keating et al. describe the globalisation debate, which relates to a set of distinct processes:

> **Economic:** Trade and interdependence; mobility of capital and labour (migrants from central and eastern Europe); transnational companies and global markets.

> **Communications Revolution:** The internet; instant links across the planet; the creation of an information society not limited by time and space; emergence of virtual communities and social and political movements divided by space but united in so many ways; no regulation by national-states, empowering groups and individuals; diversity but also uniformity and individualism; emergence of a global culture and lifestyle, especially among the young in a world of text, e-mail, mobile phones, the Internet; all of this emerging with the dissolution of old territorial communities.

> **Political Dimension:** The rise of global social movements dedicated to special causes, such as the environment and globalisation; new political spaces configured in different ways. People are operating in a global space, not just a Scottish space; their perceptions are changing and they do not see the world through the prism of Unionism. In contrast, their Scottishness may be something they hold on to in a time of dramatic change; for many, territory, borders and boundaries have less significance as their understanding is limited and these do not affect their lifestyles.

Globalisation, it is argued, is a complex set of processes with the potential to impact dramatically on supranationalism (Europe), on nation-states (the UK) and on stateless nations (Scotland) and in turn to change the relationships and dynamic between them. More importantly, it opens up new political options, gives more choice and provides the possibility of new constitutional ways forward for Scotland.

In Europe, nation-states, including the United Kingdom, are undergoing a process of transformation because of globalisation and European integration, and the consequences are profound. The nation-state and its geography; social, economic and political systems; national economies; national identity; the political community; the foundation of democracy;

and social solidarity are all affected. There is a search for a new democracy within and beyond the state, cultural regions and sovereignty.

There is an acceptance that national identity is a substitute for social class as the basis for solidarity. The attraction of class has declined and we are more likely to feel an affinity with co-nationals, i.e. a civic form of nationalism.

Are Scots more interested in economic nationalism or cultural nationalism as a basis for identity? In this context, should we talk about more than one Union – including the economic, social, cultural, political and constitutional? Increasingly important is the issue of security; the threat of global terrorism; and shifting global political alliances. In this context, would it make any sense for security to be devolved?

The bigger picture is not the best of both worlds but the best of all worlds – Scotland, the UK, Europe, global – and now a larger concept of a world without borders, boundaries and barriers – the virtual world.

Our aspirations and ambitions are only limited by our imagination and not by where we are or the place in which we live. All of this is having a profound effect on our political systems, public opinion, public perceptions, party affiliation and loyalties, political alliances and, as a result, on our governance, democracy and representative institutions.

An analogy is that the political parties are like football teams, playing the same game with the same tactics, week in and week out, while the fan-base is crumbling, new attractions are taking supporters away and fewer are doggedly loyal.

There seems to be a consensus in the European debate that we are moving from a world of sovereign nation-states to a plurinational and post-sovereign political order which recognises nationality and shared sovereignty.

Transformation of the nation-state is possible because public opinion is not insisting on unitary nationality or traditional statehood and, as we can see in the United Kingdom, nationality is being accommodated in a new form of asymmetrical state. The evolving European order, using the new Europe for self-affirmation and political action, will increasingly dominate our political and constitutional thinking.

The United Kingdom is an explicitly multinational state, as indicated in its very name, created in the successive unions of England and Wales in 1536, with Scotland in 1707 and with Ireland in 1801. It was never a unitary state on French lines, nor a federation like the United States of America. Michael Keating points out that:

> Its founding constitutional principle was that of parliamentary sovereignty, uniting political authority but not challenging the existence of the four nations.

England was the dominant nation with London the centre of economic, political and cultural power. Each of the other nations related to this centre in distinctive ways and each had its particular brand of society, politics and administration. While constitutional authority was unitary there was a large degree of diversity across the various national civil societies.

In Scotland, national identity was carried on by institutions that survived the Union of 1707, notably the education system, the established Church of Scotland and the law, and was reinforced by the tendency, especially from the late 19th century, to set up special Scottish institutions to handle new government tasks. In a telling and deeply incisive commentary about Scotland, Keating says:

> The hesitancy looks like a legacy of Scotland's recent institutional past, in which politics, culture and economic development were for political reasons kept in separate compartments. Scotland is still presented as a place where things might happen rather than a dynamic society giving birth to distinctive forms of social relations and collective action.

Labour is still reticent about invoking Scottishness as a mobilising theme for fear of giving heart to the Nationalists and jeopardising the Union. The Nationalists for their part cling to Scottish Independence as the solution to the nation's problems without attending too much to the need to build the nation as a system of collective action to meet the challenges of globalisation and European Integration.

Politicians make few claims about how a sense of national identity might be mobilised to pursue social or political ends with the nation-state of the United Kingdom or to face the challenges of globalisation beyond it. Gradually, however, an understanding may be emerging about the relationships of culture, economics and politics and the need for a distinctive Scottish synthesis. This should be part of our political renaissance in Scotland.

The Union seems content to drift while change is being embraced in Europe and elsewhere. The Union seems often wedded to a past that no longer exists.

CHAPTER 13

Old Nation, New Ideas: the Unionist Challenge

IT IS WORTHWHILE TO expand on the thinking behind the work of Keating and his colleagues in the academic community as it helps to reinforce the need for a much wider type of debate at the present time. While the focus is on Scotland and its current role in the Union there are other issues which need to be addressed if sensible arrangements are to be worked out for the long term sustainability and success of the whole of the UK over the next 50 tears. Short termism is a curse of British politics. Rarely is a subject addressed in the context of depth, evidence or long-term consequences and that is why the SNP pursuit of Independence has been met in such a typical and uninspiring way. Context is vital if we are to understand the deeper implications of change. Old nations and their nationalist movements go back at least to the 19th century yet they re-emerged in strength in the late 20th century, with some new features.

Keating says they tended to be:

- Inclusive rather than ethnically exclusive.
- Committed to a civic nationalism based on common values and culture.
- Open to newcomers and fully embracing free trade and European integration.
- Committed to forms of self-determination different from state-hood in the classic sense.
- Not remnants of the past but harbingers of a new form of politics.
- New nationalisms and new movements.

Critically, Keating asks 'whether these new movements can be accommodated within this post-sovereign political order, by means short of independent statehood while respecting the principles of liberal democracy.' He argues that 'nations do not have to be states to achieve self-government' but then asks whether this can take full account of nationality questions.

In general terms, the academic debate accepts that a new era is opening up in which these issues are being reframed, and in the process creating new possibilities.

The doctrine of sovereignty is, however, crucially important and the political theorists argue that:

- We need to separate the concepts of state, nation and sovereignty.
- The nation is a sociological concept based on community which represents a reality based in social institutions and practices and often carries with it claims for self-determination.
- Despite nationality, people can have multiple identities.
- Nationality claims are more than pleas for cultural recognition.
- Sovereignty is not an absolute concept; there can be multiple sites of sovereignty below and above the state.

This issue of sovereignty is core to the whole debate and remains the main stumbling block at the present time for the United Kingdom Parliament and the Coalition government, as it was for the previous Labour Government. The sovereignty of Westminster remains sacrosanct but, as the new debate evolves, this position is being increasingly questioned and other alternatives and points of view are being put forward. This is more about how the world actually is rather than how we think it is.

Rethinking sovereignty will help loosen up the debate and lead to solutions which do not fall at the first hurdle on a notion of running a country based on the conclusion of the 30 Years War and the Peace of Westphalia in 1648. There are alternative traditions of sovereignty. Public opinion is not an obstacle to this and can embrace multiple identities without making rigid distinctions between sovereign Independence and other forms of home rule.

The emerging transnational and global movements, especially the European political order, provide new opportunities for nations to project themselves without becoming nation-states.

Setting aside identity, multiculturalism and ethnicity, Keating's thesis is about the ways in which nationality underpins political order. The argument is that we cannot resolve nationality issues by giving each nation its own state; but neither can we, nor should we, seek to eliminate nationality as a basis for political order. Rather, we need to embrace the concept of plural nationalities and shape political practices and institutions accordingly.

A central argument of Keating's book is that we are moving from a world of sovereign states to a post-sovereign order in which states share their prerogatives with supra-state (Europe), sub-state (Scotland) and trans-state (global) systems.

In the UK, there is a general acceptance of the idea of national diversity and a rather relaxed attitude, indeed indifference on the part of the English majority, towards the constitutional aspirations of the other parts of the state. In recent years there have been indications this might be changing as anti-Scottish sentiment and a negative view of Scotland have emerged.

This has not, however, developed into a coherent or positive view of England's place in the Union and there is some evidence Englishness may be being appropriated by the xenophobic Right. This is an issue with worrying potential, similar to the European debate, where the agenda in the UK has largely been hijacked by anti-Europeans, Euro-sceptics and other right-wing groups and much of the right-wing press.

Scottish Labour notably accepted Scottish sovereignty in the 1988 Declaration of Rights but denied this in government, even though the Scottish people had enjoyed unbroken sovereignty between 1707 and 1999.

There are some important points worth mentioning:

Sovereignty

Many Unionists may be happier with secession than devolution because sovereignty would not be compromised.

Catalonia has shared sovereignty and multiple spheres of action.

For over 100 years, the principled objections to asymmetry provided the intellectual basis of British Unionist opposition to home rule, firstly for Ireland and then for Scotland. Unionists have rarely denied the right of secession to the state-less nations but insisted that short of taking up this option they must respect the untrammelled sovereignty and unity of parliament. Home rule has to be about a devolution of powers, not the sharing of powers. This is an issue that will not go away and only with a more mature and less defensive position can Westminster remove the obstacle of absolute sovereignty. This remains a powerful block on any serious debate. The UK may not be able for much longer to play the sovereignty card and dictate the nature and extent of constitutional and political change in Wales, Scotland and Northern Ireland. This is an enormous issue of principle.

Central Institutions

Another important dimension concerns the representation of the constituent nations in the central institutions of the British state, especially in the second chamber. Proposals for the reform of the House of Lords have been around for 100 years, without any great result. The current proposals for an 80 per cent elected chamber are unlikely to make any progress and will remain a contentious issue for the Coalition. Despite the concerns of Westminster about strengthening the Union through its constituent parts, there has never been, at any time, discussion of the second chamber – elected or unelected – being made up of members from the English regions or the nations of the UK. This is clearly a move that would strengthen the Union but would be tainted by the idea of federalism.

Europe

The use of Europe by Scotland is another key consideration. In other countries of Europe, there are in place effective and binding agreements given to region-states about their participation in the European Union. Alongside economic policy, taxation and the social security system, Europe has to be the other big issue at the heart of the debate on new powers.

Independence

The final chapter of Michael Keating's book fleshes out the new ideas and concepts which we are giving prominence in this volume. Keating argues:

Of course, many of the stateless nations suffer from the same illusion, that there can be a defining moment in which the issue will be resolved. The Parti Québécois has staged referendums in 1980 and 1995, albeit on very ambiguous questions, without resolving the issue and propose a third in due course, giving rise to gibes about the 'referendum-neverendum' or the strategy of pestering the people with the same question until eventually they answer 'yes'.

The Scottish National Party is about to embark on a referendum on Independence and the evidence suggests that the response might be the same as in Quebec: that the Nationalists could win an election, as they did in 2011, but fail to convince the people on Independence.

Again, the prospect is for the endless revisiting of the Independence question.

Keating puts this issue into context by suggesting that:

> We cannot capture the plurinational state in a definitive constitutional settlement... there are many in the United Kingdom who believe they can resolve all the constitutional issues in one comprehensive settlement.

Such reasoning is linked to an urge to define and nail down the principle of sovereignty and the distribution of power. Yet the search for sovereignty is more like the physicist's quest for the ultimate particle, a search that will never end. Knowledge is advanced not by finding the definitive answer, but by repeated rounds of questioning and exploration.

So a better way of proceeding is to see constitutionalism as a dialogue or conversation, linking the various deliberative spaces and allowing for mutual influence and learning.

Blue print

Keating argues that there is no blueprint for constitutional reform, but an evolving political practice, in which issues of plurinationality can be worked out through politics. They do not have to be treated as absolutes, as non-negotiable items or matters to be settled once and for all, but as part of a continual process of adjustment.

There is no shortage of ingenious devices involving federalism, second chambers, charters of rights and intergovernmental relations. What is missing is a philosophy to bind them together and give them a democratic rationale. Neither the SNP nor the Unionist parties have a narrative for this. The general principles of this should be: respect for difference; of suspending belief in old doctrines of sovereignty; and of putting the nation-state in proper perspective should help in managing conflicts in places where they are difficult. None of these principles are evident in the approach of the UK Parliament or government.

'Triviality of Interest only to Nationalist Cranks'

305 years on from the Treaty of the Union, there are some interesting historical points to make on the question of sovereignty and the English view of Scotland:

> In search of the ancient constitution, arguments go back to the Middle Ages, when the Norman Welsh historian Geraldus Cambrensis sought to justify suzerainty over the whole of Britain, against a vigorous defence on the part of Scottish historians like Hector Boece, first principal of the University of Aberdeen.

The most influential school of historians in the nation-state tradition were the Whig historians of the 19th and 20th centuries. A central feature of this history was its focus on England. Almost all the works were entitled Histories of England, tracing British history directly from England, with the peripheral nations putting in only occasional appearances and joining the central narrative only after joining the Union.

AJP Taylor insisted that the distinction between English and British was a 'triviality of interest only to Nationalist cranks'. Instead, the Unions of 1536, 1707 and 1801 are treated as mere incidents after which English history continues.

The seeds of irritation were clearly sown early! A consequence of this was the notion that parliamentary sovereignty was absolute, since this had been established in 16th and 17th century England, and this is one part of the modern problem. The other is the view of Scotland as a materially and intellectually impoverished and dependent country.

The stateless national movements such as Catalonia and Scotland have rethought their aims and strategies in light of more modern developments:

First, there are those who believe that their respective transnational regimes (the European Union) permit sovereign Independence at a lower cost than in the past.

Second, a strand of opinion that is less overtly Separatist and holds that some continuing link with the original state will be necessary.

Third, the position of the radical 'post-sovereigntists', who have embraced globalisation and transnational integration to the extent of believing that sovereignty in the classic sense has little meaning anymore. They are more concerned with maximising the degree of autonomy and influence open to nations than with the trappings of sovereignty and are usually ambivalent as to their ultimate aims, preferring to see how the world evolves before they commit themselves.

Fourth, along with the acceptance of transnational integration and the limitations to sovereignty, the tendency among most of the movements to a more inclusive definition of the nation and a conscious adoption of a civic nationalism. Such a de-ethnicisation has enabled Nationalists to extend their appeal as well as burnish their liberal credentials.

Less radical forms of national affirmation can gain the assent or active support of broader strata of society and this is what is clearly happening in Scotland at the present time. This is evident by the fact that only when Scottish identity is challenged can it be mobilised behind political objectives. This becomes important in terms of the Union and its attitude and behaviour towards Scotland.

Scottish opinion appears to be committed to self-government as a process. There are strong aspirations to national autonomy and Scotland is seen as more than a self-governing region within the UK state. There is an appreciation that the constitution is evolving, with both Scottish and European levels being strengthened, but an unwillingness to stress or define any end point.

CHAPTER 14

The Vision, The Alternative and The Second Question

AT THE START OF 2012, nearly 13 years after the opening of the Scottish Parliament, the constitutional question sparked into life. The Conservative and Unionist Prime Minister David Cameron had a 'Westminster we have a Problem' moment, and, following weekend briefings from Downing Street and an appearance on the Andrew Marr show, he arrived in Scotland to convey his new-found enthusiasm for a referendum on Independence. All of a sudden, the Coalition Government was in a mood to take on Alex Salmond and the SNP.

The reality of the intervention was in sharp contrast to the rhetoric of David Cameron, who had shown little interest in Scotland or the constitutional question. Faced with the relentless rise of the SNP, Alex Salmond's domination of Scottish politics, Westminster's crumbling grip on Scotland and the total failure of all the Unionist parties to heed the warnings of the May 2007 and 2011 Holyrood elections, it was little wonder that the Prime Minister had come to the unremarkable conclusion that the Union's relevance to Scotland was now being seriously challenged.

We should not under-estimate this watershed in the relationship between Scotland and the Union of the UK. The stakes have been raised. David Cameron does get angry, he is prone to opportunism and he does not understand Scotland – neither its current role within the Union nor the changing impact of identity and nationality on contemporary politics.

Scotland has moved on since 1999 but, curiously, the Unionist parties have not and now find great difficulty in adjusting to new politics and making up for the five lost years since the SNP election victory at Holyrood in 2007. Cameron's intervention could have been seen as a sign of desperation, seeking to influence the process but not willing to engage in the substance of this political and constitutional issue.

Praise for the Cameron intervention has come from those who felt some impetus and urgency was required at a time when the Unionist parties were sleep-walking into a real crisis and had learned absolutely nothing from the success of the SNP and their stranglehold on Scottish politics and the constitutional debate.

Since David Cameron's call to arms, there has been feverish activity in Scotland, largely revolving around two consultation papers published by the Scotland Office – on behalf of the Westminster Government and the Scottish Government – dealing with the procedure and conduct of the Referendum on Independence. And recently, the launch of the SNP's 'Yes for Scotland' campaign and the 'Better Together, United Kingdom' pro-Union campaign have set the scene for the battle for Scotland and the looming day of destiny. Westminster and Holyrood are still arguing about the details of that historic struggle, but the campaign launch titles say a great deal about the nature of the debate ahead!

Lack of Choice

A growing number of Scots are concerned about the attempt by the Unionist parties to narrow the choices for the Scottish people and limit the alternatives that will be available in what will be a momentous vote. This chapter takes a look at how the debate is shaping up and considers some of the key issues which lie at the very heart of this historic referendum about Scotland's future.

Scotland needs a bigger and better debate than that which has so far been evident. One which takes us beyond the narrow, devolution-plus Calman versus Independence. These are the extremes of a limited debate. There are alternatives which could be better for Scotland and which would satisfy the needs of the majority of Scots who want far more powers, a greater degree of fiscal autonomy as part of a newly defined Union.

There is a compelling political and intellectual logic to this idea, but one which is not shared by the Unionist parties north or south of the border and as a consequence may not appear on the ballot paper in 2014. Nevertheless, it will undoubtedly play a role in the campaign and may even help decide the outcome.

There are early stirrings that the opposition parties are beginning to see the weakness of their tactics. The prospect of an alternative – which may be more popular than the two choices currently on offer – not being on the ballot paper is beyond the bounds of credible politics and would be an astonishing slight to an electorate increasingly disillusioned and dissatisfied with politics.

The electors need to be taken seriously and treated like grown-ups. Our new politics demands vision and a more inspired debate. The polarisation of the debate around these two limited options helps the Conservative party who have little interest in constitutional change. From the days of Margaret Thatcher to William Hague – who famously said 11 days before the referendum in 1997, that a Tory Government might scrap the Scottish Parliament if it didn't work out – to David Cameron who has shown little interest until his New Year outburst. The Conservatives are at best ambivalent about the role of Scotland in the Union and at worst dismissive of the whole idea.

There are real long term dangers for Labour in any pact or deal with the Conservatives to fight Independence. Labour can be part of the solution to the constitutional question, if they seize the opportunity, but the Conservative party remains part of the problem.

Involving the Conservatives in the overall campaign for the Union is questionable. They remain a very unpopular brand in Scotland, unwilling to bend to the mood of Scottish people and are becoming even more unpopular as the Coalition at Westminster embarks on policies which are alien to Scotland's political culture.

Saying NO to Independence is not enough. Opinion polls confirm consistently that between 60 and 65 per cent of the electors do not support Independence. After an intensive campaign, the gap between support for the Union and Independence is likely to be much narrower. Defeating Independence is only the start of building a new Scotland within the Union, it cannot be a solution in itself. The Union must change and modernise.

Both Ed Miliband and David Cameron agree that the United Kingdom has been a success and that it is worthy of preservation. We have a shared history of which we can be proud and few people will disagree with these sentiments. But what will a shared future look like?

The Union is in great need of a transformation and a political make over. Caution should be exercised about the ties of history as most Scots are concerned about their future, not the past and this applies particularly to young people, concerned more about dreams than memories. The Facebook and Twitter generation represents a whole new world of interests and aspirations, which needs to be inspired – not talked down to or ignored.

The defeat of Independence will only be one step on Scotland's journey. Is there a settled will of the Scottish people in terms of our future role within the Union? What is clear is that we urgently need an alternative to a tired Union and an outdated concept of Independence. Maybe we need to think of the constitutional question in a different way. The SNP and the status quo Unionists (Westminster Conservatives) are offering extremes, which through political neglect and lack of interest on the part of the media and the other parties, especially Labour, have now become so embedded in our popular politics that no other alternatives have been able to emerge as serious runners.

It is a measure of how political fortunes have changed, that the Unionist parties want to say no to Independence but have little to say about the Union. The SNP and Independence should not be the focus of this campaign. The future of Scotland, the transformation of the Union and Scotland's role within it are what matter to the vast majority of Scots.

In the first edition of this book, *Scotland the Road Divides*, published after the 2007 Holyrood election and co-authored with Tom Brown we said,

> Despite the narrowness of the current debate, the hope is that it can be opened out to include the third way of a more flexible modernised Union that is confident enough to embrace the new politics of the 21st century. This requires the Mother of Parliaments to understand that transferring more powers is not a sign of weakness but of strength and confidence in the constituent parts of the United Kingdom. Without that the paradox is that the impetus for the break-up of the Union may be created at the very heart of Unionism itself.

This has more resonance today that it did five years ago. No one should have a monopoly on the future of our country. If the SNP didn't exist we still need a vision for the future of Scotland and that would include how we are governed!

The Early Skirmishes of 2012

During the long drawn-out 'phoney war' over the Independence referendum, the UK government and the SNP Scottish government jockeyed for position on constitutional technicalities, processes and timetables. Two very different consultation papers dominated the debate. Throughout this period, the catchphrase used by the coalition government in London, almost *ad nauseam*, was 'a legal, fair and decisive referendum'.

Meanwhile, what the public wanted was for them to get down to the brass tacks of a substantial debate on the good or ill effects of Independence.

In their foreword to 'Scotland's constitutional future – A consultation on facilitating a legal, fair and decisive referendum on whether Scotland should leave the United Kingdom' in January 2012, Prime Minister David Cameron and Deputy Prime Minister Nick Clegg said:

> We believe passionately in the United Kingdom and recognise the benefits it has brought to all of its citizens. For over 300 years the United Kingdom has brought people together in the most successful multi-national state the world has ever known.
>
> We want to keep the United Kingdom together. But we recognise that the Scottish Government holds the opposite view. In May 2011, the Scottish National Party won a majority in the Scottish Parliament; this was a significant electoral victory, which the UK Government has openly acknowledged.
>
> The Scottish National Party entered the May 2011 election with a manifesto pledge for a referendum on Independence. They have campaigned consistently for Independence, and while the UK Government does not believe this is in the interests of Scotland, or the rest of the United Kingdom, we will not stand in the way of a referendum on Independence: the future of Scotland's place within the United Kingdom is for people in Scotland to vote on.

The questions of legality and fairness remained in dispute, but Scottish Secretary Michael Moore insisted that, for the referendum to be decisive,

> There must be a single, straightforward question; and that question must be asked as soon as possible.
>
> We live in uncertain times, with the global economic situation

creating challenges for increasing investment and jobs in Scotland. The question of Scotland's constitutional future is increasing that uncertainty. We can answer that question and at least on this one issue, end the uncertainty. It is irresponsible to allow this question to hang over Scotland, when it is in our power to end the doubts and allow Scotland to move forward with a clear constitutional future.

As the wrangling over technicalities continued, there were only occasional hints of the development of a real debate on Independence. During the on-going debate about separation, the SNP's fallback position has been to argue that Scotland would continue being part of UK institutions. Moore cited First Minister Salmond's statement that a separate Scotland would keep the pound and use the Bank of England as the lender of last resort: 'What's curious is that in these early stages of the great debate, every time reality has bitten, those in favour of Independence have defaulted to the protection of the United Kingdom.'

As well as the pound and Bank of England, he cited the SNP claiming that other countries would bail out Scotland's bank if there was another financial meltdown. 'That's an odd notion of Independence,' he added.

Moore called on the SNP to start providing 'credible answers' on tax and spend in an Independent Scotland, and suggested taxes would have to go up post-separation to pay for the SNP's promises on public spending. He said the Separatists have failed to make clear what kind of economy a separate Scotland would have. Instead, they have moved 'seamlessly from economic model to economic model, alighting on any system that seems to suit, then floating on to the next when it becomes expedient to do so.'

Until 2008, he said, Mr Salmond had urged Scotland to join the 'arc of prosperity' alongside Ireland, Iceland and Norway. But after Ireland's economy nosedived and Iceland went bankrupt, he said the SNP's focus moved east to Scandinavia. He accused the SNP of shifting 'from deregulated Celtic Lion to social democratic haven in one inelegant rhetorical flourish.'

But the Scottish Secretary questioned whether Scandinavian levels of public services could be afforded without income tax, corporation tax and VAT increasing in a separate Scotland. While the UK Government takes around 37 per cent of income in tax, that figure increases to 41.1 per cent in Norway, 47 per cent in Sweden and 48.1 per cent in Denmark.

Moore said the latter figure is the equivalent of more than £2,500 for every man, woman and child in Scotland. 'Getting there would require a radical overhaul of the Scottish economy and hard choices that cost money,' he added.

The SNP Vision

For the SNP, their crushing election victory in the 2011 Holyrood election boosted their ambition of holding a referendum in the life-time of this Parliament. Their consultation paper, 'Your Scotland, Your Referendum' was about, 'the Scottish Government's proposal for a referendum on Independence'. Instead of talking about leaving the UK, Alex Salmond talked about a 'new partnership with the rest of the UK... when nations co-operate on shared interests' and 'Her Majesty the Queen will remain as Head of State'.

The consultations left no one in any doubt about the tone and the intent of the opposing forces. The clearest exposition of Alex Salmond's vision of post-Independence Scotland was given in a keynote speech at the London School of Economics on 16 February 2012 – a speech that, despite its significance, was poorly reported, inadequately scrutinised and received scant commentary.

His theme was that Independence is the key to Scotland's future economic growth, and he identified specific measures that an independent administration needs to boost economic growth. These included responsibility for taxation, greater control over investment in energy and borrowing powers to stimulate capital investment and making best use of Scotland's 'unparalleled energy resources':

> An independent Scotland would pursue policies of ambition and responsibility. We would use Scotland's natural resources and skilled workforce to build a sustainable economy.

He expanded on previous declarations about the benefits to the United Kingdom of a successful independent Scotland:

The rest of the UK has much to gain from the emergence of a secure, prosperous ally to its north. An independent Scotland would seek to make a responsible contribution on the European and world stage – and that would benefit all of the nations of these islands.

The main purpose of his speech was to set out how Scotland is economically constrained by its current constitutional position, and to outline 'key economic opportunities to support growth and promote jobs that Scotland could seize when she becomes independent'.

Given the venue of the London School of Economics and the expertise of his audience, he could hardly avoid addressing the financial consequences of Independence:

Some people say a currency union could prevent an independent Scotland from using its fiscal powers. We would undoubtedly need to demonstrate fiscal responsibility – as any sensible nation does.

But Scotland is easily prosperous enough to stand on its own two feet. Indeed, the Government Expenditure and Revenue Scotland report demonstrates that from 2005 to 2010, Scotland was in a stronger relative fiscal position than the UK by a total of £7.2 billion. A study by the independent Centre for Economics and Business Research confirmed that Scotland receives no net subsidy from the rest of the UK.

Scotland would therefore be able to meet any fiscal obligations of a currency union. In addition, Scotland and the rest of the UK are very similar economies in terms of prosperity levels. Even in the non-oil economy, Scottish productivity is virtually identical to the UK average. Therefore a currency zone for Scotland and the rest of the UK would be a very, very different creature from the Eurozone, which covers territories from the Ruhr in Germany to Kalamata in the Pelopponese.

A sterling zone would make sense for Scotland and for the rest of the UK. Indeed, recent opinion polls have shown majority support for that in both Scotland and England.

So let's assume that no sensible person would argue against a currency zone. What Independence would give Scotland is the ability to set our own fiscal and economic policy, within the context of a stable monetary policy. It would give us the flexibility to provide specifically Scottish policies for specific challenges. And above all, it would allow us to promote sustainable economic growth.

An independent Scotland would pursue policies of ambition and responsibility. We would use Scotland's natural resources and skilled workforce to build a sustainable economy – based on producing goods and services that people actually want, rather than living off the illusory profits of periodic asset booms.

The end of the phoney war holds out the prospect of a substantial and informed debate about Scotland's future. What is not clear is whether the debate will concentrate on the single issue of Independence or will be expanded into a much more enlightened and progressive exchange of ideas on a new future for Scotland within a transformed union of the UK.

Why the limited Debate?

The PM's visit to Scotland earlier in 2012 and his carefully-crafted and reasonably well-received speech provided a timely reminder of how fragile and vulnerable the case for status quo Unionism could prove to be in the rapidly changing politics of Scotland and the UK.

Whether by design or by accident, Cameron gave a marginal boost to those who want a bigger and better debate, outwith the narrow constraints of Independence and no-change Unionism.

First of all, his actions underlined the fact that constitutional change is a process and not an event, killing off the idea that the status quo is a tenable political proposition.

Second, Cameron confirmed that Scotland could get more powers, however ill-defined at present. Even though this came in the form of a political bribe to cut the support for Independence, you are never quite sure with Cameron whether what he says is based on opportunism or progressive thinking. Either way, he will now be held to account for his remarks by the people of Scotland.

Third, he publicly acknowledged that saying NO to Independence is not enough, and will not sustain a campaign or a strategy over the next two years. Again, the PM prevaricates by pretending this new debate about powers has to be suppressed until Independence is out of the way. It is hard to imagine Scots seeing the sense of this.

Fourth, the PM has raised some doubts about the strength of the Unionist case by conceding so early to the idea of more powers in an attempt to persuade Scots that not only do we have a shared history, but we could also have a shared future. It is worth remembering that devolved power is not shared power.

Fifth, David Cameron has given, unwittingly, some shape and substance to the importance of a second question and its place in this whole debate. This is a remarkable development because at the highest level of government we now see that an alternative option for the future of Scotland is potentially available and credible; but the Unionist parties are totally opposed to its development!

The real importance of the PM's New Year visit to Scotland was not so much about the sincerity or seriousness with which he raised the idea of more powers, it is the fact that in doing so, he has surely laid to rest the ridiculous assumption that Scots only deserve a choice between Unionism and Separatism. In fact, a more robust home rule package could be evolved, which will defeat Independence, help transform an old and tired Union and reflect what Scots really want. How novel in a democracy for the people to have an effective say in their own future!

At this early stage in the referendum campaign, there are a number of views as to where we should be.

There is a desire to see Independence and Unionism fight it out in a straight 'yes or no' battle, to the exclusion of any other rational alternative. That is currently the official position of all the Unionist parties, including Labour, and destined to be a campaign in which saying NO to Independence will become the longest, most negative campaign ever devised.

The view that more powers for the Scottish Parliament are inevitable is emerging, but not strongly enough to necessitate forming a second question. It is therefore being left until after the defeat of Independence in the referendum. This lacks credibility because few people trust politicians, political parties and Governments – especially Conservative led Coalitions – to deliver on promises. In any case, another referendum may take years to set up. Add in the uncertainty of who runs Britain after the general election in 2015 and the need for Scots to control their own destiny, waiting for Westminster makes no sense.

There are those who see two questions being asked at the same time as both logical and sensible. Question one is the straight 'yes or no' on

Independence. If Scots vote for Independence, then we can return to our day jobs and prepare for separation from the UK.

The second question would ask whether Scotland should have more policy powers and a greater degree of fiscal powers if it remains part of the Union. A vote for the Union would then either be strengthened by a vote for more powers, or if Scots said NO to more powers, the status quo would endure. There are a number of variations to this proposition, but the important point is that this is achievable. Unionist opposition to this is based on a number of factors, but logic, political common sense and an intelligent regard for Scotland's needs, seem to be lacking.

A positive vote by the Scottish people for more devolved powers would be a formidable mandate for change which could not be cast aside by any of the political parties. The provision of this second question would also allow a more positive campaign to be maintained in the run-up to the referendum and start to shape a future which is neither the old Union nor Independence. Importantly, the answer to the first question is absolute; the second question is only about what kind of Union we want to see, if we vote to stay within it.

Labour in Scotland and in the UK should have nothing to do with a Unionist alliance with the Conservatives. Labour should lead from the front. This is as much a battle for the future success of the Labour Party in Scotland as it is for the future of Scotland and the Union. The Scottish people are well ahead of Labour and, as a party, they must catch up. In Wales, Labour First Minister Carwyn Jones has called for a constitutional shake up. The Scotsman newspaper said,

> Carwyn Jones will renew his calls for a constitutional convention for the UK... will ask how the different territories of the UK should be governed and legislatures should relate to each other within the UK. He has already proposed an idea where a reformed House of Lords could have equal representation from the four nations, similar to the model used by the US Senate. He will also appeal to Scots to reject Independence and choose a future for the UK which is politically diverse, looser, and combines several centres of democratic account-ability... the relationship between the devolved nations and the UK government needs to be reset.

His words reflect the ideas in this book and illustrate how a successful

Labour party, in a country initially less enthused about devolution, is now talking up progressive federal ideas, including a looser UK .

The Unionist dilemma is straightforward enough. If Independence is defeated and there is no second question on the ballot paper in 2014, the parties of the Union will have to devise the tactics of how changes after the referendum can be delivered and guaranteed if Scots throw away their control of the issue and cede responsibility to Westminster and Holyrood. How then, will the Unionist parties individually and collectively organise some form of consensus around the scope, content, delivery and timing of any new powers for the Scottish Parliament?

This seems like the art of the impossible when you consider the stark realities of who will control Westminster and Holyrood after the 2015 General election, the ambivalence of the Conservative Party and whether or not Scotland's future could be a pressing priority at Westminster. The fundamental question is whether Scottish voters can trust Westminster with the future of devolution and powers for the Scottish Parliament.

The prospect of some electoral pact on the constitutional question or some binding agreement involving all the parties, after Scotland says no to Independence, seems like a pipe dream which defies the reality of our tribal and highly partisan politics. No amount of gesturing, vague promises and ill-defined commitments could ever be a substitute for Scots having a second question and being able to control their own destiny in Scotland without recourse to the politics of the unknown at Westminster.

A new vision for Scotland, an alternative to both status quo Unionism and Independence and a second question are achievable and capable of inclusion in the ballot of 2014. The real motives behind those who would contest this achievable political outcome should become obvious as the campaign unfolds!

The Home Rule Challenge – There is an Alternative

While the option of a second question remains open, the debate for Scotland's future is still narrowed by the notion that either Independence or status quo Unionism must be defeated before we can turn our attention to anything else. This makes no sense. We need to redefine Scotland's role in the Union. We need an alternative that takes us beyond the uninspiring and narrow options of devolution plus Calman versus Independence. In contemporary politics, these are extremes which currently exclude one significant alternative, Devo- enhancement. This home rule concept brings together two different options which are popularly referred to as devo-max and devo-plus.

After proper debate and technical analysis, these could form the core of an alternative which, if opinion polls are anything to go by, could be popular, workable and modern. These alternatives embrace maximum devolved powers with key issues such as Defence and Foreign Affairs and some Treasury matters remaining at Westminster, with further debate about pensions and social security to be considered, and different degrees of fiscal autonomy in Scotland and our relationship with the UK.

Opinion polls show that without being debated to any great extent, these ideas have captured the imagination of the electors. Ipsos MORI carried out a poll for Reform Scotland in July 2012 and the findings contain a remarkable degree of cross party support for a Devo-Plus alternative and a second question. In a choice between Devo-Plus, Independence and Status Quo, 52 per cent of Labour voters think Scotland should remain in the UK under Devo-Plus and 28 per cent of SNP voters believe the same. 10 per cent of SNP voters and 24 per cent of Labour would be more likely to vote 'no' if it would lead to Devo-Plus. Almost three-quarters of Labour voters want Unionists to campaign for more powers for the Scottish Parliament.

These are remarkable findings and reinforce the trend in recent opinion polls to support a new and radical package of measures for the Scottish Parliament and by definition, a rejection of both the Status quo and Independence.

It would be a constitutional and political outrage if, at this early stage, an alternative was not given serious consideration by all of the political parties in the run up to the referendum. These are the very basic outlines of an idea which requires a great deal more work to be done.

If a credible and substantive case for home rule can be put forward, then regardless of whether it is on a ballot paper in the referendum, a devo-alternative might still have a very significant impact on how people might vote.

There has to be a technical and legal dialogue about how all of this could be captured as an alternative in the form of a second question on the referendum ballot paper. Cynics currently argue that it is too complicated, it will just muddy the waters, and the Scottish people cannot deal with more than one question – which is both patronising and insulting to Scottish electors. These arguments are about tribalism, ambivalence, a lack of intellectual effort, a downright hostility to any further powers and a fear of what Scottish voters might do, nothing more. It is up to the Scottish people to decide the questions they want to be asked.

The politics of a Home Rule within a new Union makes a great deal of sense and should force the Union to define what it is FOR – a form of federalism, nationality and identity, diversity and difference, reform and renewal – and what it is AGAINST – break-up and separation, 'large-N' Nationalism and Independence, division and discord, uncertainty and insecurity. Currently, Independence has a sense of purpose and novelty to it, regardless of whether you support it or not. Unionism doesn't and we are left defending the past without any vision for the future. The Save-the-Union campaign is shaping up to be remarkably backward looking, because so far there is nothing being projected about the future and while fear and scaremongering do win votes, there has to be a place for inspiration, idealism and a vision. Unless and until the Union believes in the need to do any of that, their campaign is destined to be negative.

There currently appears to be no new model for the future of the Union, and the reluctance of Unionist parties to move from simply saying no to Independence means that it may fall to non-party political Scotland, civic Scotland, think tanks, the Trade Unions, the churches and others to carry the banner of a 'third way'.

The people of Scotland now have a chance not only to select a new future for their country in 2014, but also to influence what choices they will have before them.

Surely this debate can be opened out to include the idea of a more flexible and modernised Union which sees transferring more power and responsibility as not a sign of weakness, but strength and confidence in the constituent parts of the UK. There is now a unique opportunity to write a new chapter in Scottish politics. But time is running out.

This is the moment to take greater control over the future of our country and to begin to exercise more responsibility for what we do and what we aspire to.

Trust the Public

In their response to the UK Government's Consultation paper, the School of Social and Political Science of Edinburgh University made some telling points which cut through the so-called complexities and difficulties of having a debate on a reasoned alternative to the Independence versus Unionism battle.

They argue that in view of the SNP's manifesto commitment to a referendum in the second half of its term of office, and the need to thoroughly examine all the constitutional options and their implications as widely as possible to ensure an informed choice, a vote in the Autumn of 2014 would not seem inappropriate. Reflecting the compelling logic put forward in this book they argue,

> The Prime Minister and the Secretary of State for Scotland have indicated their willingness to revisit the current devolution settlement with a view to strengthening devolution only after the Independence referendum, should the latter result in a No vote. We are concerned that this pledge – even if accompanied by a detailed proposal for reform – would prevent voters in the Independence referendum from making a fully informed choice.
>
> 'We are concerned that a promise of reform to the devolution arrangements following a No vote may create two types of No voters, those whose No vote expresses a commitment to the status quo, and those committed to a change the Prime Minister, the Secretary of State and others have held in prospect. Just as it is imperative for the meaning of a Yes vote to be unambiguous, so too is it important for the meaning of a No vote to be clear.

This line of argument leads to another issue. How many people will simply not vote if their choice or preference is not on the ballot paper or will vote for Independence because their preference is too far removed from the Union for them to vote No?

Alex Salmond's soft political approach to what Independence means may beguile many voters into thinking that we are not leaving the Union, but merely changing the way we operate within it.

There are too many issues, especially at this early stage, which Westminster and the Unionist parties have simply failed to grasp.

Reshaping and reforming the Union may be the best option to win over those who want substantial change but don't want to leave the Union. They are already asking why their views are being ignored. Why should Scots lose control over their future by allowing the Unionist parties to think and talk about more powers in the future but deny Scots a chance to vote on it in 2014?

Concluding their submission to the UK Government, the School of Political and Social Sciences of Edinburgh University deal with the view that a two-question referendum is too complicated to be put before a Scottish electorate – an electorate that has been voting in significant numbers since the great Reform Act of 1832! Again, they argue with conviction, evidence and common sense when they say,

> We share the desire for a referendum to produce an unambiguous outcome, but believe that this is possible with the insertion of an additional option in the referendum ballot.
>
> There are a variety of systems used outside the UK which have delivered unambiguous and intelligible outcomes from multiple options. Among these, a system especially pertinent to the Scottish debate is that which has been used in referendums on electoral reform in New Zealand – and the forthcoming referendum on Puerto Rico's constitutional status – which includes two questions posed simultaneously: the first question is to solicit consent for a change to the existing arrangements, and the second to determine the form that change could take. The second question is only applicable if the first question produces a majority for change.

It seems difficult to believe that the second question has been so easily dismissed by the Unionist parties, bearing in mind the experience of other countries. The idea that Scots could not navigate more than one question seems both ridiculous and insulting, and begs the question of whether the Unionist parties are genuinely interested in any further constitutional change, or is a long, evasive, weary and torturous period of procrastination and evasion the prize awaiting Scots after the vote in 2014?

Reinforcing the strength of this argument, Professor Michael Keating, in an article for the *Holyrood* magazine, 'Maxing the Debate', combines international experience and new definitions of sovereignty, explores ideas of devo-max and fiscal autonomy, and makes a case for considering new forms of constitutional change. The clarity and expertise of his writing, the range of his work and the depth of his experience uniquely equip him to give us advice and insights into sub-national government and ideas for the modernisation of our increasingly dated systems of governance.

The way we conduct our debate on political and constitutional change in this country suggests issues and problems unique to Britain, when in fact they are commonplace in Europe. British exceptionalism, our obsession with the sovereignty of Westminster, and the ambivalence and disinterest we show to the outside world all help to feed into the complacency of the political parties at Westminster and our politics generally. Keating captures much of this current debate in his book, *The Independence of Scotland* (Oxford University Press) which reviews Independence and devolution options including the need for an alternative and the danger of dismissing, too early, ideas that with a bit of political and intellectual effort, could be much more attractive to Scots than the Union unchanged or Independence.

Keating's thinking reflects the debate about a third way and makes the following points about what this would involve.

Philosophy The philosophical basis lies in the idea of 'post-sovereignty', that in the globalised world and the European Union, the traditional concept of Independence is redundant. Sovereignty is shared at multiple levels and in complex ways.

Devo-Diversity When it comes to the details, there are several different versions. One would provide for the devolution of everything except the currency, defence and foreign affairs, taking us back in many ways to the old union between 1603 and 1707, or the union between Sweden and Norway between 1815 and 1905. A less ambitious version would retain some common regulatory responsibilities and certain social entitlements like pensions.

More Powers Proposals for fiscal autonomy have usually been accompanied by a further devolution of competencies, notably in social security, which is the only major domestic spending programme not already devolved. Keating argues that any of these proposals would represent a massive transfer of power to Scotland, allowing the big decisions about the balance between taxes and spending to be made here.

Sharing of Revenue There is, however, a series of questions to be posed. Would there be a system of fiscal equalisation or sharing of revenues among the nations and regions of the United Kingdom? Even the most decentralised federations have such a system to deal with 'asymmetric shocks' or economic problems hitting one territory harder than others.

Avoiding Confusion The Unionist parties, on the other hand, refuse to countenance the second Question, arguing that it confuses matters. Unionists have also argued that one cannot logically have a referendum on 'Devo-Max' since it requires the assent of both Scotland and the rest of the United Kingdom, whereas Independence can be unilateral. This argument is, I think, a weak one.

Avoid a Polarised Debate Evidence from opinion surveys shows that a large body of Scots (usually the largest) is opposed both to Independence and to the status quo. It also shows that they, like citizens in other stateless nations including Quebec, Catalonia and the Basque Country, do not make a sharp distinction between Independence and advanced devolution, but rather see these as lying on a spectrum.

Keating makes a compelling case for change which recognises that traditional concepts of Independence are outdated and sovereignty and power have to be shared. Equally important is the idea of raising our constitutional horizons and acknowledging the progressive thinking that is taking place in Europe and elsewhere in the world. There is no escaping the conclusion that our constitutional debate is uninspiring, poorly informed and lacks meaningful context for electors to make effective choices about the future of Scotland and its role in the Union.

Devo-Max and Devo-Plus

This section looks in a bit more detail at the two options which are emerging as reasonable and practical alternatives to Independence and the Status Quo Unionism. Without being embraced by any of the Unionist parties or forming part of a second question, there are early signs that a number of politicians, think tanks, elements of civic Scotland, the Trade Unions and, more significantly, Scottish electors, have shown an interest in a third way or a new alternative.

Devo-max and Devo-plus are radical proposals for the future of

Scotland, and, as such, require careful consideration and a much greater scrutiny if they are to impact on the debate which has just started. It seems self-evident that, even if the Unionist parties do not wish to engage with these alternatives, they will nevertheless make an impact on the debate. The constitutional landscape is complex, and is in danger of leaving the public confused as they genuinely try to come to terms with ideas that will shape their own destiny as well as their country's.

There are also early signs that there might be some movement on the part of the political classes to temper their outright hostility to any argument or idea which runs contrary to the prevailing party mantra. Some Labour MSPs are now openly expressing their interest in these new alternatives. The Lib-Dems are looking at a policy for home rule which, as Professor John Curtice said recently, 'is devo-max by another name'. The Lib-Dems' historical commitment to federalism should encourage them to be taking a lead in Scotland and creating some distance between themselves and their deeply unpopular London leadership. And, despite the new Scottish Tory leader Ruth Davidson's uncompromising position against further devolution, some of her MSPs do not share her views. So there is considerable potential for a growing number of people to be breaking party ranks as the opportunities and benefits of new ideas start to emerge.

Further Alternatives

What are the other alternatives to Independence and status quo Unionism? Reform Scotland, the Independent think tank, have produced some good work, identifying the various terms being used in the constitutional and political debate and spelling out the alternatives.

> **Asymmetric Devolution:** A system in which different constituent states possess different powers; one or more states have considerably more autonomy than the others, although they have the same constitutional status. The UK has had an asymmetric model of devolution since 1999.
>
> **Calman Commission:** The Committee on Scottish Devolution, Chaired by Sir Kenneth Calman and established by collaboration between Scotland's main Unionist parties. Commonly referred to as

the Calman Commission. The Commission's remit was to review the Scotland Act 1998 as a whole, including the financial accountability of the Scottish Parliament. The Commission published its report in June 2009. Much of the Commission's work was incorporated in the Scotland Act 2012.

Confederalism: A system in which sovereign countries choose to cooperate with others through treaties, commonly in areas such as defence and currencies.

Devo-Max: Where all the taxes are raised and controlled in Scotland and money is sent to Westminster by way of grant to pay for activities Westminster carries out on Scotland's behalf, such as defence and foreign affairs. Westminster would not be accountable for raising the money it spends in Scotland.

Devo-Plus: Where each layer of government from Westminster to Holyrood to local authorities is responsible, as far as possible, for raising the money it spends. This could see the Scottish Parliament take control of most taxes, with the exception of VAT and National Insurance, to raise the income necessary to meet the Scottish Parliament's expenditure responsibilities. Westminster would continue to raise the money it spends in Scotland through VAT and NI.

Federalism: Federalism is used to describe a system of government in which sovereignty is constitutionally divided between a central governing authority and constituent political units.

Full Fiscal Freedom: See Devo-Max

Independence: Scotland would become a separate independent state with its own currency and its own head of state.

Independence-Lite: Scotland becomes constitutionally independent but maintains a currency Union with the UK and retains the Queen as head of State. It could enter into shared services for defence and foreign affairs if mutually agreeable.

Scotland Act 1998: The Act which established the Scottish Parliament.

Status Quo: The current devolved arrangement, whereby the Scottish Parliament is responsible for 60 per cent of all expenditure in Scotland, but only 6 per cent of all tax income raised in Scotland.

Unitary State: The situation in the UK before devolution to Scotland, Wales and Northern Ireland, in 1999.

West Lothian Question: Question regarding the fairness of the current devolution settlement which allows MPs elected from Scotland to vote on legislation which only affects the rest of the UK, whilst MPs from the rest of the UK cannot vote on legislation which only affects Scotland.

Reform Scotland then set out their interpretation of the realistic alternatives facing Scotland at the present time.

1   Current Status: Holyrood responsible for raising only 6 per cent of all income raised in Scotland despite being responsible for 60 per cent of all expenditure.

2   New Scotland Act: New limited powers on income tax. Stamp duty, land tax and land fill tax devolved from 2015. There would be a significant lack of financial accountability.

3   Devo-Plus: Both Westminster and Holyrood accountable for what they spend in Scotland. Taxes transferred to Scotland would include income tax, Corporation tax and a Scottish geographic share of oil revenue and other taxes. Taxes retained by Westminster would be National Insurance and VAT, and some small transfers such as TV licenses.

4   Devo-Max: Holyrood responsible for raising all income from Scotland. Holyrood pays a grant to Westminster for reserved services. There would be the potential for major disagreements over defence spending in particular.

5   Indy-Lite: Constitutionally separate state. There would be a Currency Union, with the Queen as Head of State. No grant to Westminster but cooperation on embassies etc.

6   Full Independence: Fully separate state with a new Head of State, a Scottish President for example. No currency Union with the pound.

The Real Battle

Although these alternatives are presented in a highly simplistic way – four of them are complex scenarios that would be challenging to implement – they do illustrate the main thrust of the arguments and the principles upon which they are based. We should also bear in mind the analyses of both John Curtice and Michael Keating, who have raised the important politics and different visions of Scotland that are motivating some of the key advocates of change.

Curtice argues that much of the demand for more devolution is coming, not from the centre left, but from the centre right of Scottish politics. In his column in the Holyrood Magazine 'Shifting Sands', he said,

> This is certainly true of the principal advocates of Devo-Plus, the think tank, Reform Scotland. They, along with many others of similar persuasion, believe that a Parliament that does not raise the money it spends lacks sufficient incentive to behave in a financially responsible manner. Holyrood they argue, should have every reason to promote a healthy private sector that generates buoyant tax revenues and a responsible public sector that is intent on spending effectively.

Curtice concludes by suggesting that more devolution is not simply another manifestation of the notion of social democratic consensus, but also the product of some hard-headed market economics.

For Labour and the Conservatives in Scotland, there are real challenges. Scottish Labour leader Johann Lamont has already expressed her concern over whether more devolution would promote social justice or a more entrepreneurial society. There is no reason why it couldn't be both! Some Conservatives see some benefit in the argument that more fiscal freedom could revive their fortunes. This was very much the theme cultivated by Murdo Fraser, who sought a more distinctive post-devolution identity for the Conservatives in his failed leadership bid.

This is, then, the paradox that lies at the heart of constitutional politics in Scotland. Ideas that tick most of the boxes of a progressive and potentially popular way forward for the Scottish people are largely being ignored by the Labour, Conservative and Lib-Dem parties. Instead, Scotland seems destined to have a two-year debate about saying NO to Independence, a one-question ballot paper that excludes the potentially more popular third option, and a series of vague promises and commitments to possible further change to be handled at Westminster, not Holyrood, in the years that lie ahead. This is neither an inspiring nor a sustainable position.

Devo-Plus would put Holyrood in full control of income tax, corporation tax and most welfare spending. This allows Holyrood to be responsible for funding all its spending. Unlike the Devo-Max alternative, pensions, VAT and national insurance would remain in Westminster hands, but Scotland would control its share of UK borrowing. It would also receive a 'geographical' share of oil revenues.

It is worth highlighting, for comparison, the key principles of Devo-Max. This is based on the principle that economic policy levers should be devolved to Scotland, except in instances where there was a clear economic or strategic reason for those levers to remain at UK level. The Scottish Parliament would raise all tax revenue in Scotland and would also set tax rates. Any changes to tax rates and other fiscal measure would be made in a way that complied with EU rules. For example, VAT would still be set at UK level to meet EU requirements. The Scottish Government would have access to borrowing powers subject to the constraints of the market and consistency with macroeconomic stability at the UK level.

Scotland would be responsible for all areas of welfare other than certain elements where a unified provision was agreed. This is different from Devo-Plus where pensions would be retained at Westminster.

The UK Government would be responsible for defence and foreign policy. Scotland would fund its share of those services by a payment from the Scottish to the UK Government funded from tax revenue in Scotland. This is a major departure from Devo-Plus where the UK Government would raise and spend income on its 'reserved powers'. The payment to the UK Government could also cover a Scottish contribution to a UK-wide cohesion fund which would support solidarity and equalisation, such as funding initiatives for economic development. There would be agreements with the UK Government about such matters as assets and liabilities assigned to Scotland and economic and financial policy.

The differences between Devo-Plus and Devo-Max are significant, but both alternatives do form the basis of a radical and substantial devolution of power from London to Edinburgh. These options are very different from Independence. While at different points on the constitutional spectrum, there is a real sense of combining fiscal responsibility for spending with the raising of income, having more economic powers to tackle distinctive Scottish problems and providing a real expression of national pride and identity in a way that would deliver sound government and also help the Union out of its long-term decline.

Comments from England, a thoughtful newspaper and a cynical columnist!

An Article by Simon Jenkins in the Guardian

'Over the years, UK politicians have allowed the question of Scotland's constitutional future to slip from their hands to such an extent that David Cameron's visit to Edinburgh, early in 2012, was an unusually high profile, and even a high risk, event. Mr Cameron offered his views on Scotland's place within the United Kingdom with which a majority of Scots broadly agree, if the opinion polls are to be believed.

He made a significant new commitment to consider new developed powers for Scotland in the event of Scots voting against Independence in the planned referendum. The most logical deal would be one in which there is a single-question referendum on Independence-but with assurances. If Scotland votes yes to separation the route is clear. If Scotland votes No that should be followed reasonably quickly by a further vote on some sort of home rule or 'devo-max' option. **The outline content of that latter option should be made clear before the Independence vote** (if not then there could be a reaction against voting No). Mr Cameron avoided four important traps. He avoided the trap of sounding colonial. He avoided the trap of negativity. He avoided the trap of getting bogged down on procedural arm wrestling. The other UK parties need to raise their own games too. He avoided the trap of sounding like Mrs Thatcher.

There is a legacy of political and media indifference towards Scotland. Mr Cameron will never win a reasoned argument against Independence on his own. If there is a positive Scottish Labour and Liberal case for the Union, or for deeper devolution within it, then it is time it was more authoritatively made. Scottish voters deserve a rich and serious debate.

Here we go again. Ireland gone. Scotland going. Next is Wales. And then where? Cornwall? The Isle of Wight? There is no knowing what the ineptitude of London politics may do to the British confederacy. The latest row over yes or no to Independence is mere play acting. The real issue is option three, 'devo-max'. London hates it. Scotland craves it.

The longer London derides the aspirations of parts of the UK the stronger those aspirations will grow.

Today, Cameron on Scotland is like George III on America, 'astonished at the rebellious disposition which unhappily exists in some of my colonies'

Most baffling of all is Cameron's horror of Devo-Max, the one measure that might mitigate the UK's current centrifugalism.

Meanwhile the Scots, Welsh and Ulster economies are more akin to that of Greece, with spending decisions detached from taxing ones to the point of irresponsible dependency. Scotland gobbles English money and nationalist politicians win votes, by spending on student grants, health prescriptions and wind turbines. There is no English advantage in letting this dependency continue and it stands to the credit of Scots majority opinion that it wants it to end. Maximum devolution would repatriate fiscal responsibility to Adam Smith's home country. It would bring down to earth the spendthrift populism of Alex Salmond's nationalists, probably lose them the next election and damage the cause of full Independence. It would demand a drop in the number of Scottish MPs at Westminster. All this is to the advantage of Cameron's Tories.

This piece is amusing, but deadly serious in putting forward the case for Westminster (read England) to be shot of Scotland and with the added political bonus of many fewer MPs, especially Labour ones.

It is no longer enough to make a case **against** Independence, Nationalism and populism, it is necessary to make a case **for** identity, diversity and progressiveness.

Change is Inevitable

Britain remains an over-centralised State and, whether or not Westminster is fed up with the constitutional question, it won't go away. This is why it would be comforting and convenient and less intellectually and politically challenging to pretend that defeating Independence will be an end to the nation's search for a better constitutional future within a transformed Union. This is not going to happen, so why should the Unionist parties cling on to this position and waste the period up to 2014?

Labour is in danger of allowing the SNP to continue its domination of the constitutional issue. This does not make any sense to Labour voters and potential voters, the majority of whom believe that both the Union in its present guise and a rather tired Independence are eclipsed by some form of Devo-Max or Devo-Plus option.

There are compelling reasons for a second question and a bigger choice for Scots.

Scots are not inspired by the current alternatives and much of the opinion polling suggests that the idea of more devolution within the Union is a sensible and supportable idea. There seems little point the day after the Referendum realising we are absolutely no further forward than we are today about the future of the country. In the autumn of 2014, do we then start the whole process again? In our democracy the Scottish people should retain control of the constitutional debate. The current thinking of the Unionist parties is to promise the earth at a later stage – but only if you defeat Independence first.

Edinburgh University's School of Social and Political Science, in their submission to the Westminster consultation, said, 'we believe that the referendum on Scotland's constitutional future is an appropriate opportunity to revisit the constitutional settlement established following the 1997 referendum on Scottish devolution by determining the constitutional preference of the Scottish people, including a stronger form of devolution in the UK.'

And Professor Michael Keating at the University of Aberdeen said, 'evidence from opinion surveys shows a large body of Scots (usually the largest) is opposed to both Independence and the status quo. It also shows that they do not make a sharp distinction between Independence and advanced devolution, but rather see these as lying on a spectrum. Devo-Max is a difficult idea and, as usual, the devil is in the detail, but to dismiss it out of hand is to polarise the national debate needlessly and (Unionists beware) to provoke people into voting for Independence as their second best option'.

There is an overwhelming case for a second question to give real choice to the Scottish people and if, as everyone says, the Yes vote should be unambiguous so too should be the meaning of the No vote!

The Declining Power of the People

The single most important challenge facing our democracy is the continuing decline in the numbers of people voting in elections.

Those inside the political game, whether Nationalists or Unionists, tend to see life through the prism of party colours and often have a distorted understanding of what the 'man or woman in the street' actually thinks. Today's politics is rooted in unreality as a volatile electorate is making up its own mind, and, in the process, making clear to politicians and parties that they are fast losing the trust and confidence of the people they seek to serve.

The importance of all of this for the referendum campaign and poll cannot be overstated.

There have been four Referendums in Scotland since 1973 and the turnouts in Scotland have been less than inspiring. First, the European Economic Community poll in 1975 had a turnout of 61.7 per cent, with three areas of Scotland registering 50 per cent or less. Second, the ill-fated Devolution for Scotland poll in 1979 had a turnout of 63 per cent with two areas registering 50 per cent or less. Third, the poll on the establishment of a Scottish Parliament in 1997 when the turnout was only 60.2 per cent with nine council areas with less than 60 per cent, including Glasgow where just over one person in two bothered to vote. Fourth, the Alternative Vote Referendum in 2011, when the turnout was 50.74 per cent and where Northern Ireland, Wales and Scotland, already operating a form of proportional representation, registered the highest turnouts.

These referendum polls took place when the overall voting in ordinary elections was much higher. It is inconceivable that the 2014 referendum turnout could be lower than current election turnouts. Or is it? There is such a massive disconnect between voters and politics at present that anything is possible.

The mere holding of a referendum, if the past is anything to go by, will not of itself guarantee a larger turnout. This is the state of Scotland and Britain today. Unless the political parties can fire the imagination of the voters, and persuade and inspire them to turn out, Independence, Unionism and Devo-Max/Plus, will have little meaning, credibility or legitimacy.

CHAPTER 15

The Growing Divide

IF THE LAST 13 YEARS is an indication of what the future might be like, then some fundamental decisions have to be made by Westminster and Holyrood on how to deal with the current political and constitutional situation in Scotland. Labour will continue to be at a competitive political disadvantage relative to the other parties in Scotland – especially the SNP – until the issues within the party are resolved. There are likely to be continuing strains and tensions, which for most people may only be evident at Scottish elections but which, in reality, will be a permanent feature of the post devolution debate.

Political Change

The Holyrood Election outcomes in 2007 and 2011 were dramatic and have changed the face of Scottish politics forever in a way which was barely conceivable in 1997, when Labour's White Paper so convincingly won support across the political divide and was subsequently endorsed in a two-question referendum. Since the early days of post devolution Scotland and the eight years of Labour-Lib-Dem control of the Parliament, there have been seismic changes which are posing real and extraordinarily difficult challenges to the Unionist parties as they continue to struggle with a constitutional agenda largely created and dominated by the SNP over the last five years.

Over this whole period, and probably reflecting the narrative over the past 80 years, three issues stand out more than any other: the rise of the SNP since 2007; the continuing decline of Scottish Labour; and the failure of the Unionist parties, in recent years, to understand, influence or deal with the political and constitutional question.

For Labour, establishing a new post of Leader in Scotland, the election of a new Leader, Johann Lamont, the Review of the Scottish Party undertaken after the election defeat in 2011 and the helpful noises being made by senior party figures about the need for more sweeping reforms have helped the party and this was given tangible effect in the better-than-anticipated local council elections, especially in Glasgow. While celebration was more than tinged with a relief beyond belief outpouring of emotion, Labour is still uneasy with the issue of the constitution and Scotland's changing role within the Union.

Labour, despite its history, should be comfortable with constitutional politics but this is conditional on the political divergence north and south of the border being accepted, and political, organizational, party decisions and party philosophy being made in Scotland to accommodate this.

The Conservatives never fail to disappoint as they continue their long decline since 1955 when they were the only party to achieve 51 per cent of the popular vote in Scotland. It remains doubtful as to whether the election of a new leader, Ruth Davidson, will improve their prospects, especially when the party continues to take a tough Westminster approach to Scotland's role in the Union and is less convinced about more powers being devolved.

The Lib-Dems also face an uncertain future as the idea of Coalition continues to blight their prospects. The loss of 80 seats in the council elections in 2012 and the humiliating result at Holyrood in 2011 underline their unpopularity and their failure, at least for now, to get any electoral benefit out of working with the Conservatives. Being in Coalitions with the SNP in key parts of Scotland has only added to their unpopularity as many of these councils were incompetent and unwilling to take heed of the wishes of local people.

Future of the Union

The issue of the Union is not whether it has been good for Scotland over the last 300 years. It is whether the Union in its present form is fit for purpose in the 21st century, against the background of the significant political change brought about by devolution, global and European influences, the shifting alliances and loyalties of the electorate and, for England, the need to tackle some emerging problems.

There are two fundamental issues: the politics of Scotland and the future of the Union. A Union of limited devolution, along with the sovereignty of Westminster and a fundamentally centralised ethos of power and responsibility, is now faced with demands for more radical constitutional change, competing claims on sovereignty and calls for identity, nationality and democracy to be dealt with in new and different ways. To meet these challenges, the Union can change and become more flexible. At the same time, this newfound sensitivity and modernity may help focus public and political opinion on the real meaning of the Union and Independence in a modern society. The many unions, not the one Union of the United Kingdom, are a useful starting point.

The First Minister tacitly acknowledged this line of thinking with his comment that he wished to repeal the Treaty of Union but would leave intact the Treaty of the Crowns. This raises, then, questions about the social union, the economic union, the cultural union and the constitutional union – and, in turn, the role of Scotland and the Union in terms of globalisation and European integration. It begs the important question of whether the Union in its present form or the Independence being promoted by the SNP are as relevant today as they once were.

This gives rise to the question of whether there are genuine alternatives. Why will the Unionist parties not entertain the idea of a workable alternative which stops short of Independence but demands instead, a Union fit for purpose and a total transformation of how this would operate in the new political and economic world? Now seems an appropriate time to challenge this mindset and open up the political debate to new ideas which will help both recast the Union and reshape the Independence aspiration into something more meaningful for Scots.

Unprecedented Change

This chapter brings together comment and analysis on an unprecedented period of politics in which the pace of political change has intensified and accelerated. Politics is the product of the context and climate of society and the economy at a point in time. In other ways, it is influenced by events, and if we believe the comment of the late Harold Wilson – Labour Prime Minister in the '60s and early '70s – that a week was a long time in politics, then we have witnessed a lifetime of constitutional and political upheaval in the past 15 years. The question is, what does this mean for the future of Scotland and the Union of the UK as we embark on our date with destiny? What is the state of preparedness of politicians and political parties in the run-up to the European Elections in 2014, the

Westminster elections in 2015 and the Holyrood elections in 2016 – and, of course, the Referendum on Independence to be held in the autumn of 2014? What is the mood of the public and how will this shape Scotland's choices? The electoral challenges are immense and so are the political consequences.

The key issues and events between 2007 and 2012 have been:

- A Conservative-Lib-Dem coalition at Westminster
- The global banking, financial and economic crisis
- Recession and Austerity
- The expenses scandal at Westminster
- The Murdoch, media, hacking crisis and the Leveson Inquiry
- 2007 and 2011 as momentous years in the politics of the Holyrood Parliament, Scotland and the United Kingdom.
- The end of ten years of the Blair government and the subsequent changes at Westminster.
- A new Labour Prime Minister, Gordon Brown at Westminster and a new SNP First Minister in Scotland, first as minority and then as a majority Government.
- Unionism and Republicanism in government in Northern Ireland; Labour and Plaid Cymru in government in Wales in 2007.
- New Labour leaders in Scotland after 2007 and 2011.
- Commemoration of 300 years of the Treaty of Union in 2007.
- The White Paper on Independence and the national conversation from the SNP in 2007.
- The Green Paper on the Governance of Britain at Westminster by the Labour Government in 2007.
- The Reform Treaty of the European Union, now agreed by heads of government.
- The Liberal Democrat refusal of participation in government in Scotland and Wales
- Polls in Scotland showing rising support for the SNP but declining support for Independence.

- Competence and Scottishness being seen as more important than constitutional change and separation.
- A remarkable 305 years of the old Union, while bringing to an end the beginning of devolution and inspiring new events, ideas and issues as Scotland begins to see a distinctive flavour to its 'new politics'.
- The Calman Commission and the passing of the Scotland Act 2012 at Westminster
- The election of new Lib-Dem and Conservative party leaders in Scotland in 2011
- The publication of the SNP Governments consultation paper, 'A referendum on Scotland's Constitutional Future'
- The publication of the Coalition Government's consultation paper, 'Consultation on the Scottish Government's proposal for a referendum on Independence'
- The launch of the SNP's Independence campaign in May, 2012
- The launch of the Union campaign, 'Better Together'
- The Scottish Council elections in 2012

An Uncertain Future

Our politics and democracy are experiencing seismic change and the consequences will be far-reaching and create a future of great uncertainty and unpredictability as far as election outcomes are concerned. Assessing the mood of Scotland 15 years on from 'Yes, Yes' reveals the shifting base of public opinion in Scotland and a new political dynamic. Political parties have been slow to adapt to a very different Scotland after 13 years of the new parliament and Scottish government.

The Union has to face challenges as it finds itself in a period of dramatic change in terms of Europe, the international sphere and the devolved nations and regions, and there is a pressing need to create a new debate between the two extremes of Unionism and Independence.

The SNP government's White Paper in 2007 on an Independence referendum calling for a new 'national conversation' was actually an audacious launch of a strategy designed to alter the face of Scottish politics and create the conditions for change. The SNP is a party with a plan for government but also a party with a political plan for the country – in contrast to Labour, which was too absorbed by governing to give any real consideration to the changing nature of public opinion and the mood of the nation. For understandable reasons, Labour had failed to notice the country had moved on. The party that developed and delivered devolution between 1997 and 1999 was focused on making devolved government a reality and could be forgiven for overlooking the need for continuing debate and further development. All the evidence since 2007 suggests the rise and rise of the SNP has been well-planned in order to take full advantage of the new politics evolving in Scotland. The questions to be answered are:

- What now are the options for change and where are we in relation to the deeper and wider debate that Scotland needs?
- What are the academics in Europe discussing in terms of sub-national government and regional policy? How can they enrich our own debate when the language of academia is highly technical, complex and out of the reach of the ordinary voter?
- What is the future for the Union, what does it stand for and what does it mean in a changing world? Can it adapt to cope with a radically different future? Why is it so hung up on the sovereignty of Westminster? Why can it not recognise the legitimate aspirations of identity, nationality and democracy? Is the future of the Union dependent on how it can change, rather than on what happens in Scotland, Wales or Northern Ireland?
- Is there a failure to grasp the bigger picture because we are letting history, Britain's view of itself as exceptional, highly centralised and out-dated, blind us to the new world of opportunity, where national, sub-national and regional politics have enormous potential waiting to be tapped?

The bigger picture includes responsibility in the modern world and two completely different visions for the Union – one saying 'no more devolution, the event has taken place, no significant further concessions', and the other saying 'Scotland should leave the political union and become independent' – and public opinion is not overwhelmingly supportive of either. The battle lines are being drawn, embodied in the personalities and beliefs of two institutions and two rigid and unconvincing alternatives. We are now locked into a constitutional struggle which will have dramatic consequences for Scotland and the Union. There is at the heart of this battle an astonishing paradox; left to their own devices, the three Unionist parties in Scotland will fight to exclude an alternative which by all accounts is supported by the electors and would give Scotland the best of all worlds. The outline of such an alternative is; the defeat of Independence; fiscal credibility and responsibility; the full range of devolved powers consistent with a form of federalism; the prospect of transforming the Union and in the medium term dealing with the English question; where devolved power becomes shared power and the sovereignty of Westminster is also shared; and all of this is recognised and safeguarded by written guarantees in the form of a new Treaty of Union or a new constitutional agreement.

There is a compelling case for this to be taken seriously as we plunge into a long campaign in which we refuse to discuss a possible best deal for Scotland because the Unionist parties want to defeat Independence first and then – on the back of reassurances, vague promises, and undeliverable manifesto commitments from the parties – the Scottish people lose control of their own future and that of their country for Westminster to consider the matter once again at some unspecified time in an unspecified future. This makes no sense unless you are willing to wait until something like 2020 for another referendum to decide what could be done in the next two years. There is, of course, the possibility that 2014 will make the discussion of Scotland's role in the Union somewhat academic if Independence beats the odds and wins! There are many pressing problems that require attention now and cannot wait until we spend decades seeking a resolution to the constitutional status of Scotland.

Other important factors are the 'English question' and devolution for the English regions; the Barnett formula and the West Lothian question; the unresolved reform of the House of Lords; globalisation; and European economic and political integration. Unresolved is the question of what the Union actually means in 2012 – whether social, economic, political, constitutional, cultural or monarchical. After over 300 years of the Treaty of the Union, there is no reason why it cannot be reassessed with a view to further radical change in the political and constitutional make-up of the United Kingdom. There is no doubt that demands for change will come from Wales, Northern Ireland and London in addition to Scotland. Wales has already made substantial progress, in particular winning primary legislative powers from Westminster. Westminster persists with sovereignty without appreciating that its attitude and response to developments and issues in the regions and nations could be a decisive issue for the future status of Scotland in the Union.

The next step in devolution – 'devo-plus' or 'devo-max' or some variation of the two – will be about the powers of the Holyrood Parliament and whether they should be extended.

Political parties underestimate the importance of Scottishness and Scottish interests reflecting the importance of identity and nationality. Questions about why these are so important and why the opposition parties do not appreciate their significance or try to be more Scottish, cut across and undermine their political philosophies and Unionist links. In other countries and contexts, there do not seem to be the same internal conflicts and agonies over multiple identities, shared sovereignty and nationality not Nationalism.

Not normally discussed, two other considerations are worth mentioning. The psychology of Independence is an interesting subject: could such a shock to the system provoke Scots into taking ownership of their own destiny and becoming able to tackle their deep-seated problems, without being dependent on anyone else or blaming anyone else for their shortcomings? An interesting body of literature exists that links the external or internal shocks a country experiences with the success and achievements it ultimately wins, with a number of examples – such as Finland, Ireland, Japan and Germany – where change or some kind of stimulus brought about a radical transformation in the prospects of a country. Obviously, some of the shocks were one-offs but these examples show how effective economic change can take place and how a nation responds to the conditions in which it finds itself. Setting aside its recent set-backs, Ireland may not have had an external shock but it established itself as one of the smartest countries in the world, with a highly productive economy and a vastly improved quality of life.

The question for Scotland is whether, without some dramatic event, a new level of economic and social performance can be achieved, and whether such an event could be a collective decision of the Scottish people to become independent, regardless of the financial and economic conditions their country inherits. Could that be what it takes to become world-class, confident and ambitious, with an abundance of self-belief, a highly competitive attitude and a high level of personal responsibility, replacing old cultural traits of dependency on the government, being risk averse, always seeing the glass half-empty, being suspicious of success and being a nation that rarely encourages but is quick to detract? The prospect of not blaming or scapegoating some-one else for our national short-comings, especially England, would be a welcome change!

The other unmentionable consideration is whether it is possible that a future Westminster government would be willing to cede Independence before it would cede sovereignty or share sovereignty or power with Scotland.

Sovereignty has become so deeply embedded in the DNA of Westminster that a growing impatience with Scotland and the different political culture which is emerging could, with the ascendancy of right-wing thinking and anti-Scottish sentiment within the Westminster bubble and the media, create a mood that considers sacrificing Scotland or ceding Independence preferable to ceding sovereignty.

This may be dismissed as a scaremongering scenario, impossible to imagine but it is conceivable under the Coalition and the Conservative Prime Minister, particularly with Scotland contributing one MP to a Tory majority and English MPs representing the interests of four-fifths of the people of the United Kingdom. In such a situation, it might not be Alex Salmond and the SNP who take Scotland out of the Union; the break-up of Britain could happen outside Scotland at Westminster if the less intellectual, knee-jerk type of politics were to hold sway. The pursuit of 'English votes for English laws' as one answer to the West Lothian question is an example of how fragile the issue remains at Westminster. Looking for short-term technical and procedural solutions make little sense when you are dealing with matters that are political and constitutional. Of course, this is thinking the unthinkable – but it is sometimes as well to do so.

Thus, the role of the Union and Unionist thinking is a powerful factor in the politics of Scotland. It is why we have to widen out the debate here and in Wales and Northern Ireland to the whole of the United Kingdom.

In working out the implications of all of this, we also have to recognise developments in Europe, where the sharing of power and sovereignty is more common and the issues of multiple identities, diversity and plural nationalities are fully understood. These are accepted aspects of the way configurations of regions, nations and nation-states are being reordered in their new politics.

This book has attempted, first, to define the transitional debate and, second, to argue for a rethink of the Union and the current attitude and approach of the Westminster Parliament and government. It is not now a question of whether the constitutional programme evolves; it is a question of how, when and to what extent. There are real and substantial choices for Scotland now emerging between the polarised positions of the Union with no more devolution and Independence with no more Union.

The political leaders of the Unionist parties in Scotland have to make a choice between either taking ownership of the debate and working out a viable alternative for Scotland's future or continuing to be dragged along by the SNP, who currently drive the agenda. Labour can stamp its imprint on the constitutional question, but only if it believes in a way forward which is not predicated on responding or reacting to the SNP but instead, focused on Scotland.

There is a third-way scenario that sees Scotland move radically forward in a completely transformed Union but stopping short of Independence. The SNP White Paper published in 2007, and subsequent comment and debate, recognised the need for progressive thinking. This raises some important questions about what Independence means in the modern world and whether Scots can achieve everything they desire within a new Union.

Fifteen years on, there is a new politics in most parts of the Union, but one of the big challenges will be deciding what is to be done about the English question. The reaction of the Unionist parties to the SNP government's White Paper was revealing; even before it was published, they had responded predictably by condemning a referendum on Independence, but more surprisingly, they acknowledged the need to embrace new powers for the Holyrood Parliament. This unity declaration in the form of a press release was followed up by a formal meeting involving senior politicians from the Liberal Democrat, Labour and Conservative parties.

The SNP managed to establish within their first 100 days of minority government in 2007 a degree of competence and authority, as well as giving enhanced stature to the office of First Minister. This has continued for the last five years. Setting aside the novelty factor, the fair-minded nature of the Scottish people willing to give the SNP a fair wind, the constraints presented by a Unionist majority in the 2007 parliament and the fact that the opposition parties are still licking their political wounds after the elections in 2007 and 2011, the impact of the SNP has been considerable both in tone and style, but also in terms of creating a new excitement in Scottish politics by apparently making devolution work.

There is no doubt that it is early days for the SNP Government, but the ingredients for success are obvious and could be replicated by the opposition parties. A Scottishness, an uncompromising defence of Scotland's interests and competent government have ensured success after success. Why the Unionist parties don't understand this is hard to explain, other than to reflect on the long devolution narrative which shows a great deal of heart-searching to even get to their current state of ambivalence, fear and unease about the C question. Trademark or signature issues of the SNP's period in government have been that they have not continually had to look over their shoulders to Westminster; they have been able to make devolution work, giving a bigger and louder voice to devolution within the Union. They have been competent and have acquired stature for the office of the First Minster.

The reaction to this has been illuminating. Opinion polls show a significant bounce in favour of the SNP yet an equally significant reduction in support for Independence. The lessons for the other parties are obvious. The distinctive nature of Scottish politics is taking shape, in that Scottish voters may want to see an avowedly Scottish party like the SNP govern Scotland, but still continue to support Labour in their attempt to govern the United Kingdom. In doing this, the electorate paradoxically continue to reject Independence and see their future within the Union.

All of this could change, but what is currently happening in Scotland is also happening elsewhere in Europe and is therefore a long-term possibility. There was no 'Brown bounce' in Scotland in 2007 as there was in the rest of the United Kingdom following the very successful start by the new Prime Minister. Is this another indication that the road is dividing?

As they adjust to these new realities, the opposition parties north of the border may wish to ponder the question of whether an SNP administration at Holyrood is a bigger short-term threat than full Independence. If both issues are left unchecked, they may come together in the medium to long term to change Scottish politics for ever.

The inability of the Westminster government in the form of the Scotland Office to either understand or be concerned about the direction of Scottish politics has existed for many years. A number of new scenarios give Scots real choices on the political and constitutional future of the country, stopping short of Independence but building beyond Westminster. A rigid Unionism – unwilling to change and struggling to find a philosophy, a strategy and coherence – is a real threat to itself and to the need for stable-state politics in Scotland.

The opposition parties have to re-engage with the constitutional process, feel comfortable in doing so, and accept that radical constitutional policies are not the preserve of one party and will not inevitably lead to Independence. They should be confident in their own ideas about Scotland's future and be undeterred by the attitudes of UK political parties and Westminster. Embracing passion, pride and patriotism and wrapping them up in the Saltire is a predictable ploy for a party seeking Scottish Independence. That does not make them Nationalists, nor appear to be selling out their socialist or social democratic credentials. Scottishness is not the monopoly of one party and it is remarkable that the SNP has hijacked this for so long without meeting any resistance. This constitutional debate is about the future of Scotland, not the SNP. If the SNP did not exist, the Unionist parties would still need a strategy and vision for Scotland within the Union. The Union is currently not the perfect partner, and again if there was no threat from the SNP the Union would still have to reinvent itself. These self-evident truths are not the subject matter of nuclear physics; they are elementary politics.

Consensus is important in a democracy and vital if the case being made is to impact positively on Westminster and provide sensible and unifying solutions for our country. Currently, this is difficult to achieve and we are in danger of drifting into a referendum campaign saying No to Independence, but not offering anything which is positive and inspiring. Politics needs to have a constructive narrative which raises expectations, builds hope for the future and captures the best in people.

The success of the SNP has revolved around the fact that they have a purpose, a cause, a conviction and now a campaign for what they believe in. The Unionist parties are often too busy being negative that they have forgotten to be positively enthusiastic about anything. The level of public disenchantment with politics can only increase if this continues.

There is the bigger issue of what needs to be done to tackle issues and solve problems that have stubbornly endured and are deep-seated. This is where a more radical transfer of powers may be needed in reserved areas where it is felt that Westminster-based solutions have not worked or where Scotland simply wants to move quicker, do more or do things differently. This is where the debate needs to be focused; rooted in practical policy areas that impact directly on people and the issues facing the nation. Too often, the constitutional and political debate is abstract and immersed in lofty concepts such as nationhood, fiscal freedom and patriotism, and important though they are, they rarely are defined or discussed in a way that is inclusive and relevant. Hopefully, the referendum campaign will deal more seriously with the practical aspects of the alternatives before the electors.

There are three areas of particular significance, but to move into these areas, the case for doing so must first be demonstrated (without that proviso, you are dabbling in Independence politics and not practicalities).

First: The economy and taxation, where the strengths and weaknesses of the Scottish economy and what is needed to achieve real success should dictate the new powers. There is a compelling case that, without access to all the levers of economic power, the Scottish Parliament and the Scottish government will never be fully responsible for the Scottish economy. The ideas of fiscal responsibility and the creative and competitive economy are key drivers behind a review of these reserved powers.

Second: Social security and employment law, where they interface with workplace participation rates, skill training and education and, increasingly, the issues surrounding economic migrants from Central and Eastern Europe. There are a number of important social and economic problems that have stubbornly resisted attempts to tackle them and it is vital to ask the question whether or not reserved powers should be transferred to Scotland so we can find our own distinctive solutions. This should be one of the important tests used to determine the transfer of powers from London.

Third: Europe, where there are examples that could usefully be looked at as the European Union increasingly impacts on our future. Sentiment in the more pro-Europe Scotland diverges from the rest of the United Kingdom on the key issues of the Euro and the Treaty of Reform and in our attitude towards inward economic migration and further social and economic integration in the EU.

Any review would also have to look at the new global challenges such as energy, our carbon footprint, the environment and global warming, and the increased expectations of a population with more lifestyle choices. Does Scotland have bigger ambitions than Westminster? Or is it simply that Scots are unhappy with the outcomes from Westminster and want to do things differently?

Embroiled with the issue concerning powers is the question of the sovereignty of the Westminster Parliament; in the absence of a written constitution and checks on the power of the executive, the writ of parliament is questionable but unassailable. There should be a debate about the fact that Westminster could abolish the Scottish Parliament with a one-line Bill as there are no safeguards written into the Scotland Act to prevent this or other changes to reserved and devolved matters.

Why should Westminster also be able to legislate for Scotland in devolved areas? The issue of sovereignty is a major stumbling block to shared power instead of devolved power and the stability of the Scotland Act will always be at risk if the ability of Westminster to legislate on devolved Scottish matters is not curbed or removed. There is a powerful case to be made for sovereignty in different sites and in relation to different powers and responsibilities.

For Labour in particular, never completely at ease as a party with the devolution or the constitutional debate, the basic attitude has to change radically, quickly and urgently. It is Labour that has the most to gain from a new way forward; it also has the most to lose if Scots continue to drift away as public sentiment and perception change and Labour is perceived as too strongly linked to Westminster, not Scottish enough and continuing to ignore the calls for more informed choices in the forth-coming referendum campaign and vote.

Why has the SNP been allowed to hijack the notion that it is the only party prepared to be uncompromising in the defence of Scottish interests?

Why is the SNP now pushing the envelope of the existing constitutional settlement to the limits, with only a 'we will say no' response? Why is the SNP driving the constitutional agenda? Why is the SNP able to make great political capital of its embrace of Scottishness (over which it actually has no monopoly)? The answer to all of these questions is not so much about the political skill or greater sense of purpose of the SNP, although that is partly true; it is about the failure of the Unionist parties, especially Labour, over the past five years in particular, to understand the crisis that has engulfed them and the changing nature of society, our politics and the electors in Scotland.

Is the explanation the not-so-invisible hand of UK Labour, MPs and the Westminster Parliament and government, as Scottish Labour fails to establish its own identity and therefore appears ambivalent about the need to revisit the settlement? The relationship or modus operandi between Scottish Labour/Holyrood and UK Labour/Westminster has to be reviewed and rewritten to reflect the fast emerging realities of Scottish politics and the changes that are taking place in Scottish society. Despite some limited progress after the 2011 Holyrood election, there is more work to be done. Labour's failure to acknowledge the importance of nationality, identity and diversity could ensure the continuing decline in its fortunes. A substantial part of Labour's support has moved on but the party has not moved with it.

Labour's base in local government, the trade unions and the electorate is shifting and elector/party alliances, allegiances and loyalties are loosening and changing as different constituencies of interest are being created.

The party needs to renew and refresh its approach and attitude towards Scotland's political future and resolve the tensions and conflicts between London and Edinburgh. There is no reason why Labour should not take ownership and lead the debate on Scotland's political and constitutional future.

There would seem to be five preconditions for this to happen: a new mindset with a confident and ambitious approach to change; an embrace of Scottishness which is neither grudging or hesitating: a new look for the Union at Westminster; more Independence for Scottish Labour and its MSPs; a renewed commitment to progressive centre-left politics with fairness at its core and a new sense of what the party stands for and has to offer an electorate suffering from austerity and growing disillusionment with politics; and the development of a third way, loosening the present constraints of the Union and the current settlement with the aim of providing greater fiscal responsibility, more extensive powers and shared sovereignty for the Scottish Parliament. This essentially means moving to a distinctive form of federalism. To put further pressure on Westminster to respond and reform the Union, the obvious political and strategic step is to seek a review of the Treaty of Union and the Scotland Acts. This would be a powerful statement of intent and in sharp contrast to the SNP, which wants a repeal of the Treaty of Union. This would highlight Labour's embrace of the political agenda, consistent with the stated aim of radical reform *within* the Union.

It is worth remembering that current opinion polls suggest there is no great enthusiasm for Independence, and that should give Labour the confidence to run with the grain of constitutional and political thinking in Scotland.

What is more difficult is to use that substantial base of public opinion and shape an intelligible alternative to Independence that will capture the imagination of the electorate, guarantee stable-state politics and meet the aspirations of individuals, families and the nation while convincing a sceptical public that the political and constitutional future of their country is safe in Labour's hands.

That would be the point where the SNP could be tested on what Independence actually means. Labour could in turn extol the virtues of a radical blueprint that achieves all the stated benefits of Independence within the Union, without the uncertainty, instability and anxiety that repealing the Treaty of Union would bring.

But the case will have to be made, as Labour will be aware of an alternative scenario where the debate remains polarised, narrow and tribal, the SNP remains in power for much longer than anticipated as a majority government or in coalition, more popular opinion spills over from support for the Nationalists' credible performance in government to support for Independence, Westminster continues to project a hard-line Unionism or the result of the 2014 referendum is either a narrow majority for Independence or a narrow majority for the current devolution settlement. Either way, the Unionist parties will be seen to be losing or to have already lost public confidence and Scotland will move slowly but perceptibly towards a different future.

It is reasonable to say that running the country for eight years has meant the political and constitutional agenda in Scotland has not been the main focus for Labour. Developing devolution from 1997 to 1999 and delivering the outcome between 1999 and 2007 may have resulted in not enough thought being given to the bigger picture. As a result the constitutional debate has largely been closed down within the Labour Party, so that for nearly a decade it seemed as if the business had been completed.

Perhaps the differences and tensions between London and Edinburgh over devolution have helped create a *Fawlty Towers* 'don't talk about the constitution' complex. The lack of real interest in a next phase of devolution has reflected the somewhat schizophrenic approach to devolution throughout Labour's history since the early part of the last century. Some may have thought that the Scotland Act would kill off the SNP and others hoped devolution was an event, not a process.

Whatever the reason, Labour has demonstrably lost ground and needs to engage and re-establish its hard-won credibility as the party that delivered devolution in government and can now be trusted to drive the agenda forward, either with or without Westminster.

The changing dynamic in Scottish politics means the electorate are now 'boxing clever' as they get to grips with proportional representation, list systems, second votes, coalitions and tactical voting.

A politically-aware electorate, exercising more political judgement than politicians and journalists give them credit for, have created in Scotland a very distinctive situation which may continue to diverge sharply from election results at Westminster. When shifting party loyalties, changing expectations, an embrace of single issues and changing economic, social, employment and learning considerations are thrown into the mix, no one should be in any doubt that Scotland is on the move. While destinations are still unknown, the constitution and political future of Scotland will remain a live issue.

This reality must also be recognised in London, where the stakes for the future of the Union are high. If the UK refuses to be flexible in the face of demands for further progress to be made on the devolution settlement, every Scottish election will become a battlefield for the forces of Unionism and Separatism. This is where we are.

If, however, it is recognised that the case for change and more devolved powers is compelling and based on substantial consensus, Westminster could loosen up and progress be made within a more flexible Union. The UK parliament could go further and see the merit in tackling some of the outstanding English questions, taking seriously the wider future of the Union in the new circumstances of post-devolution Britain. An even more radical reform of the Union is possible, where concepts such as sovereignty, identity, nationality, diversity, pluralism, respect, culture and democracy are given new meaning.

At the heart of any future debate, the concepts of Independence and Unionism should be put under the microscope and subjected to a thorough and detailed examination of what they mean in 2012 and whether they still have relevance to the problems and challenges faced by Scotland and the United Kingdom – or whether there are better and more effective ways of achieving social and economic outcomes in the future.

Serious consideration must be given to the philosophy and purpose of the Union in the 21st century. It has to be recognised that the mere existence of the Union in its current form is not in itself a rationale for its continued unreformed existence, nor an explanation of its relevance and importance.

The Union has now to become the focus of a far more critical review and, once and for all, the idea that the constitutional issue is essentially 'Scottish business' has to be dropped. The totality of extraordinary change and our concern to shape a new future are issues for everyone.

The public have to be engaged in the debate, which requires that an often abstract and 'jargonised' discussion of constitutional change should be more rooted in their day-to-day personal and national aspirations. The debate has to be relevant and aimed at the hearts and minds of people; there is a tendency for politics and politicians to operate above the level of people, in a dialogue between parties and within parties – never truly entertaining a serious contribution from those who really matter in the political process.

In fact, on the evidence of the Green Paper prepared by the last Labour Government in 2007, there appears to be a new determination to further buttress the Union by more centralisation of power at Westminster, reconfiguring the tier of regional administration, providing local government with some new powers, more enthusiastically embracing Britishness – while, at the same time, closing the door to any further political and constitutional devolution in England and to any further powers for Scotland, Wales or Northern Ireland.

Overall, the Green Paper seems to be on a collision course with the view that the Union has to change and be more flexible, and that the long-term future of the UK is inextricably linked to further political devolution, especially in England. Every statement and proposal in the Green Paper seems to reflect a firmly-held view of the future of the Union. The attitude and performance of the Conservative-led Coalition has done nothing to dispel the feeling that, to them, devolution is more of a curse than a blessing.

It ignores the real possibilities that Westminster will continue to cede powers to the European Union and, at the same time, transfer more powers to the devolved governments. There is little mention of the challenges of the new global agenda, which transcends territorial boundaries and national borders, nor does there appear to be recognition of the poor condition of our democracy, where voting is fast becoming a minority activity. A new political era is opening up – but this is not obvious from reading the Green Paper.

The Holyrood Parliament is becoming older and wiser and now has a maturity which it could not have had in 1999. This allows the real prospect of a new political culture and will generate a new understanding of the potential of devolved government. It will also provide a more credible base for arguing for further changes and more powers. The experiences of Wales and Northern Ireland only serve to illustrate the potential of breaking the Westminster mould. There is more that unites the parties at Holyrood than divides them. Majority Government should not encourage a return to the bad old ways of Westminster where partisanship, tribalism and intolerance remain the order of the day.

But the potential interest in new ways of doing things will not be fully realised unless other factors are part of the mix. Leadership is essential in all parties.

They need to have a strong belief in the benefits that devolved government and a more flexible Union can provide. They need a vision for our democracy and our country and to embrace big ideas to encourage people to engage with politics. In short, they need an all-party determination to move Scotland in a new direction.

For the pragmatists, there are doubts, shared by those who are arguing for a more intellectually-inspired and informed debate about our political and constitutional future. Are there new forms of national self-determination and self-expression in this new century which do not require separation or Independence? Indeed, are these outdated concepts? Would Scots and Scotland be better off exploring new ways of gaining sovereignty and promoting identity, nationality, diversity, freedom and security? What will the world be like in 10 or 20years?

There are other options than static Unionism or total Separatism. Surely Scotland and its political parties have to recognise that the United Kingdom is also facing challenges and change; simplistic notions of the future may become increasingly irrelevant. It may well be that Scots will find new ways of expressing themselves that are not based on territory or borders.

If we are uncertain of the answers to these questions, why are we so certain about the future government of our country? We live with hard practical realities and day-to-day decisions but these should be seen in the context of a broader understanding of on-going change and future needs.

One hindrance that must be overcome is the rigid mindset in Scotland concerning nationality, sovereignty and identity, and the doggedly traditional ways of expressing these in political terms. There has to be a better way, looking at individuals and their needs in Scottish society and losing the obsession with geography and endless talk about differences and divisions. Change in the world is making much of this redundant.

Cooperation, collaboration and collective action are features of the new global politics. That is why it is important to keep asking the question, what does Independence mean in the 21st century? If the on-going debate is to make any sense, then it has to acknowledge the fact that there may be other futures for Scotland which embrace different ideas and structures and require new ways of seeing the world and our role in it.

It also requires our political, business, media and civic leaders to work more closely together to change attitudes and project a more positive and ambitious vision for the nation. There is no other way forward if we are to tap into our talent and potential, making Scotland the internationally-recognised learning and knowledge workshop it should be. 'Smart, successful Scotland' was a slogan that tripped easily off the tongue, but much has to be done to make it so. To compete at that level, Scotland has to turn the world-class resources it undoubtedly has into world-class assets and then world-class achievements.

The country's constitutional and political future within the Union is inextricably linked with Scotland's practical performance in a rapidly changing world.

It is essential that the Scottish state of mind should also change, and it should not underestimate the effort and sacrifices that will be required. The success of Ireland, however temporarily eclipsed, Denmark, Norway, Finland, Singapore, Bavaria and US states like Virginia was achieved by their being focussed, confident and determined in the pursuit of economic and social objectives. Scots have these qualities but as yet do not apply them in any sustainable form. Also lacking is the unity of national purpose that is so important, and this can only be attained by defining identity and aspirations – not by anachronistic comparison with England or old fashioned ideas of nationalism. Scotland should only be constrained by talent, imagination and ambition.

At present, the Scottish state of mind seems uncomfortable with the language of global success, with the emphasis on competitiveness, productivity, growth and aggressiveness where necessary. There is uncertainty about how Scots can shake themselves free from the complacency and apparent lack of drive that are holding the nation back. Most successful countries have needed some kind of crisis or stimulus – internal or external – to create the conditions for change. In the absence of anything as dramatic, Scotland must reach that tipping-point that creates radical change.

Can this come about within the existing Union or is Independence or some other drastic alteration in thinking and structures of government required? Whatever the choice, taking more responsibility for successes and failures has to be the Scottish way forward. There is a pressing need to learn from the experiences of other countries and the sub-national structures that exist throughout the world in various forms of devolution. It is important to think beyond the UK and acknowledge that devolved government with significant power is commonplace elsewhere. It is difficult to transfer a complete model from overseas, but there are ideas and experiences which could provide lessons and could enrich the efforts to obtain improvements in the governance of Scotland.

This chapter brings the debate on Scotland's constitutional future to the start of the referendum campaign. For Scots, the next two years will see the future of the nation placed at the heart of the political agenda.

Scottish Labour, Scotland and the Union will take centre stage as the nation scrutinises in detail what is on offer. After 100 years of debate, we are fast moving towards a tumultuous decision on the future of our country. The next chapter will look at the big issues that are likely to dominate our date with destiny.

CHAPTER 16

Rethinking the Union, Building a Better Scotland

THE LAUNCH OF THE 'Better Together' campaign brings to an end a few months of feverish activity and sets us on a path towards 2014 when the constitutional and political future will be decided by the Scottish people in a nation-wide referendum. This will be the fourth referendum held in Scotland in the last 40 years, and by far the most important. The way ahead is not clear.

While the fate of Independence will be decided in the forthcoming vote, there is not much more that can be said with any certainty in the new world of Scottish politics. As we have seen, the rise of the SNP and the fall of Labour in that period have altered the electoral map of Scotland and reshaped our politics.

Regardless of the fate of the Independence vote, Scotland is on an inevitable path towards a much more radical and substantial home rule settlement within the Union. There is a compelling logic to what is happening and for the first time in a generation there is a real edge to a constitutional and political debate which will not go away. There is a growing gap between the aspirations and the expectations of Scottish people on the one hand, and politicians and political parties who are not listening to calls to change the Union and Scotland's role within it on the other. This debate is about the future of the Union: Holyrood, Cardiff Bay and Stormont are not out of step with modernity, progressiveness or the electors, but Westminster is!

This referendum has to be about the future, not the past, and this is the where the 'Better Together' – only saying NO – campaign will be at its weakest. Austerity Britain, continuing recession, high levels of unemployment, a Tory-led coalition at Westminster and disillusionment with UK politics at record levels does not provide the best backdrop for promoting a positive 'what the Union can do for you' campaign. That is why a powerful and positive message on Scotland and the Union makes sense. Scotland cannot wait until 2014 and the defeat of Independence for a 'new Union, new Scotland' package of proposals to appear. This makes no sense.

As this book goes to print, the Unionist parties, Labour in particular, are beginning to appreciate their position and may see the sense of a new alternative or 'third way' which will serve the interests of the Scottish people much more effectively than Independence or status quo Unionism. The grasping of this reality and its compelling political logic will nevertheless be hostage to issues of timing, political uncertainty, strategic considerations, political courage and the continuing failure of Westminster to understand what is happening in Scotland.

Ed Milliband, speaking at the Royal Festival Hall in June 2012, was right to argue that Labour had been too reluctant to talk about Englishness and the issue of national identity and this may be the portent of new thinking. However, there was little reference made to what is happening in Scotland.

Labour and the Legacy

An alternative to status quo Unionism and Independence in the form of devo-max/plus, leading to some progressive federal structure for the UK, will be the elephant in the constitutional room. It will continue to intimidate, tempt and influence Labour and the Lib-Dems into having the sense to avoid wasting two valuable years by suggesting that there is not a workable alternative to be placed before the Scottish electors in a referendum. This is a question of political will, not practicalities.

In the process of defeating Independence, there is an opportunity to prepare the political ground to build a positive and popular alternative which could form the basis of a second question and make the whole referendum experience more sensible and relevant to the voters. The unambiguous defeat of Independence is surely not conditional on having nothing positive to say about the further reform of the Union, especially when this alternative might be more popular with the electors than what is currently on offer to them.

It is unlikely, especially bearing in mind the lack of trust and confidence in politicians and parties, that the electors will be bought off by vague promises, unenforceable commitments and assurances that there will be more devolution jam tomorrow only if we defeat Independence today.

The public are much smarter than many politicians think. In the absence of a more thoughtful and attractive alternative, electors could end up either not voting, as they have been denied the choice they want, or voting for Independence as being the option closest to their idea of real change and reflecting more their idea of identity and Scottishness.

Equally important, it would be a strange electorate that would wish to lose democratic control over the future of Scotland and pass it over to Westminster, not Holyrood, to decide what may happen next. Scotland's electors must retain control over their own future. The second question becomes an important part of that ambition.

It is one thing to deny electors a valued alternative, but it is much worse to then suggest they are not up to navigating two questions on the same ballot paper. Adding insult to injury would take on a new meaning in Scottish politics! There is a real danger that we are embarking on another phoney war where choice for the electors is being restricted because of narrow party political considerations, and not what is best for Scotland.

The road to 2014 has been long, complex and challenging for the parties of the Union, less so for the SNP who have embraced Independence as a cause in the early days, as a campaign in recent times and now in the form of a commitment to a referendum as the majority party of Government since 2011.

The current positions of the four main parties in Scotland are very much a product of their individual journeys, especially Labour who have always felt ill-at-ease with the issue of Scotland's role within the Union. Labour's position continues to be at times confused and contradictory. The torch of constitutional change has occasionally burned brightly. Keir Hardie's home rule commitment, the referendum of 1979 – despite the defeat of the proposed Scottish Assembly at the hands of a wrecking amendment – and the passing of the Scotland Act 1998 and the Scotland Act 2012, were very much driven by the Labour party in Scotland.

Yet in 2012, two years away from our date with destiny, the Party seems divided, unsure and lacking in confidence. Lacking a coherent narrative and vision for Scotland's future is problematic in itself, but there is also a lack of passion, energy and empathy for radical change, as if this issue of constitutional change was in some way alien to Labour's thinking and damaging to Scotland's future and the Union.

Time is running out. Labour needs to resolve the differences between Westminster and Holyrood, within the Party in Scotland and to reconnect with the Scottish people who have embraced the spirit and soul of constitutional change to a much greater extent than they have. This is the context in which an alternative future is vital.

The second question will avoid the need to waste the next two years in an outpouring of negativity and the squandering of a valuable opportunity to shape the future of our country in partnership with the Scottish people.

The defeat of Independence is only one part of the story. For those who believe this will be the outcome, there is a compelling moral, political, philosophical and democratic case for a different future for Scotland to be designed, developed and delivered by the time the Scottish Government starts to legislate for the referendum in 2013.

For Labour, there is more at stake than just the constitutional question. What happens in the referendum campaign has to be viewed as part of a wider strategy to regain ground lost to the SNP, as well has writing a new narrative for a more centre left and progressive Labour party in Scotland in order to deliver positive results in both the Westminster and Holyrood elections in 2015 and 2016. There are significant prizes for Labour to win if they grasp the importance of constitutional change and lead from the front.

Traditional Politics in Crisis

Political parties have to acknowledge that there is growing public disenchantment with politics, especially the Westminster kind. A political volatility and a breaking down of party allegiances and alliances is emerging, and the credibility and integrity of our elections and democracy are being undermined by dramatic reductions in voter turn-out.

How all of this impacts on the voters will have a direct bearing on the result both in 2014 and the subsequent elections. Westminster turn-out figures are down from 71.3% in 1997 to 63.8% in 2010. Holyrood turn-out figures down from 58.16% in 1999 to 50% in 2011. This presents a statement on the relevance and credibility of the ballot box as the essential focus for representative democracy. Elections without voters make no sense.

What kind of democracy is this? What kind of politics is on offer to generate such indifference? What are the factors behind so many people being disenfranchised? Could this growing disconnect have unintended and unforeseen consequences at the referendum ballot as Scots cast their votes on a wide range of concerns, feeling and sentiment that run counter to narrow party political considerations and traditional tribalism?

The Unionist parties have most to lose if the credibility of our political parties continues to decline. The SNP, in Scottish elections, have managed remarkable victories, not by increasing the overall number of people voting but by winning votes from other parties. So while people are fed up with traditional politics, the SNP have been able to bring some excitement to Scottish politics by combining populism, positive leadership, a sense of purpose and an embrace of identity. This is not rocket science. This is about the ability of a party to better understand the mood of a nation and seize the opportunity to build on sentiment, Scottishness and credible Government.

Why has this been allowed to happen without a convincing response from Labour, especially after the crushing defeat at the Holyrood elections in 2007 and 2011? Scotland wants to be seen as a nation, a state of mind, something to believe in, an idea, a vision, a reality outside the Union, a new politics, a source of inspiration, enthusiasm, pride and passion, but all of this seems too problematic for Unionist thinking, and especially for the Labour Party.

Being distinctively Scottish, and ambitious for Scotland's future, seems inconsistent with being part of the Union or being a Social Democrat, Liberal or a Conservative. Seeing a different Scotland in a different Union, however, and the transformation of Scotland's role within that union, are all achievable and realistic objectives. Labour in Scotland and in the UK has nothing to fear from the SNP, nor from the Scottish electors, if they build on the need to reconnect with the Scottish people. A new narrative is needed. This should embrace Labour's philosophy and values, framing the arguments and the language in a way which is relevant and inspiring, with a commitment to stand up for Scotland, and to be seen as doing so, and a commitment to a radical and substantial package of home rule powers for the Scottish Parliament. Labour should be demanding radical changes for the Union and Westminster, and above all, it has to accept the new political realities.

First, at this point in time, the overwhelming majority of Scots want to stay in the Union. Second, there remains a huge potential vote for Labour in Scotland. People left Labour and voted SNP, not because of the SNP's embrace of Independence, but because they no longer knew what Labour stood for and were tired of being taken for granted by a party that seemed remote from their needs and aspirations.

Third, Scots want a progressive, left-of-centre party which builds its politics and its core beliefs around fairness, justice, competence, virtues, values and vision: tackling economic inequality, addressing social justice and creating social mobility. These issues have largely disappeared from the political agenda and public discourse, but they still matter, especially at a time when just 50 per cent of the electors bother to vote.

Fourth, Scots are beginning to embrace a form of federalism. This is an attractive agenda and would help Labour push forward on a new and more credible political narrative.

For Labour, this should be a time of real opportunity and renewal. The constitutional question has to be a vital part of Labour's long-term political strategy in Scotland and will have considerable implications for Labour in the UK, but it has to be made in Scotland. Labour should not just see the referendum as the final struggle against the SNP and the forces of Nationalism, but as an opportunity to prepare for the parliamentary struggles ahead in 2015 and 2016, reconstructing the Labour brand for a new era in which the political landscape of Scotland will change dramatically, even if Independence is defeated.

On the constitutional front, we are once again addressing the issue of a referendum on what the settled will of the Scottish people might be. The picture is understandably confused. Labour is at an early point in seriously re-engaging with the whole devolution process but there is some evidence to suggest that public opinion is well ahead of where they are. Opinion polls in particular show considerable interest in more powers for the Scottish Parliament and the idea of a second question.

Labour should keep an open mind if it is serious about listening to the electors and understanding better what they want their country to be and where their sense of identity now places them in the debate about the future of the Union. Labour has agreed to set up another Commission to look at the future of Scotland and its Governance. The Commission should not be used to close down new thinking and debate within either the Labour party or in Scotland generally nor an opportunity for the wider party and Trade Union movement in Scotland to be sidelined until the commission completes its work. The future of Scotland is political not technical. A Commission could be part of the debate, but not a substitute for the debate.

Labour has lost so much constitutional ground to the SNP, allowing them to not only dominate the debate, but to monopolise it. Winning back this ground will require stamina, sustainability and the ability to resist the temptation to become negative or personal.

There are also significant problems to be tackled at Westminster where many still see the constitutional debate as a particularly Scottish issue. This is not the case. A transformation is required at the very heart of the Union which makes more sense of Scotland's ambitions, but in turn seeks to discuss England, the West Lothian Question, Wales, Northern Ireland, London and a rebalancing of the Union in ways that shed its tired and dated appearance and make it more fit for purpose in the modern era. In this context, a more powerful devolution settlement for Scotland would strengthen the Union, not weaken it, and inspire more ambitious change at Westminster.

The UK is out of step with Scotland, not the other way around! Westminster is obsessed with centralised power, preoccupied with exceptionalism, constrained by sovereignty, unable to share power and remains insensitive and ambivalent towards devolution. There is an attitude problem at Westminster which, if left unchecked, could threaten the very Union it seeks to defend and promote. Ed Miliband deserves credit for trying to open the debate up to include England and the wider Union.

Convincing the people of Scotland that they are serious about transferring more powers – reserved, fiscal and economic – to Holyrood and seeking more responsibility requires Labour to prove that their new approach is not one of political expediency, political necessity or a grudging acceptance of a need to do something in the aftermath of the SNP advance. This is not just about the colour of the ink on a Commission report, Government white paper or parliamentary Bill. Labour can only win public support for constitutional change if it actually believes in what it is saying and doing.

The Battle for Hearts and Minds

The narrative is clear. Independence IS the SNP. It is the basis of their DNA. The SNP is committed in the next two years to win a majority vote for Independence in a referendum. Despite the spin and briefing to the contrary, this is the purpose of nationalism and Alex Salmond. This is an opportunity for the Labour to strike at the heart of SNP thinking. But Labour has to make a clear distinction between,

What Labour is FOR in Scotland:

Progressiveness;

A centre-left party;

The politics of the common good and common purpose;

The Politics of justice, fairness, virtue, equality and economic competence;

A new embrace of social mobility, tackling inequalities and dealing with material deprivation;

The politics of a new Union, shared power and sovereignty;

A narrative that is not framed on hatred of the SNP and it's Leader;

Policies and priorities that are positive and do not reflect an obsession with the SNP agenda. Distractions, from the main agenda, encourage negativity.

New, radical and substantial powers for the Scottish Parliament;

Fiscal responsibility and more economic powers;

A form of federalism;

An embrace of identity and nationality;

Diversity and difference;

Stability and sustainability;

Political equilibrium; and

Reform and renew the Treaty of Union: a new Treaty

And what it is AGAINST:

Populism;

The politics of fragile coalitions of electors needed to sustain a broad and unstable base for Independence;

The politics of breakaway/separation;

'Large-N' Nationalism

Independence;

Division and discord;

Uncertainty and insecurity;

Political turbulence; and

Tearing up the Treaty of Union

These are the philosophical, constitutional and political differences at the heart of Scottish politics and should be central to the Referendum campaign. For Labour, the politics of 'who they are' and 'what they stand for' and 'what is their vision for Scotland' are vital at a time when so much is at stake and when public trust and confidence in politics is at such a low ebb. Partisanship and tribalism make little sense in a world desperate for solutions to practical problems.

Some serious questions and doubts have been raised regarding the role of the political parties and these should put into sharp focus the need to renew our politics and our democracy which could lead to a realignment of thinking and political parties. This is the progressive dilemma that Labour faces in Scotland: the need for progressive instincts, long term radicalism, the embrace of identity politics and an inspiring narrative for Scotland within a transformed Union.

But for all of this to happen, Labour must acknowledge and accept an uncomfortable set of truths. Notwithstanding the fact that other parties and countries are experiencing similar challenges, electoral turn-outs have slumped, party membership figures have collapsed, party loyalties and allegiances have weakened, voter patterns are changing, there is a crisis of confidence in our politicians and political institutions and a continuing and corrosive onslaught on the value of political and public life on the part of certain sections of the media.

Devolution is also changing the face of our politics and governance. The 'Balkanisation' of the Labour vote in Britain in 2010 resulted in only Wales, Scotland and the North of England remaining loyal to Labour.

Inspiration and Vision are key to this debate, but are currently in short supply. How people vote in the referendum will depend on a variety of factors including the condition of their lives, which campaign makes sense of the issues that matter to them and whether or not people can work out which vision of the future is likely to help tackle some of Scotland's most enduring problems.

Inequality Matters

For many Scots on the margins of Scottish society, and despite the rhetoric to the contrary, we are a very unequal nation. The referendum may give them a chance to register their identity by voting in more significant numbers to make a protest against their exclusion from many aspects of Scottish life and to see Independence as a way forward in which they have nothing to lose. The poorest areas of Scotland have dismal turnouts but this may change.

In his new book, *The Soul of Politics*, published in the US, Jim Wallis, a new-wave Christian intellectual, talks about the relationship between politics and morality being absolutely vital for the future and argues that,

> Too many people are not making it and are being left behind. Neither the injustices built into our social system nor the irresponsibility this generates is tolerable any longer. Controlling the poor is not the only alternative to abandoning them.

Outlined in stark terms, his book asks the question, 'Is it possible to evoke in people a genuine desire to transcend our more selfish interests and respond to a larger vision that gives us a sense of purpose, direction, meaning and even community?' Although speaking about the US, his comments could equally apply to Scotland and Britain where the increase in economic inequality since the 1980s has no counterpart in the advanced world.

Despite the serious commitment of Labour governments to tackling inequality – especially child poverty – and the relative indifference of the Conservatives, the inequality gap is growing. There are serious doubts about our commitment to justice, fairness and equality, as fundamental issues at the heart of our politics and our democracy.

Since ancient times – when philosophers such as Plato, Aristotle and Socrates sought to understand society, exploring ideas of governance and politics and giving meaning to the lives of individuals – political debate has rightly been preoccupied with the values, ethics, virtues and principles which should drive any form of progressive politics. This debate seems sadly lacking in Britain and Scotland today. We see the poor as outside the mainstream and as a burden on society and unemployment is often seen as just an economic variable akin to inflation or interest rates.

The relationship between our politics, our ethics and our public life remain at the heart of this inequality story. Many people do recognise that the nature of injustice-inequality-poverty has changed from the era of Beveridge and his five giants of Disease, Idleness, Ignorance, Squalor and Want. In Scotland, our dismal voting turn-outs provide a powerful reminder of how those who do not feel part of society can be seen not only being materially disadvantaged but politically disenfranchised. Indeed, in the recent Holyrood elections the lowest voter turn-outs were seen in the poorest areas, and nearly 70% of eligible voters didn't vote in five of the most impoverished areas of Glasgow.

This was recently taken up by Daniel Dorling in his book *Injustice, Why social Inequality Persists*. He argues that injustices are now being recreated, renewed and supported by five new sets of beliefs which have old origins but have taken new faces. In this context, five beliefs give new life to upholding injustices: elitism is efficient; exclusion is necessary; prejudice is natural; greed is good; and despair is inevitable. Those who uphold these beliefs find it hard to see possibilities beyond the current situation and are allowing injustice and inequality to continue. This is a debate about justice, fairness and equality of opportunity and how these philosophical issues play out in the way we conduct our national affairs. This is why the issue has such significance and resonance for a modern society and democracy such as ours.

The founder of the department store John Lewis, in a BBC broadcast in 1957, said:

> Capitalism has done enormous good and suits human nature far too well to be given up as long as human nature remains the same. But the perversion has given us too unstable a society. Differences of reward must be large enough to induce people to do their best but the present differences are too great. If we do not find some way of correcting that perversion of capitalism our society will break down.

Nearly 60 years on, the position has, if anything, worsened. People accept that effort deserves reward and usually they discriminate between different types of effort. Throughout history, the philosophical debate has been about important principles. Our society, though, has got it dangerously wrong. Without a rethink of the enormous excesses and staggering differences of income, health, life chances and wealth in Britain and in Scotland, we will undermine solidarity, destroy trust and mutual respect, undermine the motivation of the many and continue to undervalue certain important aspects of our economic and social well-being. The inspiring idea of the common good is in danger of slipping off the political agenda.

Scotland is a very unequal society and as such has a disproportionate number of social problems. Compared with the Nordic countries and some of the states in Western Europe, we are relatively undeveloped in our thinking, our vision and our actions towards inequality and the wider society. We need to move beyond the rhetoric of Socialism, Red Clydeside, Equality and Collectivism and acknowledge that talking a good game is no substitute for a radical agenda of health, education, employment and economic reforms to tackle modern-day poverty.

Unequal Scotland may well see an increase in the referendum vote involving the people who rarely, if ever, vote. People who now feel they have nothing to lose in pointing Scotland in a new direction.

Idealism, Inspiration and the Young Voter

The death of Apple boss Steve Jobs was a timely reminder of two important things. First, the brilliant innovator and visionary, who, at the heart of an on-going technological and communications revolution, had touched, in a very practical way, the lives of millions of people, and second, the remarkable speech he delivered to graduating students at Stanford University in 2005, which was memorable because of its idealism, inspiration and faith in the future of young people.

Why in Britain and Scotland do we seem incapable of having a positive vision for the future which seeks to capture the imagination, idealism and the hopes of young people for a better and brighter future than is currently on offer to them? Young people grow up today in a society of gloom and despondency, a glitz, glam and celeb culture where superficiality and owning more things seems the order of the day, and where greed, lack of responsibility and lack of respect are constant reminders of a hopeless decline in our values and vision.

There are also many people now questioning what meaning there is in our day- to-day lives, where consumerism has advanced at the expense of citizenship and where a lack of soul and spirit is reinforced by cynicism and negativity. This is aided and abetted by a relentless assault on the senses by newspapers, advertisers and powerful institutions which have a vested interest in money and finance. Surely there is a life beyond austerity, deficit reduction and a mindless and empty political and business rhetoric that often dominates our national discourse? Young people and children exposed to all of this deserve better.

Looking at today's society does not inspire confidence. But politics is only part of the story as there is little inspiration or idealism to be found anywhere. Robert F. Kennedy, speaking in 1968, said that in arguing, Americans had come to value the wrong things. 'Even if we act to erase material poverty, there is another greater task. It is to confront the poverty of satisfaction... that afflicts us all. Americans have given themselves over to the mere accumulation of things.'

There must be few countries in the world where children and young people are described by politicians as being 'feral' and living in 'sick' communities. Which other countries would criticise students and children for their consistent record-breaking exam achievements as we seem to do, as certain newspapers cynically claim that exams are too easy and are being 'dumbed down'? Why can't we, as a society, acknowledge the achievement and the efforts of our young people?

More to the point, how as a very acquisitive society, can we be content with 1 in 5 children and young people living in poverty and, as a result of inequality and the lack of social mobility, becoming isolated on the margins of our society at an early age? What is this doing for their confidence and ambitions? And what about the relentless onslaught on young people generally, where we are in danger of taking the actions of a few that deserve criticism and then, by lurid headlines and sensationally inaccurate reporting, tar a whole generation with the same brush?

Has it always been like this? The '60s seemed different. While it can be dangerous to reminisce about the past and confuse fact with fiction, substance and sentiment, there was a better feeling around. More hope, vision and ambition infused the political scene. Strong leadership and vision for a better tomorrow in our politics was evident on both sides of the Atlantic. John F. Kennedy promised to put men on the moon by the end of the '60s, an ambition accomplished after his death. The 'white-hot heat of the technological revolution' was firing up British politics. Martin Luther King was talking about taking black people in the hate filled southern states of America to the promised land, a dream that was partially realised by the legislation of Lyndon Johnson. The Beatles were on the scene, the Mersey beat was there to be enjoyed and Simon and Garfunkel were singing about a 'Bridge Over Troubled Water'. The Beach Boys were surfing and the song 'God Only Knows' was espousing the idea of friendship. Flower power was alive and well and San Francisco was the place to go, as long as you had 'a flower in your hair'.

Sentiment and nostalgia are powerful but it is the sense of hope, a concern for each other, idealism and inspiring people that can create a positive mood and a sense that we are all part of a future that we all have to build. There is little of this around in Britain or Scotland today. We are a unique species with the ability to think, innovate, be creative, and debate the future we want to achieve. Young people are a vital part of this.

This is where the inspiration of Steve Jobs has a unique message for all young people. Speaking at Stanford University he said,

> Your time is limited, so don't waste it living someone else's life. Don't be trapped by dogma – which is living with the results of other people's thinking. Don't let the noise of others' opinions drown out your own inner voice: and, most important have the courage to follow your heart and intuition. They somehow already know what you truly want to become. Everything is secondary.

That is what young people want to do but they have to be valued and encouraged to do so. Are they asking too much for the idealism, hope, enthusiasm, inspiration and leadership that can take them and us to a better future? Will this referendum campaign reach out to young people and inspire them to vote? The number of 18–25 year olds voting is consistently low and declining across all elections, so a great deal more effort has to be made to help and encourage them to shape their own future and the future of their country. In the context of declining poll numbers, young people have a bigger role to play but it is up to the older generation to take them seriously.

Independence

The autumn of 2014 is some way off and the campaign will be a major test of the political strengths, endurance and resolve of all the political parties. The substance of the arguments for and against Independence will be important. Of significance, though, will be the context or the social and economic conditions in which the ballot and the later stages of the campaign takes place. This is where the unpredictability of events and how they play with the voting public may become crucial to the outcome.

While the economic and financial outlook may change, it will be difficult to erase from the public consciousness the genuine anxieties and fears that people have built up around austerity, deficit reductions, the Euro-zone crisis and what all of this means for standards of living and the quality of life of families and individuals.

Fear and apprehension may influence many people to resist further dramatic change and uncertainty at a time when optimism and confidence are in short supply. Independence is such an ambitious step to take that many electors may, despite broadly supporting the cause, decline to say yes to Independence because of the Global, European and UK economic outlook.

Some people may see things differently and feel their prospects could not be any worse in an Independent Scotland. Overall, the timing will not reflect a Union or a Scotland where economic prospects will have improved to any great extent. Key considerations are:

- The fallout from the Euro-zone crisis
- The implications of the banking and financial crisis on small countries
- The lessons from Europe, suggesting that economic and financial integration requires political union, and what implications this has for a Monetary and Currency Union with England, post-Independence
- The fear and anxiety hang-over from austerity measures and recession

- The impact of unemployment, wage restraint and lower pensions on the outlook of Scots
- A sense that identity, nationality and progressive sub-national politics don't require Independence or separation from the UK
- A feeling that both the unchanged Union and Independence positions only serve to reinforce the case for an alternative way forward which stops short of Independence but provides all the practical economic and social benefits people are seeking for themselves and their families.
- In a world of interdependence what does being Independent mean?
- Does political and constitutional Independence, where everything else stays the same, really add up to a credible alternative?
- Despite extensive debate about Independence, what is the vision for Scotland and how will this deal with outstanding issues any more than Devo-Max or Devo-Plus or some fusion of the two?
- What does being a Nation State mean in a globalised world where borders and boundaries have less importance?
- Within the SNP, which is a broad church of different opinions about the future of Scotland, is there the possibility of the 'devo enhancement' option attracting support?

Many or all of these will be important influences in the campaign and will add to the certainty or uncertainty of the referendum outcome.

The Union

So far there has been very little constructive or serious criticism of either the Union or Independence. Evolving an intelligent and coherent alternative to Independence requires a solution that will secure all the practical benefits of Independence while remaining within a Union of the United Kingdom, will stop well short of Independence as a political or constitutional reality, offer the prospect of a radical renewal and reform of both Scotland, the Union and the relationship between them.

Progressive politics in Scotland can confront the SNP with a popular constitutional alternative which appeals to Scots who are still lukewarm to the idea of Independence, but may over time and in the absence of a credible alternative, start to warm to the softer, less aggressive and more inclusive approach of the SNP leader.

The distinction between 'soft' and 'hard' constitutional politics will play an important role. This is the real danger for the 'No to Independence, Yes to the Union' campaign. The campaign will inevitably focus on questions about the social union, the economic union, the cultural union, the political union, the monarchical union and the constitutional union-and in turn the role of Scotland in the rapidly emerging Global and European Unions.

The allure of simple and easily-explained extremes is a danger in a modern democracy, where the media is content to deal with partisanship, confrontation and controversy in selling arguments to the people. There are, however, very sound reasons – practical, tactical, patriotic and political – for the constitutional debate to switch gear and move in a new direction. The settled will of the Scottish people should drive our constitutional debate. We should be talking about creating something better.

The 'Better Together, United Kingdom' campaign in its current form is far from being clear about its vision and purpose. What is the vision for the future of the Union? Why would Scots want an unchanging Union to envelop their country for the next 25 years? What is our shared future to be?

These are the big questions for the forthcoming campaign. Supporters of the Union talk about a shared history but what is likely to be our shared future? The Union has provided political, economic and financial stability and security over a long period of time. Shared sacrifice has also been important as two World Wars, in the defence of Britain, cost many lives. The Monarchy has been the focus of national unity and a sense of pride for many Scots. We have enjoyed the single market of the Union and the cultural, social and family ties between Scotland and England remain strong and enduring.

The backdrop of human rights, individual freedoms – often taken for granted – rule of law and democratic institutions have all played their part in securing high and improving standards of living for all. As Scots today, though, do we feel inspired, excited or enthused about the United Kingdom, the Olympics, the Diamond Jubilee celebrations or the idea of Britishness?

Is there a real sense or awareness in Scotland of solidarity, common purpose, ambition or identity within the Union? What would we put down on a blank piece of paper as our vision for the Union over the next 20 years?

There is no doubt that much of the sentiment towards the Union has diminished over the past 20 years, and certainly in the post devolution era. This was probably inevitable in the kind of world we live in and of itself is not a significant problem. It does, however, highlight the potential for a radical realignment of thinking and the prospect of Scotland as a nation becoming a much more significant focus for Scots as they consider their future and their vision for Scotland and not the Union. The importance of the UK may remain but the emotional and sentimental links with the UK are likely to weaken.

A great deal has changed since 1999 and the setting-up of the Scottish Parliament. We are diverging from Westminster and we have pushed difference to the forefront of our social policy agenda. The ban on smoking in public places, personal care free at the point of need, free tuition fees, minimum pricing of alcohol and new criminal justice reforms have made Scotland much more distinctive, innovative and modern. This process of radical change will continue and again raises the possibilities of what could be achieved if more radical fiscal and economic powers were made available to a more progressively minded parliament and Nation.

New powers are inevitable, the only question is when. Despite the improvements being made in some areas, there are many deep-seated and enduring problems where little progress has been made and where talking a good story has been no substitute for positive political action.

There is too much dependency on Government, we do enjoy a victimhood which allows us to blame others for our obvious shortcoming s and we do see England as a convenient outlet for a cynical blame culture which is often intended to divert attention from our own inadequacies.

More powers, responsibilities and sole ownership of our own strengths and weaknesses would help us address our demons and our problems. New powers and responsibilities for our Parliament would put Scotland to the test and give the Nation a chance to match its rhetoric with achievements. We need a shock to our system to shake us out of our collective complacency.

Scotland and England remain two of the most unequal societies in Western Europe and the consequences are all too evident in terms of our lack of social mobility, social injustices and economic inequalities. Unequal societies have far more social problems. Scotland would be in a better place to tackle those issues if we had the powers to do so and the political will to address them. Again there is a compelling case for more radical home rule.

It is, however, the state of the Union itself which is a major source of concern and likely to bear heavily on the minds of voters over the next two years. The late Harold MacMillan, former Tory Prime Minister, talking about how the fortunes of political parties could change so quickly, said it was 'events dear boy' that created the most grief. This suggests that the Scotland of today could be very different, in mood and aspiration, from that on offer in two years' time.

A deeply unpopular Coalition at Westminster and the economic storms of austerity and recession-hit Britain could influence the mood of voters and their perceptions of what might be in their best long-term interests. Scots could react in two important ways. Fearful of the economic uncertainty and insecurity, voters might opt for the status quo as the safest port in stormy times. On the other hand, many Scots, dissatisfied and depressed with what is on offer from Westminster, may think they have nothing to lose and vote for Independence.

The Union campaign should see this voter dilemma as finely balanced and measured in how much negativity they heap on Independence through fear and scaremongering tactics. Once again, there is a compelling case for a more inspirational alternative which captures the imagination of Scots, the mood of a nation in transition and provides the economic and fiscal powers that will help shape the kind of society Scotland wants to be.

Central to the debate will be the voter's views and perceptions of the Union. The Union is complex and has witnessed remarkable change over the last 305 years, yet only in the last 13 years have we seen any real and significant change to the way we are governed. The Scotland Act 1998 was by all accounts a monumental interruption to the well-ordered running of the Union by the Westminster Parliaments and Governments in London. Westminster is not an institution that welcomes change!

Trusting the Union to again immerse itself in serious constitutional change will be hard to imagine, in view of its track record over three centuries. This is one of the reasons why Scots should decide in 2014 to retain control over their own destiny without being politically hoodwinked into voting down Independence as the only condition whereby Westminster will consider further change.

Supporters of the unchanging Union will rarely own up to its short-comings and the pro-Independence lobby will normally indulge in sweeping dismissals of the Union, without much reference to real and substantial concerns that should have a bearing on how people vote.

Why should we be concerned about the current state of the Union? A recent article in the Herald newspaper had a headline which said, 'Independence is risky, but Union is even scarier'. The article, by Ian Bell, highlighted some of the weaknesses of the Union case and some of the contradictions at the heart of the Coalition Government's current brand of Union thinking. The Coalition's attitude, values and ideology are alien to most Scots. The Conservatives are taking on the appearance of right wing Republicans in America who are viewed as ideologues and unimpressed by common sense or the common good.

Currently Conservative attitudes to the NHS, Education, Europe, Health, Immigration and Welfare at Westminster are in danger of tearing up the post-war consensus on the role of the state and driving forward the market into areas where they have no legitimacy and nothing to offer.

There is little doubt that Scots would not like to see their future through the prism of the politics of the current Conservative-led coalition at Westminster and the fear that this could be their shared future within the Union!

What then, is the state of the Union and is it fit for purpose? There is a case for transforming the Union and the main areas of concern are:

- The obsession with sovereignty and how this constrains the notion of sharing power within the nations of the Union: devolved power is not shared power.

- The UK remains one of the most highly centralised nation states in Europe – with complete legislative power over 50 million people being concentrated in one Parliament in London.

- After the Empire, it remains insecure in the context of interna-tional affairs, globalisation and Europe. Britain has been described as having lost an Empire and never finding a role. This certainly reflects English ambivalence towards both devolution and Europe.

- Westminster and England are seen as increasingly hostile to the idea of the European Union and the political and economic integration which have provided prosperity, stability and security in the post war period.

- Westminster as an institution seems at best grudging of the achievements of devolved government over the past 13 years and at worst hostile, patronising and dismissive of the positive benefits that have emerged in Wales, N. Ireland and Scotland: this grudge mentality is losing the Union friends.

- There is a dated feel to the Institutions of the Union, especially Westminster where a combination of London Metropolitanism, pomp and circumstance, archaic procedures, failure to recognise the dramatic changes taking place in other parts of the Union, a sense of exceptionalism, more a sense of shared history than a shared sense of the future and a fierce resistance to change, create the impression that the institution is not fit for purpose and is being left behind by change and modernity. If Westminster was concerned about strengthening the links between London and every other part of the UK, why, in 100 years of debating the reform of the House of Lords, has the idea of creating a second chamber comprising representatives from the regions of England and the other nations never been considered? Reform of the House of Lords seems more important to Westminster than the future governance of the whole of the UK.

- The concept of democracy and power operating outside the House of Lords and the House of Commons is rarely on the agenda.

- Westminster, supported by all the main political parties, sees the strengthening of local councils and the Big Society as more important than any kind of devolution within England as it poses no threat to the established order and power exercised at Westminster.

- Westminster learns very few lessons from anyone and ignores completely the experiences and success of other European countries in developing sub-national government and more efficient forms of governance.

- Westminster finds difference difficult and feels ill at ease when the devolved areas deliver innovative policy change which clashes with their priorities and creates some envy among the citizens they represent, especially in England.

- A failure to take England – its nationality and identity – seriously. There is a growing sense that people see the Westminster Parliament as the English Parliament, which it clearly isn't. English identity is real and has to be a factor in how we reconfigure the United Kingdom. Only some form of federalism will provide a way forward.

- Does a vision for the UK really exist or has devolution put an end to thinking in this way?

- Is clinging on to Britishness as an idea not totally out of touch with the concept of national identities being embraced throughout the Union?

- Westminster is capable of developing political views that are alien to the more collectivist views of Scotland, where the politics of the common good and common purpose are still valued. Consumerism, commercialism and selfishness are too often dominating the debates about public policy at the expense of citizenship, justice and fairness. There is a perceptible philosophical and political gap emerging between Edinburgh and London.

- Negative perceptions exist at Westminster of Scotland as a dependent, troublesome, subsidy junket and Socialist aberration. If this is the collective wisdom of Westminster then the only solution is for Scotland to raise what it spends in Scotland based on the Nation's priorities.

- There is a confusing and highly complex disconnect between political parties at Westminster and Holyrood, especially the Labour Party, where a dangerous ambivalence towards devolution is in danger of ceding more political ground to the SNP and damaging the chances of reconnecting with the Scottish people.

- The Conservative-led coalition is deeply unpopular in Scotland and while there is a significant buy into the need for austerity and cutting the deficits, the policy platform of the Conservatives is generating a great deal of hostility and concern.

- A growing unease, intolerance and hostility towards 'foreigners, benefit migrants and immigrants' , which makes little sense in a world of the free movement of people in the EU, globalisation and the interdependent world that is fast emerging.

- The 'little Englander' mentality is damaging and all too evident with a powerful combination of exceptionalism, isolationism and sentimentality at Westminster about Britain's past clouding their judgement on Britain's role in the modern world: views that are not largely shared in Scotland.

- The possibility of a Labour victory in the general election will have a bearing on the mood of Scots at the referendum poll in 2014. The 2010 General election result showed clear support for Labour and a massive rejection of the Conservative party. If there is any suggestion in opinion polls in the run-up to the referendum in 2014 that another hung parliament or a Conservative majority is likely, then voters may be less attracted to the Union case.

- There is also the English question. The Barnett Formula is out–of-date. The West Lothian Question needs to be answered and the issue of sovereignty needs to be addressed. During thirteen years of devolution, the political parties at Westminster have shown little genuine interest in these matters, and are content instead to blame Scotland, Wales and Northern Ireland for the difficulties they face. These are Westminster issues and need to be dealt with in London. The trouble is, they all need a federalist solution which is well beyond the comfort zone of all the political parties in London. These are being viewed as technical, but they are highly political.

So what does the Union mean for Scots in 2012? Is there a vision for the future of the Union and what does it hold for Scotland?

The structure and vision of the Union could resemble that of the European Union where Scotland, England, Wales and Northern Ireland share common political and economic goals, support common structures of governance, but are partners in shared power not devolved power. And where sovereignty is modernised and also shared. This would better recognise identity, nationality, different ambitions and culture and reshape the Union and Westminster to reflect and respect the importance and value of all the parts of the United Kingdom and not just Westminster, London and the old Union.

How do we convince the Union that shared power is a strength not a weakness and the future of every part of the UK will depend on the success of mutuality, respect and solidarity? A sense of goodwill and inspired thinking could transform the prospects for the Union, unlock the potential of every part of the UK, boost the economies of the regions and the nations and create less dependency and more responsibility in building a shared future. Westminster doesn't need to control the Union; it should aim to facilitate change and diversity.

After 300 years it is time for a dramatic shock to the system and a constitutional shake up for the Union. The idea of difference should be inspiring, not threatening. Westminster lacks confidence and as a result remains defensive, insecure and potentially unstable. Westminster remains the biggest threat to the future of the Union.

The launch of the 'Better Together, Save the Union' campaign has exposed the central dilemma of the Unionist campaign. **There is no new model on display. There are no new ideas. There is no new vision.** It is the same old Union. It pushes the boundaries of political credibility to believe the Unionist parties, especially Labour, can campaign for two years without spelling out a new Union, a radical programme of Home Rule measures for Scotland and the new relationship between Scotland and the Union.

The partisan nature of this constitutional struggle is embarrassing. The people of Scotland are being asked to decide their destiny but the Unionist parties will not allow a proper choice to be offered to the voters.

The SNP leader has confirmed his willingness to support an alternative and a second question. Labour could pay a heavy price for putting the narrow interests of Westminster before the national interest of Scotland. The future of Scotland cannot be decided at Westminster, where the prospect of constitutional jam tomorrow if only you defeat Independence today is both insulting and bizarre.

The Scottish people should not contract out their future to London on the basis of promises made by the Unionist parties and see another two wasted years added to the five wasted years since 2007. This mind-set has to be confronted and eventually broken.

The Tactics of the alternative

For Labour and the Unionist parties, the issue of an alternative linked to a second question poses real difficulties. The tactics of dealing with the second question, if it is not included in the ballot, present a challenge to how political parties work.

If the Unionist parties, bowing to inevitable public pressure, offer the possibility of more powers outwith a second question on the ballot, what conceivable tactics could be deployed to convince the electors it would be worth ceding control over the issue to them and what practical form could this take? This becomes a very difficult matter to deal with because our democracy and the state of disillusionment with politics offers no guarantees that any deal entered into would be binding.

So what are the concerns if the second question is rejected?

- The parties agree to manifesto commitments to a new and radical devolution package of measures within an agreed time scale for the elections in 2015 and 2016. Practical politics would make this difficult and the sovereignty of Westminster could mean this is a non-starter. The public could see this as an empty gesture.

- The parties agree to another test of public opinion in the form of a referendum within an agreed time scale. All-party agreement would again be difficult. The outcome of the 2015 General Election is uncertain and again, the practical outcomes seem remote.

- A set of vague promises and commitments are made that would be worth very little.

- The parties work out new proposals during the forthcoming referendum campaign, but refuse to put them to the people in the same time frame. This would lack any logic or credibility and could be construed as an unnecessary delaying tactic to gloss over the difficulties of delivering change as well as playing for time by some who are genuinely opposed to any further change.

- Any attempt to ignore the popular wishes of the electorate could have consequences. The parties of the Union will have great difficulty in organising a convincing outcome in the context of a multi-party approach, different ideas of what an alternative should be and an unknown time frame, all based on the outcome of two elections that cannot be predicted with any degree of certainty!

- Why would the Scottish electors trust Westminster – this is a Westminster-inspired campaign – and pass control of their future to London?

- How long do we want the constitutional debate to crowd out other pressing priorities, if the Unionist parties do not take any action until after 2014 and the defeat of Independence?

The only effective solution is a second question in 2014. In this context, Scottish people should put pressure on politicians and political parties to adopt this, refuse to surrender control of the issue to Westminster and support those groups and individuals campaigning for the second question to be included in the parliamentary legislation in 2013. Scotland's date with destiny should not be the subject of any political skulduggery.

The logic is compelling: defeat Independence, but embrace a new package of devo-enhancement at the same time and retain the credibility and integrity of the referendum process and our democracy.

Social Justice and the 'Vision Thing'

There are real issues at the heart of the choice we have to make in 2014. Social justice, economic inequality and social mobility are issues which are vital to the success of Scotland and the building of a fairer, more just and stable society.

Former UK Health Secretary Alan Milburn's recent report card on the progress we are making on social mobility underlines the chronic inequality of opportunity we have throughout Britain. For far too long, these issues have been cast to the margins of our debates and indeed, under the Conservative-led Coalition, the poor and disadvantaged have become more marginalised, the focus of right-wing press coverage and ill-informed political rhetoric.

We are now back to the Victorian era where the 'deserving' and 'undeserving' labels are being implied and sometimes used to further divide society and create a 'them and us' underpinning to what is already becoming a fractured and ill-tempered United Kingdom.

Scotland and England are two of the worst countries in Western Europe for glaring and growing inequalities. And all the evidence confirms that unequal societies have far more social problems. Does an unchanged Union offer any hope that these enduring problems will ever be seriously addressed? Are the prospects any better with Independence? The referendum campaign gives us the opportunity to talk about the kind of Scotland we want to live in, the vision we want to see for our country and its relationship with the rest of the UK, the fact that too many people are not making it and are being left behind and whether the choices on the ballot paper reflect sufficiently the ideas of the common good, common purpose and common trust needed to transform both Scotland and the Union in the tough years that lie ahead. This should be the debate.

No one now seriously disputes the fact that Scotland can be an Independent country. The kind of country, the quality of life and the standard of living that new Scotland would have and aspire to is still a matter of extreme doubt.

The debate has to move onto the substance of whether, on issues like equality, the Union or Independence or some other alternative is the best way forward for Scotland. This is what the people of Scotland want to hear, not just exchanging tribal blows about whether we will have any influence on the MPC of the Bank of England or whether Scotland will see its credit ratings slump after Independence. Speculation and scaremongering were never a sound basis for informed choices.

The leaders of the Labour and Green parties in Scotland have made a positive start by talking about social justice and the need for progressive policies to tackle the injustices built into our social and economic systems in Scotland.

More fundamentally, do we wish to take a lead from England, and Westminster, as a way forward where growing inequalities, increasing intolerance and market driven consumerism dominate or do we want to aspire to the quality of life, the solidarity and civilised ways of thinking and the world class public services of the Scandinavian countries and some other states of Northern Europe?

If the debate on the political and constitutional future of our country is to be meaningful, these are the issues we should be talking about.

The lack of vision in our politics is depressing. What kind of future can we dream about? Where are the inspirational ideas that can transform our country and our prospects? There must be more to political life than we are currently getting. We are not providing any vision for our young people and seem incapable of capturing their imagination, idealism and hopes for the future.

Why are our politicians so afraid of the 'vision thing'? Borrowing from the experience of US Presidents, there is a history of capturing the mood of an era or inspiring the transformation of a society or embracing the idealism required to face new challenges and opportunities. Of course, some of the inspiring rhetoric has to give way to the more pressing needs of office.

Some of these have become iconic and inspirational and have been associated with great moments in US history. Barack Obama's powerful *'Yes we can'* slogan inspired Americans to believe in change and embrace and confront challenges and problems.

The 'new covenant' of Bill Clinton outlined in his 1992 Democratic National Convention speech talked about a new pact between citizens and government. We can go back to Theodore Roosevelt and his 'Square Deal' and Harry S Truman and the 'Fair Deal'. Franklin D Roosevelt, inspirational war and peace-time President, initiated the enduring and very popular 'New Deal'.

And in one of the greatest and shortest – 246 words – speeches of all time, Abraham Lincoln's Gettysburg Address embraced the powerful notions of hope and democracy when he said, 'government of the people, by the people, for the people, shall not perish from this earth'.

One of the most under-rated Presidents, Lyndon B Johnson, created in 1964 the notion of the 'Great Society' to describe his aspirations for his civil rights. President John F Kennedy, facing a period of transition in the 60s, used the idea of 'The New Frontier'. In his acceptance speech in 1960 Kennedy said,

> We stand on the edge of a New Frontier – the frontier of hopes and dreams, a frontier of unknown opportunities and beliefs in peril. Beyond that frontier are uncharted areas of science and space, unsolved problems of peace and war, unconquered problems of ignorance and prejudice, unanswered problems of poverty and surplus.

In Scotland, we do have unconquered problems of ignorance and prejudice and unanswered problems of poverty and surplus and we do have the capacity and potential to do something about them, but they seem to attract little priority.

In our cynical world and the management politics we indulge in, where are our inspiring ideas? We need to embrace and inspire change not just manage it. We need to fix our politics.

Our Date with Destiny...

Scotland stands on the edge of a new era of radical political and constitutional change, regardless of the fate of Independence in 2014. Scotland's journey is far from complete and the theme of a 'Stronger Scotland in a Better Union' has a much more plausible ring to it than either Independence or an unchanging Union.

The only question is when. Westminster and the voices of the Union are unwilling to commit to change, at least at this point in time, with Scots expected to be satisfied with some vague, unspecified commitments to be decided at some unknown point in the future and only if they defeat Independence first.

This kind of thinking defies the laws of credible politics and represents a challenge to the Scottish people. By Scots, of Scots, for Scots, but only if you do what you are told first, is a dangerous way to run a democracy. It is ludicrous and the Unionist parties know it. This is where the right of the Scottish people to have an alternative in the form of a second question, becomes absolutely vital. This is the elephant in the room that will not go away. Westminster has to show that it has learned something from the 13 years of devolved government.

It is time to take greater control over the future of our country and to take more responsibility for what we do. It makes sense in Scotland to raise the taxes we spend on public services provided by our own Parliament. It makes sense to devolve more reserved powers to Edinburgh. It makes sense to have control over more economic levers of change. Westminster should see this as an invitation to help transform a Union that is struggling to come to terms with the aspirations of Scotland, Wales and Northern Ireland.

This is also an invitation for the Union to take England seriously and start to deal with issues of sovereignty, excessive centralisation and ambivalence towards constitutional change. The Scottish people want Scotland to stay within the Union but how difficult does Westminster want that task to be?

Elementary modern studies would grasp the facts, that identity is not Independence, nationality is not about big 'N' nationalism, difference is not the same as disruption and ideas of Scottishness, pride and patriotism wrapped in a Saltire, are healthy components of a vibrant democracy and an electorate that brings both heart and mind to bear on issues that affect self and country.

In all of these matters, Labour in particular should write its own narrative for the future and not let it be dominated by the SNP. Labour needs to frame its argument in the context of a rapidly changing Scotland. Labour needs self-confidence and a bigger belief in Scotland. This is consistent with being in the Union; indeed it may be the key prerequisite for Scotland staying in the Union.

Martin Luther King, in a telling comment about right and wrong, said,

> Cowardice asks the question – is it safe? Vanity asks the question – is it popular? Expediency asks the question – is it politic? But conscience asks the question – is it right? And there comes a time when one must take a position that is neither safe, nor politic, nor popular, but one must take it because it is right.

Labour could be in the fortunate position of ticking all the boxes!

For the Unionist parties, an unparalleled opportunity exists, to defeat Independence, be in harmony with the Scottish people to stay within the Union, but on different terms, and see Scotland as driving forward a new and modern Union.

Looking ahead to the prospect of two years of saying No to Independence, the idea of a new alternative and a second question will begin to look attractive to a campaign already under siege from common sense, opinion poll evidence and much of civic Scotland and the academic community. The campaign for an unchanged Union, if it persists in ignoring the chorus of calls for another alternative, will damage its prospects in the referendum ballot, run the risk of a political backlash in the Westminster and Holyrood elections and further add to the disillusionment and disappointment of the public with politicians and political parties. More damagingly, a campaign in which the major political parties are not listening will only damage democracy itself and drive electors away from voting.

The formal launch of the 'Better Together' campaign took place just before this book was published. The tone, style and substance of the campaign left no-one in any doubt that few lessons had been learned by the Unionist parties about devolution, the changing face of Scotland, its politics or the mood of the Scottish people.

A Westminster-style feel to a low-key campaign launch conveyed little empathy with, or inspiration for, the achievements of devolution or the Scottish identity issue. There has to be real concern that this campaign could generate more support for Independence.

The campaign launch lacked soul, spirit and an inspiring message and in its attempts to inform may come over as very negative and slightly intimidating. Saying No, in the most dismissive of tones, to a possible currency union with the rest of the UK seems more like a punishment in waiting if Scotland votes for Independence rather than an opinion on what might happen. The tone and style of the Union campaign could create a backlash from Scots who do not think the Union is taking the matter seriously enough.

The campaign rightly praises the shared history and achievements of the Union, but rarely hints at its weaknesses and its total failure to spell out what a shared future might look like. The warning that Independence would be like asking Scots to 'buy a one-way ticket to send our children to a deeply uncertain destination' was rightly described as a jibe by the *Herald* newspaper.

Scots are a mature voting public and we should credit them with more common sense than this. Respect is important. The 'Better Together' campaign should avoid lacing comments with so much negativity.

The major weakness of the Unionist campaign is, however, the lack of an alternative. The justifications for this are deeply flawed and reveal more about the insecurity of the Unionist parties and their failure to understand what has been happening in Scotland in the post-devolution era.

The Lib-Dem leader suggested that the idea of a second question was all too difficult and that it would end up in the courts like the George W Bush versus Al Gore Presidential race! It is hard to see the connection.

Or the second question is dismissed as a ploy by Alex Salmond to have a consolation prize, after Independence is defeated. No, there are hundreds of thousands of Scots, politicians of all parties, academics, Trade Unions, business people, much of civic Scotland's leaders, showing a preference for a third way which rejects the upheaval of Independence and the complacency of an unchanged Union.

Then there was the general mantra of the spin surrounding the launch that a second question would, 'muddy the waters' and lead to confusion, generate legal challenges and cut across the idea of obtaining an unambiguous result. Where is the evidence to justify any of these assertions?

It would be foolish and dangerous if the parties of the Union started to believe their own propaganda and think the 'no' result is in the bag – a slam dunk – and that they do not need to expend a great deal of political effort in the months and years ahead.

The Unionist campaign will remain flawed and incomplete if it refuses to either adopt a second question or set out the tactics and procedures as to how Scotland's progress could be achieved without a second question. Opinion polls consistently show Scots being against Independence and for a third way of radical home rule policies that will keep us in a better Union.

The Unionist parties may have good reasons for prevaricating on this issue but having the best interests of Scotland at heart does not seem to be one of them. This is a weak position and insulting to Scots who genuinely want the best for their country and not what is best for political parties.

Scots do not want to waste two years only saying no to Independence, nor do they want to wait for Westminster to decide what happens next. Scots do not trust Westminster – that is why this referendum allows them to retain control over their own destiny. The Conservative leadership has shown little interest in devolution but Labour and the Lib-Dems have. Scotland now looks to them to break free from their ambivalence and embrace a third way.

Labour has to set out a new and progressive narrative and set out clearly its devolution and constitutional credentials. Their journey from the home rule sentiments of Keir Hardie to the present day has been long and uncertain. There is now an opportunity for Labour to clear up this confusion, identify with the need for more powers for the Scottish

Parliament and a transformation of Westminster and to reconnect with Scottish voters whose embrace of their country should be seen as inspiring, not threatening.

In the autumn of 2014, a decision will be made which may have epic consequences. Regardless of the nature of the outcome, Scotland's constitutional journey will accelerate from that point: the momentum is tangible and the mood is determined. The parties of the Union have an opportunity to put Scotland first and in doing so, help transform the UK. For this to happen, they have to listen to the people of Scotland, engage with their growing sense of identity and provide them with real choices for the future of their country.

That process has to start now. But for this to happen the parties of the Union have to show more belief in themselves, their ideas and their country. Scotland can win and so can the Union.

A Model Constitution for Scotland

W. Elliot Bulmer
ISBN 978-1-908373-13-7 PBK £9.99

Scotland is a free, sovereign and independent commonwealth. Its form of government is a parliamentary democracy based upon the sovereignty of the people, social justice, solidarity and respect for human rights...

A Model Constitution for Scotland sets out a workable model for Scotland's future and includes detailed constitutional proposals together with informed discussion on the topic.

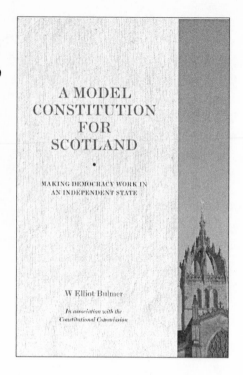

The Independence debate has to break out of political elites and address the 'after Independence' question. Elliot Bulmer's book is an important contribution to this, exploring how we make Scotland constitutionally literate, and how we shape our politics in a way which reflects who we are and what we aspire to be. Bulmer rightly argues that Independence has to aspire to more than abolishing reserved powers, Holyrood becoming a mini-Westminster, and nothing else changing. A must read for independentistas, thoughtful Unionists and democrats.
GERRY HASSAN,
author and broadcaster

Bulmer deals with fundamental rights and freedoms in a broad-minded and incisive fashion.
NEWSNET SCOTLAND

A Nation Again:
Why Independence will
be good for Scotland
(and England too)

Edited by Paul Henderson Scott
ISBN 978-1-908373-25-0 PBK £7.99

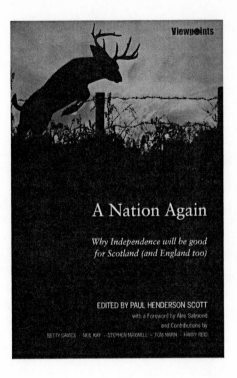

*If you believe in the Case for
Independence, this book will provide
you with a stirring endorsement of
your view. If you are sceptical, it
might well persuade you to convert
to the cause. If you are downright
hostile, this book could be dangerous
– it could prompt you to rethink.*

Suddenly Scottish Independence
is within grasp. Is this a frivolous
pipedream, a romantic illusion?
Or is it, as the writers of this
dynamic and positive collection
of essays insist, an authentic
political option, feasible and
beneficial?

As the Scottish people prepare
for their biggest ever collective
decision, this book forcefully sets
out the Case for Independence.
The distinguished authors, from a
variety of different perspectives,
argue the case for the Imperative
of Independence.

Details of these and other books published by Luath Press can be found at:
www.luath.co.uk

Luath Press Limited

committed to publishing well written books worth reading

LUATH PRESS takes its name from Robert Burns, whose little collie Luath (*Gael.,* swift or nimble) tripped up Jean Armour at a wedding and gave him the chance to speak to the woman who was to be his wife and the abiding love of his life. Burns called one of 'The Twa Dogs' Luath after Cuchullin's hunting dog in Ossian's *Fingal*. Luath Press was established in 1981 in the heart of Burns country, and is now based a few steps up the road from Burns' first lodgings on Edinburgh's Royal Mile.

Luath offers you distinctive writing with a hint of unexpected pleasures.

Most bookshops in the UK, the US, Canada, Australia, New Zealand and parts of Europe either carry our books in stock or can order them for you. To order direct from us, please send a £sterling cheque, postal order, international money order or your credit card details (number, address of cardholder and expiry date) to us at the address below. Please add post and packing as follows: UK – £1.00 per delivery address; overseas surface mail – £2.50 per delivery address; overseas air-mail – £3.50 for the first book to each delivery address, plus £1.00 for each additional book by airmail to the same address. If your order is a gift, we will happily enclose your card or message at no extra charge.

Luath Press Limited
543/2 Castlehill
The Royal Mile
Edinburgh EH1 2ND
Scotland

Telephone: 0131 225 4326 (24 hours)
Fax: 0131 225 4324
email: sales@luath.co.uk
Website: www.luath.co.uk

Printed by RR Donnelley at Glasgow, UK